Latino Boom!

Latino Boom!

EVERYTHING YOU

NEED TO KNOW

TO GROW YOUR

BUSINESS IN THE

U.S. HISPANIC

MARKET

Chiqui Cartagena

BALLANTINE BOOKS

NEW YORK

Copyright © 2005 by Maria J. Cartagena

All rights reserved.

Published in the United States by Ballantine Books,
an imprint of The Random House Publishing Group, a division of
Random House, Inc., New York.

BALLANTINE and colophon are registered
trademarks of Random House, Inc.

Library of Congress Cataloging-in-Publication Data

Cartagena, Chiqui.
Latino boom! : everything you need to know to grow your business
in the U.S. Hispanic market / by Chiqui Cartagena.—1st ed.
p. cm.
ISBN 0-345-48235-2
1. Hispanic American consumers—United States.   2. Hispanic Americans—
Population.   3. Target marketing—United States.   I. Title.

HC110.C6C365 2005
658.8'0089'68073—dc22   2005046477

Printed in the United States of America on acid-free paper

www.ballantinebooks.com

First Edition

2 4 6 8 9 7 5 3 1

Book design by Jo Anne Metsch

Dedicated to K. J. Knight, who not only came up with the idea for this book, but who also makes me a better person every day

Contents

~~~~~~~~~~~~~~~~~~~

Introduction

~~~~~~~~~~~~~

Today I am considered a Hispanic media war veteran. I started my career when Univision was still called Spanish International Network in 1985 (we used to joke about the acronym and say: "I work for SIN") and I was there when *The Miami Herald* relaunched *El Nuevo Herald* in 1987. In the mid nineties, I worked on the development and launch of *People en Español,* to date the most successful magazine launch in the U.S. Hispanic market. I have worked on so many Hispanic media start-ups during the past twenty years that my peers consider me a Pioneer; that's right, a pioneer with a capital P. But, as we all know, pioneering has its challenges.

What makes me unique in the world of Hispanic media is that, unlike most of my peers, my experience encompasses both content production in print and broadcast media as well as business acumen in sales, marketing, direct marketing, and strategic planning. Taking advantage of my multimedia, multilanguage experiences, in the late nineties I began working for some of the largest American media companies that were waking up to the need to address the growing Latino community in the United States. I have helped develop and launch several consumer magazines, and have put together many business plans for media products and services geared toward Latinos. Some have had great success; others never even got off the ground. But my primary role has always been to advise senior-level executives how to proceed in the relatively uncharted waters of the Hispanic consumer.

Not that my advice was always followed, mind you. In fact, the main reason why I'm writing this book is precisely because, when I get hired to help solve the "problem" of what to do about the Hispanic market, I often find that executives tend to repeat the same mistakes. Some of these mistakes are based on pure ignorance, and I often spend much time "educating" executives about this market. Other mistakes, however, are made out of pure stubbornness on the part of otherwise intelligent people who simply don't want to change the way they do business in a specialized market.

The presumption that Latinos behave in the same way as the general market often permeates the thinking of these executives. This attitude invariably causes their forays into the Hispanic market to fail miserably. For example, one of New York's great daily newspapers thought that one way to increase its circulation was to attract more Hispanic readers to its publication. So it decided to launch a bilingual edition that would be distributed side by side with the regular English-language edition. Sounds like a brilliant idea, right? Well, it failed miserably. Why? The paper's management did not really think through all the sales and distribution issues that would come into play in order to make a bilingual edition successful. On the sales side, they thought their sales force could just sell this new edition the same way they sold the regular paper, but they were wrong. In order to sell successfully, you need to understand what you're selling. This is a different market, with different players, and your sales teams need to be properly trained in order to succeed. To their credit, management did hire the best team of Latino journalists to work on the new edition, but even the best-written newspaper will not get read if it doesn't reach its readers. You see, the bilingual edition was distributed through the same channels of distribution that were used for the regular English-language edition, which left out many areas in the city where Latinos actually work and live. Those of us who have worked in the Hispanic print media know that Latino publications are sold through a network of independent distributors that reach bodegas and other small mom-and-pop stores that dominate Latino neighborhoods. Without access to these barrio stores, you are greatly limiting your chances of success, even in a city like New York. The newspaper's management didn't think through the distribution differences before the paper launched its bilingual edition, and found itself caught between their union and a hard place. Distribution problems forced the paper to cancel the bilingual edition only six months after it had launched, but to outsiders, the perception was that it failed because "Latinos don't read."

Unfortunately, these failed "experiments" cause much more damage to those corporations than their executives care to know. For one thing, it damages their brand image with an increasingly important population. (Changing a negative image costs twice the amount of money it would take to do it right from the beginning.) Second, it discourages other players in the industry from getting into this market and makes everyone more skeptical about the upside potential of the U.S. Hispanic market.

WHY ARE SO MANY CORPORATIONS LOOKING TO ENTER THIS MARKET NOW?

When they were released, the Census 2000 figures caused many in the business world to rethink their attitudes toward the Latino community. Why? Just take a look at these statistics.

- Hispanics are now the largest minority in the country. In 2002, Latinos outnumbered the African-American population for the first time in history—something that wasn't projected to occur until 2005! Blacks currently represent 13 percent of the total U.S. population, or 36 million people. Latinos are 41.3 million strong, roughly representing 15 percent of the total U.S. population, according to the latest Census update.
- Add to that the 3.8 million Hispanics who live in the Commonwealth of Puerto Rico, and who are *not included* in U.S. Census figures, and you'll see that this is a market no business can continue to ignore.
- Latinos are one of the fastest-growing demographics in the United States. The Hispanic population grew by almost 60 percent from

1990 to 2000, compared with a 13 percent growth rate for the general population. In fact, fueled both by high birth rates and by legal (and illegal) immigration, the Latino population increases by about 1 million persons per year!

- These demographic trends will continue to affect the population landscape of the United States for the foreseeable future. Census 2000 projections put the total Latino population at 53.7 million by the year 2015 and at 81.8 million (141 percent growth) by the year 2030. Between 2000 and 2050, the Hispanic share of the population will nearly double, from 12.6 percent to 24.4 percent.

- Finally, Hispanic buying power is also increasing faster than that of any other segment of the population. According to the Selig Center for Economic Growth at the University of Georgia, Hispanic buying power reached $686 billion in 2004 and according to Global Insight, personal consumption spending by Latinos will grow at an annual rate of 9.1 percent from 2002 to 2020—far exceeding the national growth rate of 6.0 percent. In fact, Hispanic buying power will outpace that of the African American community by 2009!

Those are staggering statistics! It doesn't matter whether you are selling Pampers, blue jeans, cars, or credit cards, the Hispanic market is a market that every business must learn to understand and start including in its business plan if it wants to grow in the future. This book is intended to be the first step in helping you understand this important market. It is a business primer on the Hispanic market in the United States. In it you will find a general overview of this growing market that will give you enough background information to begin making smart decisions on how to proceed with any Hispanic-oriented initiatives your company may have or be planning. You'll learn many important things about the geographic concentration, socioeconomic profile, and levels of education of this market, things that make it uniquely challenging and at the same time appealing to marketers. You'll also learn about the three main groups of Latinos: isolated, acculturated, and assimilated, and how they differ in size, language preference, and behavior as consumers. I am also including a section, dedicated to critical demographic trends and snapshots of the top ten Hispanic markets in the United States, that will allow you to use this book as a reference guide for your own business presentations.

Before we get started, I encourage you to test your knowledge of the Latino community. Understanding a community is a key factor in tapping into it successfully. Ask yourself what you know (or think you know) about this market. Write it down on a piece of paper, and when you are done reading the book, take it out and review it. Together we will debunk some of the most common myths and stereotypes regarding Latinos and analyze some of the real challenges facing the Hispanic community in the near future. And, of course, I'll spend some time taking you through examples and mini case studies that will help you avoid some of the most common mistakes made by others who entered this market. Finally, because I enjoy looking at the big picture and forecasting changes in the market, I will spend some time identifying trends to monitor in the future.

Because this book is just a first step, I have also included a Resource Guide that will help you take further steps on your own. The goal I had in mind when I set out to write this book was for any business owner or executive to be able to read this book on a plane trip or in a day. It is intended for people who may or may not be involved with any Hispanic project at the moment, but who need to become more knowledgeable about this market in order to make the right decisions for the future of their businesses.

Latino Boom!

1

~~~~~~

EVERY DOG HAS HIS DAY

Before we talk about the business opportunity behind the growing Hispanic market, I think some historical context is necessary. Throughout this book you will hear me talk about the strong bond Latinos have with the Spanish language and Hispanic "culture." People often say that to know a language is to know the culture of the people who speak it. But to fully understand the Hispanic culture of Latinos living in the United States, one must also realize that this "culture" is also shaped by the historical and political relationship of Spain with its Latin American brethren. So, allow me first to take you through a quick review of the history of Spain in Latin America, and how the politics and beliefs of the Spanish empire have come to influence many aspects of today's Hispanic culture, including some very deep-rooted issues of race and class. Once we have briefly explored the historical baggage all Latinos carry from Spain, I'll bring the focus back to the unique and more modern history of Latinos in the United States.

POLITICS AND ISSUES OF RACE AND CLASS

Talking about Latinos and politics is unavoidable these days. Not only was the Latino vote a "must-win" in the past presidential election, in several key battleground states *how* Latinos voted actually decided *who* ultimately won the 2004 presidential election. Democrats are still reeling from the results, but the fault does not lie entirely with John Kerry's campaign. It is clearly part of the larger problem the Democratic Party has to face, which is that the party has lost touch with its power base. Latinos have traditionally been at the heart of the Democratic Party's power base. That is why historically the majority of Latinos have been affiliated with and voted for the candidates of the Democratic Party. But as you will see in the following chapters, Hispanics also tend to be more socially conservative in their views on politics and religion, especially if they are foreign-born and Catholic. Realizing that they could appeal both to the conservative side of older and foreign-born Latinos, the Republican Party has been impressively effective in gaining political ground with the Latino community. It has also been able to appeal to the younger generation of Hispanics that are born in the United States and are quickly climbing the economic ladder.

Which party does a better job of attracting the Latino vote will continue to be very important because of the tremendous rate at which this population is growing. According to political researchers, about 750,000 Hispanics will become eligible to vote each year over the next twenty years, so the political impact of the Latino community in the United States is undeniable. Now, to better understand the perspective U.S. Hispanics have on politics and issues of race and class, one must go back to the history of Spain and its colonization of the New World. For those of you who are Latinophiles, in my opinion the best book to read on this subject is *The Buried Mirror: Reflections on Spain and the New World,* which was written in 1992 by the renowned Mexican novelist Carlos Fuentes to commemorate the quincentennial of the discovery of the Americas. In it Fuentes brilliantly uncovers the historical-political connections between Spain, Latin America, and the United States in "search of a cultural continuity that can inform and transcend the economic and political disunity and fragmentation of the Hispanic world." According to Fuentes, in spite of all the political and economic crises that have rocked Latin America throughout the centuries, the one thing that all Spanish-speaking people share is their cultural heritage.

What most people do not realize is that the same year that Christopher Columbus "discovered" the Americas in the name of the Spanish empire, Spain itself was undergoing its most significant political and religious transformation. After eight centuries of Muslim occupation, in 1492 the kingdoms of Aragón and Castile were united through the marriage of Ferdinand and Isabella. Together their armies were finally able to defeat the Moors in Granada, the last bastion of Muslim military resistance in southern Spain. With the expulsion of the Moors, the Spanish crown began an era of ethnic and religious cleansing that would shape the culture of the Spanish empire for centuries to come. Soon after the defeat of the Moors, attention was focused on the expulsion of the other entrenched culture of Spain: the Jews. That's right. For eight centuries, the Jews, Muslims, and Catholics coexisted in Spain, a country that is approximately the size of Texas. (Perhaps historians should examine that period more closely to see if they can find answers to the problems we are facing in the Arab and Jewish world today.) But as the new Catholic kings desperately tried to consolidate power in their fractured country, they decided that their "unity" would be based on achieving both religious *and* racial purity. As a result, the Jews were also forced to leave the country or convert to Catholicism. Many historians agree today that the expulsion of the Jews was one of the biggest mistakes the Spanish kings made, since the Jews were the only ones in the Spanish kingdom that had the necessary experience and knowledge in commerce and finance to keep the Spanish empire thriving.

So in one crucial year, 1492, the Spanish went from being politically divided to being united under one kingdom, from having different languages and laws for each kingdom to having Castilian be the official language of all of Spain, and to bringing back the old Roman law. And finally, after 800 years of coexistence, the expulsion of the Muslims and the Jews may have achieved the religious purity the king desired, but it also drained the intellectual, scientific, and business classes of Spain at the worst possible time: the emergence of Spain as a world power. This was the political backdrop of the discovery of the Americas. Why is this important? Because this political and religious transformation of Spain would forever mark, or should I say scar, the colonization of the New

World and therefore influence the "Hispanic culture" inherited by Latinos in the United States today.

The Spanish conquistadores who came to the Americas were often the sons of noblemen who were not going to inherit titles, lands, or fortune in Spain, so they ventured to the New World in search of new riches and titles. They were not alone, of course. With them came religious missionaries, military personnel, and seamen whose only desire was to get rich in their New World adventures. But the base of political power always remained in Spain. For more than 300 years all the decisions on how to settle, govern, and exploit the New World came directly from the Spanish court in Madrid, subjugating both the colonizers and the colonized to a higher power: that of the king of Spain and through him, of course, God. So, from the very beginning, class issues permeated the colonization of the Americas. Unfortunately, these class issues still remain today, with 90 percent of the political and economic power still concentrated in the hands of 10 percent of the population, who more often than not are the direct descendants of light-skinned Spaniards or other European colonizers.

In terms of race, Latinos have a colorful and seemingly contradictory history. Although Spaniards participated in the slave trade, it was a Spanish slave owner turned missionary who, as early as 1524, became the strongest advocate for the rights of Indians. Bartolomé de las Casas successfully convinced the Spanish crown to recognize that African slaves and American indigenous peoples had a "soul" and therefore demanded that the Holy Roman Catholic empire of Spain grant them human rights. As a result, the Spanish government recognized the rights of Indians for the first time in 1542, when the Law of the Indies was enacted. The mixing of races that ensued created the many beautiful shades of brown that now exist in Latin America. This mixture of races was once lauded as "the cosmic race" by the great Mexican writer and intellectual Jose Vasconcelos. Nevertheless, as Fuentes says in *The Buried Mirror,* the Spanish obsession with racial purity was also demonstrated by the often insulting terms used to "classify" the mixing of racial groups that went on in the New World. At the top of the list are, of course, the *criollos* or *Creoles,* the descendants of Europeans who were born in the New World. Although criollos were usually not racially mixed, they were deemed as "less than" by Spaniards since they would never have the power of the peninsular Spaniards and other Caucasian Europeans, and therefore needed to be classified differently. "The *mestizo* was the child of a white and an Indian," says Fuentes. "The *mulato* (the offensive name was derived from the Spanish word for mule) was the child of a black and a white. The *zambo* was the offspring of an Indian and a black." The terms go on and on, getting more offensive at each turn. However, although these terms were created to keep track of the racial purity of Latin Americans, in Hispanic culture "discrimination" is more pervasive than racism. Five hundred years of intermarriage and racial mixture in Latin America have created a "brown" skin tone that for many Hispanics no longer has any kind of racial implication. It's simply part of what makes Latinos beautiful. However, when Hispanics come to the United States, they are confronted with America's racist baggage. The obsession with race in this country turns even the simplest acts of life—getting a driver's license or registering your kids in school—into a black versus white paradigm that is difficult for Hispanics to understand. That is why—as you will see in chapter 5—Hispanics defy the "racial" categorizations that the U.S. government tries to impose on them, opting to embrace their "ethnic" or Hispanic identity instead.

REACHING CRITICAL MASS

Fast-forward now to the year 2000 when the press touted the crossover success of Ricky Martin, Jennifer Lopez, and Marc Anthony as a "Latin Explosion," as if Latinos had never been "visible" to the majority of Americans before. The truth is that we've been around for a while. In 1985, when I was fresh out of college, everyone was calling the eighties the "decade of the Hispanic," but nothing ever came of it, mainly because the Hispanic population hadn't reached "critical mass." Well, now, after more than 150 years of being part of the rich cultural landscape of the United States, Latinos have finally become part of the so-called "mainstream." Although Latinos are not necessarily assimilating into the big American melting pot as past immigrant groups have, they are certainly affecting and shaping the mainstream in ways that nobody could have ever imagined only a few years ago.

Already today in America national sales of Mexican salsa and corn or flour tortillas outpace that of ketchup and white bread. Clearly the influence of Latinos on mainstream America can no longer be denied. But before we get into what that really means, let's take a short trip back in modern history to better understand how current perceptions and stereotypes of the Latino community have been formed over the years.

A BRIEF HISTORY OF LATINOS IN THE UNITED STATES

Several years ago, Gregory Rodriguez, a senior fellow at the New America Foundation, a nonpartisan public policy institute, wrote an essay for *The New York Times* in which he discussed the reasons behind the lack of integration of Latinos in the United States. "While Latinos have been an integral part of the American cultural landscape since the mid-nineteenth century, only now are they beginning to gain the broad social acceptance that other groups experienced within a few generations of arriving in America. Having reached critical mass, Latinos are asserting their ethnicity more confidently than ever before. On one hand, large numbers, air travel, and the reach of global media have made the Spanish language and Latin American styles and norms far more visible on this side of the border. On the other, their growing demographic presence is propelling American-born Latino political and cultural figures into the English-speaking mainstream.

Historically speaking, the first sizable group of Latinos to become "Americans" did so through the conquest and annexation of the American Southwest in 1848. "So the first image of Latino Americans was one of defeated foreigners," says Rodriguez. "Then mass Anglo-American migration to the West turned the native Spanish-speaking population into a marginalized minority whose 'Americanness' would be challenged well into the next century."

All immigrants to the United States have had to face prejudice after their arrival but, according to Rodriguez, Latino Americans have had to endure wave after wave of anti-Latino sentiment. "Because Mexican labor has been recruited into the United States during boom times and expelled during busts, native-born Mexican Americans have suffered the fallout from campaigns ostensibly aimed at their foreign-born cousins. In the 1930s, the fear that Mexicans were taking jobs from 'real' Americans led to the deportation of more than one million people," he adds. Some scholars now believe that up to 60 percent of those "Mexicans" forced to leave were actually American citizens.

As a result of these strong and continuous waves of anti-Latino sentiment, Rodriguez says that many Latino immigrants, especially Mexicans, were forced to conceal their cultural heritage in order to get ahead. For decades, it was not uncommon for Latinos to claim to be of Italian or Spanish descent in order to avoid hostility while living in the United States.

DON'T CRY FOR ME, PUERTO RICO

Not many people realize that the island of Puerto Rico had been a military possession of the United States since 1898, when Spain ceded its colony to the American government at the conclusion of the Spanish-American War. However, Puerto Ricans were not given American citizenship *until 1917*, in part because the U.S. government was desperate to find workers who could help with the construction of the Panama Canal. From the Great Depression through World War II, Puerto Ricans came to the United States in droves, all of them in search of a better life as new citizens of this great country. After World War II, and encouraged by the U.S. government's "Operation Bootstrap," more than 1 million Puerto Ricans came to New York, quickly becoming the backbone of the city's manufacturing workforce.

In the late forties a strong movement toward independence from the United States was growing on the island of Puerto Rico. The U.S. government did not pay too much attention to this movement until 1950, when two men who claimed to be Puerto Rican "independentistas" assaulted the White House in a vain attempt to assassinate President

Truman. What ensued was a political debate that tried to appease both sides and ended up creating a unique political status for the island: the commonwealth, which is neither a state of the union nor a military possession. The Puerto Rican constitution, which was ratified by the people of Puerto Rico in 1952, and later approved by the U.S. Congress, states that as a commonwealth, Puerto Rico is "free of superior authority in the management of its own local affairs but is linked to the United States of America and hence is part of its political system in a manner compatible with its federal structure." If you are a bit confused by what that exactly means, well, join the crowd.

The truth is that, to this day, Puerto Ricans are not really considered part of the United States' population. (Even the Census Bureau counts them separately!) Although Puerto Ricans living on the island are citizens of the United States, they are not allowed to vote in political elections. However, Puerto Ricans living stateside can and, of course, do exercise their right to vote. In the Congress of the United States, the Commonwealth of Puerto Rico is represented by one, nonvoting member called the resident commissioner. The question of whether Puerto Rico should become the fifty-first state comes up for popular vote every so often on the island, but Puerto Ricans themselves are divided on this question. About half of them want the island to keep its commonwealth status because of the special tax benefits the island currently receives and because it allows Puerto Ricans to nostalgically hold on to a sense of sovereignty. The other half wants Puerto Rico to become a full-fledged state, with all the positives and negatives that becoming a state brings. (Can you imagine a Ms. Universe pageant without a representative from Puerto Rico?) Needless to say, the debate continues and may or may not get resolved in our lifetimes. But let's not get too side-tracked; let's return to our brief history lesson.

THE GRAPES OF WRATH AND THE SEARCH FOR A HISPANIC IDENTITY

Between 1965 and 1970 California experienced another surge of growth among its Mexican population, most of it due to the Bracero

Program sponsored by the state of California from 1942 to 1964. The Bracero Program allowed "guest" workers to legally come into the United States to live and work. These workers came and stayed for decades, but were never counted in the U.S. Census. For more than twenty years, a good chunk of the population of California officially didn't exist. After the program finished, most of these workers were "invited" back by their employers to become American citizens. As a result, in the Census of 1970, the population of the state of California practically doubled. Another state that literally grew overnight was Florida. In the 1960s, hundreds of thousands of Cubans fled to Miami after Fidel Castro took power in 1959. The sudden influx of many well-to-do Cuban professionals in this sleepy retirement state, until then the playground of rich and famous northerners, began to drastically change Florida forever. Thanks in large measure to the entrepreneurial spirit of its Latino immigrants, Miami has become the vibrant "Gateway to the Americas" that it is today. It may have first been the Cubans in the sixties, but soon many other Latin American exiles made Miami their home. In the late seventies and early eighties Nicaraguans began immigrating to Miami after the defeat of the Somoza regime in 1979. The eighties also brought another wave of Cuban immigration, this time by way of the Mariel boat lift, as well as a significant increase in the number of well-to-do Colombians fleeing the drug wars back home. Most recently, Miami has become home to wealthy Venezuelans, Brazilians, and Argentines, who are also fleeing the political and economic instability of their homelands. Unlike the Mexican immigration in the Southwest, the Latino immigrants in the Southeast were largely comprised of educated professionals and intellectual and political refugees escaping repressive left-wing governments in Latin America (which broadly explains why Latinos in Florida are largely Republican, whereas everywhere else Latinos tend to be Democrats).

Living the American Dream has always been the goal of *all* of the immigrants that have come to this country. Learning English and adopting American values and culture has been a commonplace occurrence with all immigrant groups that have come to this country throughout the centuries, all of them changing the face of America. But Latinos are defying the traditional melting pot theory. There are many reasons why Hispanic immigrants are not assimilating into the American mainstream as fast as other immigrant groups have. One reason is the geographic proximity of their homelands—Cuba is only 90 miles from Key West, Florida—and the relative ease with which all Latinos can come from and go to Latin America. This has also allowed for the Hispanic "identity" to remain strong with Latinos living in the United States. "It wasn't until the 1960s and early 1970s that Hispanics started to assert their ethnic identities," says Gregory Rodriguez. "They began to coin terms like 'Chicano' and 'Latino' and used them with pride to identify themselves." In his book *The Rise of the Hispanic Market in the United States,* Louis E. V. Nevaer explains how the term "Hispanic" first came to be used in the United States. The term was coined by the Census Bureau during the Nixon administration, when for the first time it set out to identify and "understand the phenomenon of a permanent Spanish-speaking population that refused to assimilate and become 'Americanized.'" In one fell swoop, the U.S. government began classifying all Hispanics under this "generic" term, which helped obscure important, fundamental differences between the three main subgroups of Latinos in the United States: Puerto Ricans, Cubans, and Mexicans. Once they were all grouped under this "Hispanic" umbrella, in the minds of other Americans, Latinos all became the same. Unfortunately for everyone, the image this term conjures in the minds of most Americans today is that of very poor, migrant workers with little or no education who come to America purely for economic reasons. No one can deny that there are some Latinos who are poor, uneducated, and don't speak English. But that group of Latino immigrants is not the *only* group of Hispanics in the United States. In fact, the largest group of Hispanics living in the United States today is made up of predominantly young, educated Latinos who were either born or raised in the United States and who are quickly becoming an important part of our consumer base. The interesting thing about this group is that although they are more Americanized than most people think, they still hold on to their Hispanic identity and heritage very strongly. But before we get into the acculturation of Latinos in the United States, let's take a look at the big picture: Latino U.S.A.

2

～～～

PORTRAIT OF A NATION:
LATINO U.S.A.

L atino, Hispanic, it's all the same, right? Wrong.

While some academics say that the difference between "Latino" and "Hispanic" is one of class and politics—where Latino denotes the working class and Hispanic someone of more sophisticated background—I prefer to keep things simple and go by the dictionary. According to *Merriam-Webster's Collegiate Dictionary,* Latino refers to people who come from a Latin American country (there are twenty-two of them), or a person of Latin-American origin living in the United States. Hispanic is a more comprehensive term that applies to "the peoples and cultures of Spain and Portugal." The term you may have heard a lot is "Chicano," which really refers only to people of Mexican descent living in the United States. But if you ask me where I am from, I'll probably say I'm Spanish (because of my mom) or Puerto Rican (because of my dad). You see, we generally don't use the terms "Hispanic" or "Latino" to refer to ourselves. These are terms used by *other people* to refer to *us.* Like most immigrants, we usually refer to ourselves by our country of origin.

As I pointed out earlier, it wasn't until 1970 that the Census Bureau for the first time included a separate question specifically asking people to identify themselves as being of Hispanic origin. According to the Census Bureau, only 5 percent of the sample of households were asked that question, and respondents who identified themselves as Hispanic were further asked to specify whether their origin or descent was Mexican, Puerto Rican, Cuban, Central or South American, or Spanish. The term "Latino" appeared on the Census form for the first time in the year 2000.

This chapter will take you through some of the basic demographic data you need in order to have a better understanding of what the future holds. First, we will go over the population growth of Latinos in the United States, which garners the most media attention these days. Then, we will briefly go over all the major statistics that define this market, such as household income, levels of education, as well as data on employment and length of residency in the United States.

HISPANIC POPULATION GROWTH

According to the 2000 Census, the Hispanic population in the United States grew 57.9 percent, from 22.4 million in 1990 to 35.6 million in 2000. By comparison, the growth rate for the total U.S. population was only 13.2 percent during the same period. In 2000, African Americans comprised 12.7 percent of the total population, Hispanics accounted for 12.6 percent, and Asians totaled 3.8 percent of the total population. But the number of Latinos is growing at a much faster rate than any other group; chart 1 gives you the latest snapshot of the racial composition of the United States today.

There has been a lot of press coverage about the fact that in late 2002, Latinos actually surpassed African Americans as the largest minority group in the United States, something that demographers said would not occur until the year 2005! Most of the press coverage I have seen on this issue has ugly racial overtones that try to pit one minority group against another. A major point to realize, and that is often missed, is that what is important here is that, taken together, all minority groups already represent one-third of the American population and that the one-size-fits-all mentality is no longer appropriate in today's business environment. Advances in technology will soon give way to a fragmentation of the marketplace such as we have never known before. With

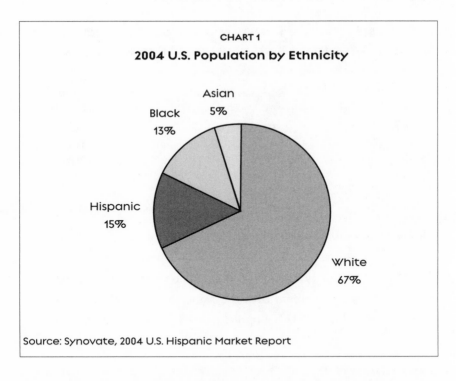

CHART 1

2004 U.S. Population by Ethnicity

Asian
5%

Black
13%

Hispanic
15%

White
67%

Source: Synovate, 2004 U.S. Hispanic Market Report

the Internet, we have seen how niche markets can not only survive but thrive. In the future, successful businesses will be defined by how well companies market their products and services to *all* groups, not just the dwindling "general market."

In March 2004, the Census Bureau released its latest projections on population growth in the United States (table 1). According to those projections, the Latino population is going to triple in size over the next half century, rising from 35.6 million in 2000 to 102.6 million in 2050, while its share of the U.S. population will nearly double from 12.6 percent to 24.4 percent. By comparison, the African-American population is projected to grow from 35.8 million in 2000 to 61.4 million in 2050, while its total share of the population will increase only slightly, from 12.7 percent to 14.6 percent. The most significant change, however, will take place among the non-Hispanic white population—the so-called general market. It will steadily decline from 69.4 percent of the total U.S. population in 2000 to only 50.1 percent of the total population by 2050. The only minority group that will outpace the growth of

TABLE 1 Projected growth of the Hispanic population
in the United States from 2000 to 2050

Year	Hispanics Number (in millions)	Hispanics Percent Share of Total Population
2000	35,622	12.6%
2010	47,756	15.5%
2020	59,756	17.8%
2030	73,055	20.1%
2040	87,585	22.3%
2050	102,560	24.4%

Source: U.S. Census Bureau. March 18, 2004

the Hispanic population will be the Asian community, which will grow an astonishing 213 percent over the same time period, jumping from 3.8 percent of the total U.S. population to 8 percent in 2050.

BREAKDOWN OF HISPANICS INTO COUNTRY SUBGROUPS

As reviewed in the last chapter, the Hispanic population in the United States has mainly been comprised of people coming from three countries: Mexico, Puerto Rico, and Cuba. All other Hispanics have been lumped together into the clumsily labeled "other Hispanics" group by the U.S. Census Bureau. This fourth group of Latinos has become increasingly more important as it has dramatically grown in size over the past decade. In fact, today "other Hispanics" represent the second largest subgroup of Hispanics in the United States (chart 2). Unlike the other subgroups, this "other" group is comprised of people from many different countries in Central and South America, so it is hard to really even consider it a "group." Nonetheless their size is important to note, and depending on what city you are doing business in, keep in mind this "other" group may make or break your efforts in reaching the Hispanic market. For example, in San Antonio, Texas, the "other" Hispanic group already represents 20 percent of the Latino market.

TABLE 2 Growth of Hispanic Population from 1990 to 2000

Country of Origin	1990 Census	Percentage of Hispanic Total	2000 Census	Percentage of Hispanic Total
Mexico	13,501,851	60.4	20,640,711	58.5
Puerto Rico	2,727,195	12.2	3,406,178	9.6
Cuba	1,050,640	4.7	1,241,685	3.5
Other Hispanics	5,096,725	22.8	10,017,244	28.4
Total	22,354,059	9%	35,305,818	12.5%

Source: Census 2000 Brief on the Hispanic Population, May 2001

When analyzing the Census 2000 data one realizes that the three main Latino subgroups actually decreased in size from the 1990 Census to the one in 2000 (table 2). The total Mexican population decreased by almost 2 percent to 58.5 percent from 60.4 percent in 1990. The percentage of Puerto Ricans was down 2.6 percent to 9.6 percent from 12.2 percent in 1990, and the Cuban population decreased 1.2 percent in 2000 to 3.5 percent from 4.7 percent in 1990. The only group that

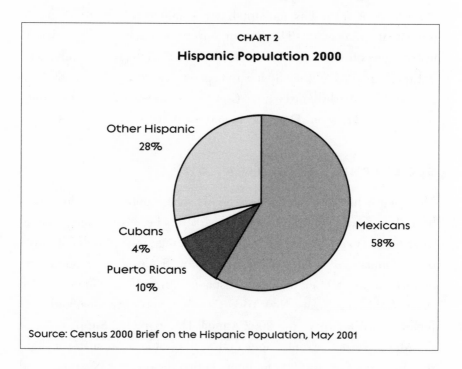

CHART 2

Hispanic Population 2000

Other Hispanic 28%

Cubans 4%

Puerto Ricans 10%

Mexicans 58%

Source: Census 2000 Brief on the Hispanic Population, May 2001

saw an *increase* in this past decade was the "Other Hispanics" group, which nearly doubled in size and now represents almost one-third of all Latinos in the United States.

However, in spite of their relative decline in size among themselves, each "country" group experienced growth rates that far surpassed the 13.2 percent growth rate of the total U.S. population. The number of Mexicans grew by 52.9 percent from 1990 to 2000, Puerto Ricans by 24.9 percent, Cubans by 18.9 percent, and Hispanics of "other origins" by a whopping 96.9 percent!

But perhaps the composition of the Hispanic population actually did not "change" as drastically as these data indicate. I believe that the fact that the Census Bureau allowed respondents to be more specific when identifying themselves actually allowed for certain subgroups to be more appropriately counted than ever before. You see, it wasn't until the last Census that people who marked the box "Other Spanish/ Hispanic/Latino," were able to *specify* their country of origin.

Interestingly, the majority of those who checked that "other" box (17.3 percent of the Hispanic total, or 6.1 million people) opted not to write in anything at all. (The Census Bureau now acknowledges that its instructions on the form were not very clear.) However, of those who did mark the box "Other Spanish/Hispanic/Latino," we know that 4.8 percent identified themselves as Central American, 3.5 percent South American, 2.2 percent Dominican, and 0.3 percent as Spaniards.

GEOGRAPHIC CONCENTRATION

The geographic concentration of the Hispanic population has always been thought of as an advantage for marketers because it enables them to target this market more efficiently. According to the March 2002 Hispanic Population Update published by the U.S. Census Bureau in June of 2003, almost 80 percent of all Hispanics currently live in only seven states: California, Texas, New York, Florida, Illinois, Arizona, and New Jersey. A quick look at the 2002 Annual Demographic Supplement to the March 2002 Current Population Study (table 3) indicates a slight shift from the Census 2000 numbers in two regions: the Northeast and

Region	Total Population 2000	Hispanic % in Region in 2000	Hispanic Population	Hispanic % in Region in 2002
TABLE 3 Hispanic Population by Region				
Northeast	53,594,378	14.9%	5,254,087	13.3%
Midwest	64,392,776	8.8%	3,124,532	7.7%
South	100,236,820	32.8%	11,586,696	34.8%
West	63,197,932	43.5%	15,340,503	44.2%
Total	**281,421,906**	**100%**	**35,305,818**	**100%**

Source: U.S. Census Bureau, Hispanic Population Update, March 2002

the Midwest. By region, the new numbers show that 44.2 percent of Hispanics live in the West, 34.8 percent live in the South, 13.3 percent live in the Northeast, and 7.7 percent live in the Midwest (table 3).

While Hispanics can now be found just about anywhere in the United States, Mexicans, Puerto Ricans, and Cubans are all concentrated in different areas. As would be expected, Mexicans mainly are concentrated in the South (54.6 percent) and the West (34.3 percent), whereas Puerto Ricans are concentrated in the Northeast (58 percent) and Cubans are concentrated in the Southeast (75.1 percent). "Other" Hispanics were found in three of the four regions, with 31.5 percent living in the Northeast, 34 percent living in the South, and 29 percent living in the West. The next page shows a breakdown of the top ten states where Hispanics live in the United States (table 4).

Growth of Latinos in Nontraditional Areas

The astounding growth of the Hispanic population in nontraditional states was one of the big surprises of the 2000 Census. Some experts argue that Hispanic growth in nontraditional areas such as North Carolina and Nevada is fueled by Latinos' willingness to do jobs that others don't want anymore. Others argue that these are safer areas for new immigrants. Either way, the fact is that in Nevada, for example, the Hispanic population grew 144 percent during the 1990s, and in 2000 Latinos accounted for 17 percent of the state's total population. Clark County, home to Las Vegas, saw the highest growth within the state. In North Carolina, Hispanics are settling in metropolitan areas located along the I-85 corridor, where the state has seen most of its employment growth. Counties that

TABLE 4 Top 10 States by Hispanic Population in 2000

State	Total Population	Hispanic Pop.	Percent	Mexican	Puerto Rican	Cuban	Other Hispanic
California	33,871,648	10,966,556	32.4	8,455,926	140,570	72,286	2,297,774
Texas	20,851,820	6,669,666	32	5,071,963	69,504	25,705	1,502,494
New York	18,976,457	2,867,583	15.1	260,889	1,050,293	62,590	1,493,811
Florida	15,982,378	2,682,715	16.8	363,925	482,027	833,120	1,003,643
Illinois	12,419,293	1,530,262	12.3	1,144,390	157,851	18,438	209,583
Arizona	5,130,632	1,295,617	25.3	1,065,578	17,587	5,272	207,180
New Jersey	8,414,350	1,117,191	13.3	102,929	366,788	77,337	570,137
New Mexico	1,819,046	765,386	42.1	330,049	4,488	2,588	428,261
Colorado	4,301,261	735,601	17.1	450,760	12,993	3,701	268,147
Nevada	1,998,257	393,970	19.7	285,764	10.42	11,498	86,288
Puerto Rico*	3,808,610	3,762,746	98.8	11,546	3,623,392	19,973	107,835
United States	281,421,906	35,305,818	12.5	20,640,711	3,406,178	1,241,685	10,017,244

Source: 2000 Census: Brief on the Hispanic Population, May 2001

*I've included Puerto Rico on this list for comparison purposes, but keep in mind that Puerto Rico is *not* included in the U.S. total figure.

are home to North Carolina's military complexes, as well as rural areas, are also seeing growth in their Hispanic communities. Interestingly, the region that experienced the greatest increase in its Hispanic population was the Midwest. Indiana's Hispanic population has seen growth in the regions of the state located closest to Illinois, particularly near Chicago, which has always been a big magnet for Hispanics. Located at the north-western border of Indiana, Lake County now accounts for 13.31 percent of the state's Hispanics. The cities of Gary and East Chicago, Indiana, are both located in Lake County. And finally, in Minnesota, Polk, Kandiyohi, Watonwan, and Freeborn counties suddenly have a high percentage of Hispanic citizens. None of these counties are home to Minnesota's largest cities, however, indicating that Hispanic communities are not only growing in urban areas, but in rural ones as well.

Latinos are Younger

According to the Census Bureau, in 2000, the median age for Hispanics is almost ten years younger than that of the overall U.S. population

CHART 3

U.S. Population Projections: Adults 18 – 34
8 States: AZ, CA, FL, IL, NM, NV, NY, and TX

2001: Total 24.7 million

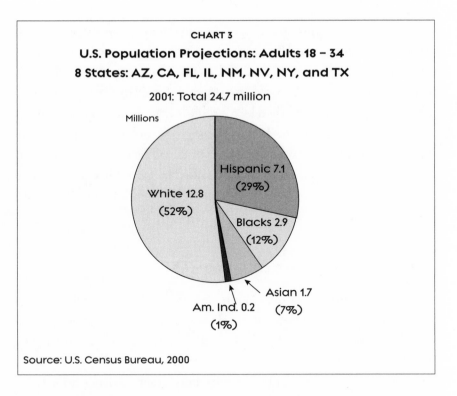

Millions

Hispanic 7.1 (29%)

White 12.8 (52%)

Blacks 2.9 (12%)

Asian 1.7 (7%)

Am. Ind. 0.2 (1%)

Source: U.S. Census Bureau, 2000

(median age of Hispanics was 25.9 versus 35.3 for non-Hispanics), while 34.4 percent of U.S. Latinos were less than 18 years of age, compared to only 22.8 percent of the non-Hispanic white population. Furthermore, a quick analysis of the Census data also shows that if you further focus on the seven states where Latinos concentrate, Hispanic adults 18–34 outnumber their hotly sought after African-American counterparts almost two to one.

According to the U.S. Census Bureau, among Latinos those of Mexican origin are the youngest, with a median age of 24.2 years. They are followed by Puerto Ricans, whose median age is 27.3 years; Central Americans, 29.2 years; Dominicans, 29.5 years; South Americans, 33.1 years; Spaniards, 36.4 years; and Cubans, 40.7 years. But the group to watch out for is definitely Hispanic teenagers. Only now are Hispanic teenagers starting to garner respect and attention from the marketing community, which finally sees them as "trendsetters." Recent Census data indicate that about 20 percent of all teens in the United States are of Hispanic descent and that as a group they spend 4 percent more (an average of $320 a week) than other, non-Hispanic teens. Furthermore, the Hispanic teen (ages 12–18) population is expected to grow 60 percent over the next twenty years compared to only a 10 percent growth for teens overall, according to a study published by Meredith's *American Baby* magazine.

The Hispanic teen market is already $19 billion strong, but the impact of the buying power of Latino youth will be most felt in the next couple of decades as those teenagers enter the labor force and become a larger piece of the key advertising demographic: adults 18 to 34. More about that in chapter 8.

HISPANIC HOUSEHOLD INCOMES

Historically, the Latino population has always been thought of as a "poor" population, but new studies show that, in fact, it is quickly climbing the socioeconomic ladder. According to the Tomás Rivera Policy Institute, the upward mobility of Latinos in the United States is often obscured by the large number of poor immigrants arriving from Latin America, especially Mexico and Puerto Rico. These recent arrivals drag down the overall Hispanic income data and paint a somewhat misleading portrait of the Hispanic consumer.

TABLE 5 Median Household Income by Race				
	2002	*2001*	*2000*	*1999*
White, Non-Hispanic	$46,971	$46,305	$45,623	$44,157
Black	29,483	29,470	29,667	27,910
Hispanic	33,601	33,565	33,168	30,746

Source: Median Income of Households, U.S. Census, 2002

According to the latest Census data, the median household income of Hispanics is $13,000 less than that of non-Hispanic whites and about $4,000 more than that of blacks. However, a study conducted by the Tomás Rivera Policy Institute in the year 2000 found that while the growth of the Hispanic middle class has lagged behind the tremendous expansion of its population, it recorded significant increases over the past two decades. The study, *The Latino Middle Class: Myth, Reality and Potential,* conducted by this nonprofit think tank, showed that while the number of Hispanic households doubled between 1979 and 1998, the number of those in the middle class grew by nearly 80 percent to almost 2.7 million individuals.

Upwardly mobile Latinos have recently become the target of major industries, among them telecommunications companies, car manufacturers, financial institutions, insurance companies, computer manufacturers, and even high-end magazines. After hiring Sonia Maria Green to run its multicultural marketing division in 2003, General Motors launched a multimillion-dollar, multimedia campaign in Spanish-language media to sell high-end vehicles (such as the Hummer) to Latinos in the United States. Although GM does not release exact figures, it is now boasting double-digit increases in car sales to the Latino community, especially to those living in south Florida.

At the height of the Internet boom, a young, enterprising Latino working for Gateway computers asked the president of Gateway stores why the company wasn't going after the growing Hispanic market. The president assumed that they were already reaching Latinos, so he gave Hector Placencia a new job and a challenge: to prove why Gateway should get into this market.

After some internal investigations, Gateway determined that less than 1 percent of its customers were Hispanic. Three years later, the percentage of Latino computer buyers at Gateway stores had increased to nearly 10 percent. "It took six months to build the proper infrastructure," explained Placencia, director of emerging markets/national accounts for Gateway. After the infrastructure was in place, the company invested $250,000 on a "pilot" Spanish-language TV advertising campaign and the response was off the charts. "Results were good enough to increase advertising budgets 100 percent in 2000," said Placencia. But the cornerstone of Gateway's success in the U.S. Hispanic market has been marketing partnerships. In 2000, Placencia signed partnership deals with Univison.com and Procter & Gamble that drove sales even higher. Between 2000 and 2004, Gateway was considered the leader in computer sales to the U.S. Hispanic market. "Right now, my biggest challenge is to continue demonstrating [to my corporate bosses] that this market is one that we need to be in, because often short-term company goals and strategy do not align with the need to continue investing in this market," says Placencia. "It's tougher now than when I sold the concept four years ago," he adds. Unfortunately, in 2005, financial difficulties at Gateway forced a restructuring that included the shut down of its Hispanic marketing efforts. This is one of the most common mistakes made by corporations: not making a real commitment to this market.

Selling to the U.S. Hispanic market does seem to be getting easier. In 2002, the Zoom Media Group launched two high-end magazines geared toward the hard-to-reach, high-spending 25- to 45-year-old Hispanic male with discriminating taste: *Loft* magazine and *Poder* (power). The magazines are already making waves, attracting more readers every day, and, more important, attracting advertisers like Armani, Polo by Ralph Lauren, and, of course, Hummer. In spite of the growing acknowledgment by business and advertising leaders that Latinos are big spenders, the popular perception of this community is still that Hispanics live in poverty, or close to it. When you analyze household income levels of Hispanics by subgroup, you start getting a better picture of the real distribution of household income among Latinos (table 6).

The magic number, of course, is $40,000. That is the figure that defines the "middle class" in the United States, the number that will open the pearly gates of consumerism to this market. According to the

TABLE 6 Household Income by Hispanic Group

Country of Origin	Mean HH Income	Median HH Income
Mexico	$41,500	$32,400
Puerto Rico	$38,900	$30,300
Cuba	$50,250	$40,760
South & Central America	$50,000	$39,000
Other Hispanic	$48,100	$37,520
Total	$43,570	$33,980

Source: Synovate, 2004 U.S. Hispanic Market Report

Tomás Rivera Policy Institute study, in 1998 about 42 percent of U.S.-born Hispanic households fell within the middle class bracket (compared to 60 percent of non-Hispanic whites). Of course, the important thing to note about that last statistic from the Tomás Rivera Policy Institute is that it is 42 percent of *U.S.-born* Hispanics, not 42 percent of the overall Hispanic community. Why is this important? Because U.S.-born Latinos, like many second-generation immigrants, tend to be better educated and more acculturated. They have the capacity to lift their average household income above those of Latinos who are foreign born. The *2002 National Survey of Latinos* conducted by the Pew Hispanic Center/Kaiser Family Foundation that was released in December of that year supports this claim as well, as you can see in table 7, below.

TABLE 7 Household Income by Place of Birth

Household Income	Foreign-born Latinos	Native-born Latinos
Less than $30,000	57%	37%
$30,000–$50,000	20%	28%
$50,000+	11%	27%
Don't know	12%	8%

Source: *2002 National Survey of Latinos*

SHIFT FROM FOREIGN-BORN TO U.S.-BORN LATINOS

The perception in the United States is that the majority of Hispanics are foreign born. While this was true several decades ago, according to the 2002 update to the U.S. Census, only 40.2 percent (or 15 million) of all Hispanics were born outside of the United States. "Among the foreign-born Hispanic population in 2002, 52.1 percent entered the United States between 1990 and 2002. Another 25.6 percent came in the 1980s, and the remainder (22.3 percent) entered before 1980," say the authors of the 2002 Census update. From a marketing perspective, the differences between foreign born Latinos and U.S.-born Latinos are huge and important to keep in mind. In 2004 Synovate estimated that 53 percent of all Hispanics were born outside of the United States, and of those who were foreign born, 74 percent were

TABLE 8 Income Level, by Age, of Foreign-Born Hispanics				
	10 years or younger	*Ages 11–17*	*Ages 18–25*	*Ages 26+*
Less than $30,000	43%	54%	61%	62%
30,000–$50,000	32	19	21	15
$50,000+	23	16	9	4
Don't Know	2	11	9	19

Source: *2002 National Survey of Latinos*

18 years old or older when they immigrated. The Pew Hispanic Center digs down even further and shows how income levels differ among foreign-born Latinos depending on the person's age at the time of immigration to the United States (table 8).

How does this compare to other minority groups? *The Media Audit* annually publishes a syndicated survey that is widely used by marketers in the United States and gives detailed information about consumer behavior in the top eighty-five markets of the United States. The 2001 report from *The Media Audit* shows that 14.3 percent of *urban Hispanic adults* between the ages of 18 and 34 had annual household incomes of $50,000 or more, compared to only 12.7 percent of urban whites or 12.3 percent of urban African-Americans. Although *The Media Audit* does not specifically track whether its Hispanic respondents are U.S. born or foreign born, an educated guess is that there is a high percentage of U.S.-born Latinos in its 18–34 "urban Hispanic adults" group.

HISPANIC BUYING POWER

In spite of its relatively low household income, the Hispanic community's buying power is soaring, giving it the power to influence just about every consumer trend in this country—perhaps even in this hemisphere—from food to clothes and cars. According to the latest estimates by the University of Georgia's Selig Center for Economic Growth, the buying power of Hispanics increased 118 percent from 1990 to the year 2000. In 2002 the buying power of U.S. Hispanics was estimated to be $580.5 billion. The Selig Center data is considered the

TABLE 9 Buying Power by Group ($ Billions)			
	1990	*2002*	*% incr.*
Hispanic	**$223.0**	**$580.5**	**260%**
African American	316.5	645.5	**204%**
Asian American	117.6	296.4	**252%**
Native American	19.3	40.8	**211%**
Non-Hispanic White	3,738.6	6,252.5	**167%**

Source: Selig Center for Economic Growth

most authoritative resource for minority buying power figures in the United States. The center's latest estimate of the U.S. Hispanic buying power was $686 billion in 2004, up 18 percent from its 2002 estimate. That change was attributed to the sharp upward revision of Hispanic population that was shown in the 2000 Census. Now the Selig Center is projecting Hispanic buying power to reach $778 billion by the year 2005 and $992 billion in 2009.

To put this in even better perspective, consider this: 40 million Hispanics in the United States have more buying power than 100 million Mexicans in Mexico! Furthermore, the buying power of the Hispanic community is growing faster than that of any other segment of the population (except Asians, whose buying power, according to the Selig Center, will grow at the same rate as Hispanic buying power), making it a key catalyst for the current and future economic growth of this country. According to the Selig Center, the disposable income of Latinos jumped 29 percent since 2001 to $652 billion in 2003, double the pace of the rest of the population. Chart 4 on disposable income is from Global Insight's "Snapshots of the U.S. Hispanic Market," an ongoing study on the quickly-evolving Hispanic market prepared for NBC and its Spanish-language sister network, Telemundo. Global Insight's projections through 2020 indicate that the disposable income of Latinos in the United States will exceed $2 trillion, much of that growth fueled by a Hispanic market transitioning from working class to middle class. Latinos are aspiring consumers, and that is certainly reflected here!

The Selig Center data are somewhat more conservative and do not project out that far, but they are updated frequently and will give you

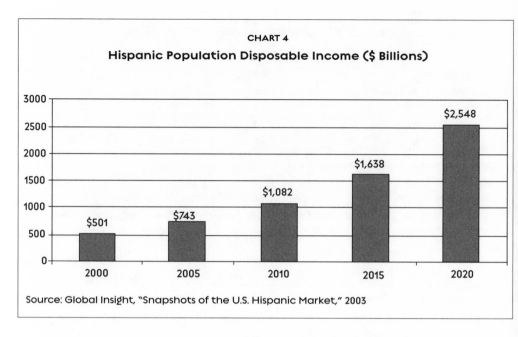

CHART 4
Hispanic Population Disposable Income ($ Billions)

Source: Global Insight, "Snapshots of the U.S. Hispanic Market," 2003

detailed information on all other minority groups as well, broken down by state and a number of other useful variables. Table 10 shows the Selig Center's top ten states with the largest Hispanic buying power. (Note that they are different from the top ten Hispanic Demographic Metropolitan Areas.)

Synovate, one of the leading research companies in the Hispanic market (formerly known as Strategy Research Corporation), also does

TABLE 10 Hispanic Buying Power by State in 2004

Rank	State	$ Billions
1	California	$198.5
2	Texas	119.3
3	Florida	63.7
4	New York	56.6
5	Illinois	31.3
6	New Jersey	26.1
7	Arizona	20.9
8	Colorado	15.0
9	New Mexico	13.7
10	Georgia	10.9

Source: Selig Center for Economic Growth, third quarter 2004

TABLE 11

D.M.A.	Total Population (000)	Hispanic Population (000)	Total HH's (000)	Hispanic HH's (000)	Hispanic Buying Power (Billions)
Los Angeles, CA	17,015.3	7,811.1	5,177.8	2,095.8	$105,047.5
New York, NY	21,005.0	4,316.4	7,356.5	1,334.8	$59,189.7
Miami-Ft. Lauderdale, FL	4,259.8	1,836.8	1,533.6	658.6	$32,926.1
Houston, TX	5,459.2	1,822.6	1,828.0	498.7	$25,072.7
Chicago, IL	9,654.2	1,838.0	3,405.3	476.3	$24,235.2
San Francisco/San Jose, CA	7,013.3	1,491.8	2,574.6	381.3	$20,942.7
Dallas-Ft. Worth, TX	6,427.3	1,509.7	2,145.4	401.7	$20,832.7
San Antonio, TX	2,144.8	1,293.7	733.0	407.8	$17,869.1
Phoenix, AZ	4,443.3	1,208.0	1,482.2	318.8	$16,686.9
San Diego, CA	2,976.5	927.6	1,055.4	240.2	$12,620.6

Source: Synovate, 2004 U.S. Hispanic Market Report

its own calculation of Hispanic buying power, but it does it by Demographic Metropolitan Area, or D.M.A. Table 11 shows Synovate's breakdown for the year 2004.

EDUCATION

The rate at which kids drop out of high school is one of the most alarming and serious challenges facing this country today. This is an issue that affects *all* minority groups, but especially black and Latino kids. According to a special report on the growing Hispanic market entitled *Hispanic Nation, Is America Ready?* published by *BusinessWeek* in March of 2004, the official figures are daunting. "While the Hispanic high-school graduation rate has climbed 12 percentage points since 1980, to 57 percent, that's woefully short of the 88 percent for non-Hispanic Whites and 80 percent for African Americans," says Brian Grow, author of the *BusinessWeek* report. According to *Losing Our Future: How Minority Youth Are Being Left Behind by the Graduation Rate Crisis,* a study published by the Civil Rights Project at Harvard University, those "official" figures are way off. "There is little, or no, state or federal oversight of dropout and graduation rate reports for accuracy. . . . Both the two most commonly used measures—the modified National Center for

Education Statistics (NCES) formula and the Census Bureau Current Population Survey (CPS) data—produce data that often dramatically underestimate the numbers of students who leave school without high school diplomas. . . . Incredibly, some states report a 5 percent dropout rate for African Americans when, in reality, only half of their young adult African Americans are graduating with diplomas." The study concludes that overall "only about 68 percent of all students entering ninth grade will graduate 'on time' with regular diplomas in the twelfth grade. While the average graduation rate for white students is 75 percent, only approximately half of all Black, Hispanic and Native American students earn regular diplomas alongside their classmates."

There are many reasons why Latino young adults drop out of school. "Latinos have long lagged in U.S. schools, in part, because many families remain cloistered in Spanish-speaking neighborhoods. Their strong work ethic can compound the problem by propelling many young Latinos into the workforce before they finish high school," says Brian Grow in his special report. But what worries experts is how to fix the problem and what long-term effect this problem will have on this nation's labor force if this trend continues.

The Pew Hispanic Center/Kaiser Family Foundation's 2002 *National Survey of Latinos* supports the findings of the Civil Rights Project and, once again, helps us understand the nature of the problem by comparing educational levels of foreign-born Latinos to those who are U.S.-born. The results, as you can see in table 12, are very telling.

Data from *The Media Audit* survey, which was conducted between January 2000 and March of 2001 and consisted of 122,000 phone inter-

TABLE 12 Level of Education, Foreign-born Latinos vs. Native-born Latinos		
Level of Education	Foreign-born Latino	Native-born Latinos
Less than High School	55%	23%
High School Graduate	29%	35%
Some College	9%	29%
College graduate or more	7%	13%

Source: *2002 National Survey of Latinos,* Pew Hispanic Center/Kaiser Family Foundation

CHART 5
Hispanics with College Degrees

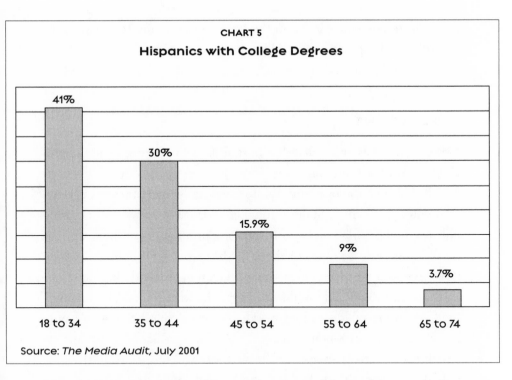

| 18 to 34 | 35 to 44 | 45 to 54 | 55 to 64 | 65 to 74 |

41% · 30% · 15.9% · 9% · 3.7%

Source: *The Media Audit,* July 2001

views in the top eighty-five metropolitan markets in the United States, showed that "urban Hispanic adults" were graduating from college in much greater numbers than those of previous generations. According to *The Media Audit* survey, 18.9 percent of all adult urban Hispanics had a college degree in 2001 and 41 percent of urban Hispanics with degrees were between the ages of 18 and 34.

"Hispanics lose ground—in both affluence and education—as the age group gets older," according to the survey.

The Media Audit survey also showed that only 4.6 percent of Hispanics age 50 or older have annual household incomes of $50,000 or more, while that percentage among the general adult population is 11.6 percent. "The relationship between education, income, and occupation stands out in the survey," says Bob Jordan, co-chairman of the thirty-year-old firm that produces *The Media Audit,* "and this relationship dispels any thought that the increasing affluence among Hispanics is solely attributable to longer hours worked or multiple income households." Jordan is also quick to point out that his company's survey only covers Hispanics living in the top eighty-five metropolitan areas and that the Hispanic community in each of those urban areas is often distinctly different.

EMPLOYMENT

Critics and bigots argue that the constant flow of poorly educated, non-English-speaking immigrants undermines the U.S. economy when, in fact, it does just the opposite. While the number of Latino immigrants who enter the United States—roughly 400,000 every year—is reportedly the highest flow of Spanish-speaking immigrants in the history of the United States, not all of them fit this profile. Of course, most of those who *do* fit this profile are undocumented and therefore not included in the official number of Hispanic immigrants. The reality is that the influx of low-skilled workers in the United States not only keeps gardens and houses clean, these immigrants (regardless of whether they are Hispanic, Asian, or Eastern European) do the jobs nobody else wants to do but everybody needs done. In fact, according to another study by the Pew Hispanic Center, Hispanics accounted for 50 percent of the job growth in the United States between 2000 and 2002, even though they represented only 13 percent of the total population! Adrienne Pulido, contributing editor for research and trends at *Hispanic Market Weekly,* one of the leading Hispanic trade publications, digs further into this phenomenon: "Latinos are fueling the growth of many industries that need young labor to bolster productivity. Cities like Pittsburgh, Cleveland, Portland, Nashville, and Louisville, Kentucky, are trying to attract more immigrants because they do not have enough young people in the labor force to help their economies grow." In her special report, *Hispanic Job Growth Alters the Marketplace,* published in October of 2003, Pulido goes on to say, "The combination of Latino immigration and youth are a lure to business communities that are encouraging Latinos to bring their skilled relatives with them. It has been an open door to Hispanics who were eager to work, prove themselves, and move up the economic ladder. It is also

TABLE 13 Change in Labor Force 16 Years +					
	Change (000)			Percentage Change		
	1980–90	1990–00	2000–10	1980–90	1990–00	2000–10
Hispanic	4,574	4,648	5,579	74.4	43.4	36.3
Black	2,875	2,863	3,439	26.5	20.8	20.7
Asian	2,177	2,034	2,950	87.9	43.7	44.1
White	10,185	5,144	6,155	11.6	5.3	6.0
Total	18,900	15,023	16,858	17.7	11.9	12.0

The "civilian labor force" consists of employed and unemployed persons actively seeking work, but does not include any armed forces personnel. Data is based on latest Current Population Survey, not the 2000 Decennial Census.

a calling-out for growing businesses and communities to prepare for lasting change in the American workforce."

In fact, when it comes to workforce participation, the truth is that Latinos will be replacing baby boomers over the next two decades! According to projections released by the Department of Labor's Bureau of Labor Statistics (BLS) in November of 2003, Hispanics have the highest rate of labor force participation across any race or ethnicity. The BLS estimates that between 2000 and 2010, 16,858,000 more persons over the age of 16 will be added to the U.S. workforce (table 13). Of these, approximately 57 percent (or 9,545,000) will be members of ethnic groups, of which 5,579,000, or 33 percent, will be Hispanic.

In table 14, once again, the Pew Hispanic Center's *National Survey of Latinos* gives us another good look at the breakdown of Latino employment between blue-collar and white-collar jobs, foreign-born and U.S.-born Latinos.

TABLE 14		
Occupation	Foreign-born Latinos	Native-born Latinos
White Collar	31%	69%
Blue Collar	65%	28%
Other	3%	3%

Source: *2002 National Survey of Latinos*

TABLE 15			
Occupation	Spanish-dominant	Bilingual	English-dominant
White Collar	23%	61%	66%
Blue Collar	74%	35%	31%
Other	3%	3%	3%

Source: *2002 National Survey of Latinos*

When the Pew Hispanic Center drills down even further to examine occupation by language (which I will get into shortly), you again see the stark differences between Hispanics who are Spanish-dominant and those who are bilingual or English-dominant (table 15).

Where Latinos are still most invisible is in corporate America. But hopefully that too will change as more executives like you learn to understand the importance of having Latinos in senior management positions and sitting around the boardroom.

LENGTH OF RESIDENCY IN THE UNITED STATES

Length of residency in the United States is one of the key factors you must keep in mind when addressing this market. Although it varies from person to person, length of residency has become a good proxy for the level of acculturation and language preferences your target market may have. The less time Hispanics have been in the United States, the less acculturated they are and the more Spanish-dominant they tend to be. A good rule of thumb is that a person must be in the United States between five and ten years to become acculturated. There's one huge caveat to that last statement. The speed with which they acculturate depends on many different factors, such as where they are living (in a densely Hispanic neighborhood or not), what their educational background is, their age at the time of immigration, whether they are in school or not, etc. So acculturation will vary from person to person. But level of acculturation will be a key indicator of how to approach your target market.

According to Synovate's 2004 U.S. Hispanic Market Report, the average length of residency of foreign-born Hispanics is fifteen years.

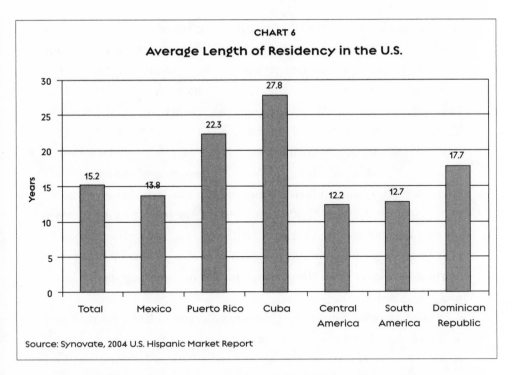

CHART 6

Average Length of Residency in the U.S.

Source: Synovate, 2004 U.S. Hispanic Market Report

Not surprisingly, the two groups with the longest length of residency in the United States are Cubans and Puerto Ricans. Chart 6 illustrates what we already know, that the most recent Latino immigrants are of Central or South American descent, including Mexico. Dominicans constitute the latest wave of immigration from the Caribbean.

LANGUAGE PREFERENCE

Language usage and preference is perhaps the most controversial of all the key factors you must understand when addressing the Hispanic market, since it goes to the core of how to speak to your consumer. A word of caution is necessary here. Much of the research that exists about the Hispanic market is sponsored by or paid for by companies who have a vested interest in Spanish-language media. The truth is that Spanish-language television networks, Spanish-language radio stations, and Hispanic advertising agencies that depend on Spanish-language advertising for growth and survival have, for decades, funded the majority of the research that currently exists about the Hispanic market, including most of the studies I am quoting in this book. Their motivation, of course, is to demonstrate to mainstream advertisers the power of reaching Hispanics through their native language. And their efforts have paid off. Hispanic media companies, like Univision and Telemundo, are the darlings of Wall Street today mainly because they are the only media companies that have experienced double-digit growth in this difficult economy. Not surprisingly, their research studies tend to skew toward Spanish-language dominance and preference. While Spanish-dominant Latinos are certainly an important group, they are certainly not the ONLY group worth reaching in the Hispanic market. Today, a growing number of marketers and media companies are starting to acknowledge the growing importance of English-dominant and bilingual Latinos.

Unlike all other immigrant groups who come to the United States, Hispanics have been able to hold on to their native language for a longer period of time. There are many reasons why Latinos have been able to preserve the Spanish language in this English-speaking country. One is the proximity of their homelands and the ease with which they can travel back and forth. Technology has also made staying in touch easier. And let's not forget the critical role a vibrant and growing mix of Spanish-language media has played in keeping Spanish alive. Although many other immigrant groups created media outlets, some of which still survive today, Latinos are the only minority group in the United States that has three national television networks, and now more than sixty cable networks available in Spanish twenty-four hours a day, seven days a week. And that's only counting the television industry! In addition, there are more than 600 Spanish-language radio stations nationwide, thousands of newspapers and magazines, and countless numbers of online sites.

How to measure language usage and preference is where the debate on language gets ugly. This is the statistic you will see vary the most often from study to study, mainly because there is no one way of defining language preference and usage. In July of 2003, the U.S. Census Bureau released its data on "language usage" by household. Based on the number of persons five years of age and older counted in the 2000

Census, there are 10.8 million households in the United States where Spanish is spoken (at least some of the time). Of those almost 11 million households, 24 percent—roughly 2.5 million—are linguistically "isolated," meaning everybody in the household over the age of 14 has some difficulty speaking English. For the first time, the Census also broke down language usage and ability between foreign-born Latinos and U.S.-born Latinos (table 16). Keep in mind that the U.S. Census Bureau counts the 3.8 million Puerto Ricans who live on the island as "Native Born," which in my opinion slightly skews the Spanish language usage because Puerto Ricans are mainly Spanish-dominant.

TABLE 16				
Language ability	Native Born		Foreign Born	
Speak Spanish	14,760,788	100%	13,340,264	100%
Speak English "very well"	10,598,734	72%	3,751,062	28%
Speak English "well"	2,631,784	18%	3,187,624	24%
Speak English "not well"	1,313,595	9%	3,816,895	29%
Speak English "not at all"	216,765	1%	2,584,683	19%

Source: U.S. Census Bureau ST4, July 2003

In its *2002 National Survey of Latinos,* the Pew Hispanic Center asked respondents a series of questions about their language ability. In particular, the 3,000 Hispanic respondents who were included in this study were asked about their "ability to carry on conversations" and their "ability to read" in both English and Spanish. According to their answers to a series of questions on language, Latinos were grouped into three categories: Spanish-dominant, English-dominant, or Bilingual, with the following results (table 17):

TABLE 17	
Primary Language	Percentage Among Latino Adults
English-Dominant	25%
Bilingual	28%
Spanish-Dominant	47%

Source: *2002 National Survey of Latinos*

The Pew Hispanic Center also asked its respondents to identify themselves as foreign born or U.S. born, but contrary to the Census, it put Puerto Ricans in the "foreign-born" column because, like immigrants from Latin America, Puerto Ricans grow up in a Spanish-dominant culture. When you break down language usage by this criteria, you see that language usage varies widely from the overall figures quoted on page 37 (table 18).

TABLE 18		
Primary Language	Foreign-born Latinos	Native-born Latinos
English-Dominant	4%	61%
Bilingual	24%	35%
Spanish-Dominant	72%	4%

Source: *2002 National Survey of Latinos*

Yet another perspective on language comes from Synovate, which tracks language usage by the person's surroundings: at home, at work, or with friends. According to Synovate, the most important measure for language fluency is the person's comfort speaking in a certain language, and their 2004 survey finds that 67 percent of all Hispanics feel most comfortable speaking Spanish. So you see, the question is quite complex.

Language is also heavily tied in to culture and therefore identity. By keeping their language alive in the United States, Latinos also keep their culture alive. In his book, *The Rise of the Hispanic Market in the United States*, Louis E. V. Nevaer espouses the idea that Hispanics, in fact, "self segregate" linguistically as a means of keeping their distance from American cultural values they may disagree with. We will get deeper into the issues of language and culture in chapter 5, but I think it is safe to say that America is already becoming a bilingual nation, which is a good thing both for this country and for the nations in this hemisphere. Keep in mind that by 2025, 50 percent of all the consumers *in the Americas* will speak Spanish. Most Americans do not realize what a double standard they live by when they demand that English be spoken everywhere they go in the world, but won't allow other languages to be spoken in their own backyard. As Nevaer cor-

ARE THERE SPANISH DIALECTS?

By Roberto Ruiz, Partner Consumer Contacts

A question that many clients ask frequently is what is our agency's point-of-view on Spanish *dialects,* and specifically how to handle this issue in communicating with the U.S. Hispanic market. We all know that Hispanics in the United States are a heterogeneous mix of people from Mexican, Caribbean and Central and South American origins. The issue arises when someone points out that different countries use different "dialects," and asks whether an ad should be written in that specific "dialect."

The idea of considering the Spanish spoken in Mexico as a "dialect" is shocking to me, as it is equivalent to saying that American English is a dialect. According to Webster's dictionary, a dialect is: "*A regional or social variety of a language distinguished by pronunciation, grammar, or vocabulary, especially a variety of speech differing from the standard literary language or speech pattern of the culture in which it exists: Cockney is a dialect of English.*"*

If we follow this definition it would be possible to have many dialects of Spanish. However, the definition is vague in terms of how much variation is needed to qualify for the term. As Webster's was of little help, I contacted other experts. Mila Ramos-Santacruz, who holds a doctorate in linguistics from Georgetown University, gave me some good advice. She explains that the word "dialect" has political connotations because it subordinates one language to another; hence the term is seldom used. Also, from a linguistic perspective, the Spanish language is an absolute reference that nobody actually uses. What people use are local variations of the language. Thus Mexican Spanish, Argentine Spanish, etc., are all local variations of Spanish, as opposed to dialects of it. For example, in Mexico a bus is called *camión,* a word that in other Latin countries means "truck."

From a communications perspective we recommend using a variation-free Spanish when targeting the whole market. In those cases where

*Source: The American Heritage® Dictionary of the English Language, 4th Edition Copyright © 2000 by Houghton Mifflin Company

marketers are trying to reach a specific segment, say people of Mexican origin, using terms that are exclusive to this group can make the message stronger by striking a chord of familiarity and generating a more emotional bond. However, in those cases, one has to be careful in their choice of words so as not to alienate or insult other groups by using words that may have different meanings or interpretations. In any case, we all have to be sensitive to using the Spanish language in a way that preserves its integrity but reaches our target consumer. After all, Spanish is the strongest link that unites this community, and if we damage it, we will weaken our cultural bond forever.

rectly points out, "In the debate over the surreptitious spread of Spanish in the United States at a time when English is spreading in other countries, there are unintended, but delicious ironies."

THE THREE GROUPS: ISOLATED, ACCULTURATED, AND ASSIMILATED

In addition to country of origin, U.S. Latinos can also be divided into three main groups that differ in terms of level of acculturation and language usage or preference. Spanish-dominant Latinos, the group most Americans put all Hispanics in, actually only represent about 35 percent of the total Hispanic population. This group of Latinos is also considered "isolated," in the sense that they do not know English well enough to function in that language and must depend on Spanish-language media in the United States for their survival. "Isolated" Latinos are made up of both recent immigrants who are relatively young and older immigrants who have been living here for decades. While these two very distinct segments make up the community of "isolated" Latinos, they are united by their lack of English-language proficiency. They are not to be confused with many older Latinos, like my parents, who speak English perfectly well, but *prefer* to watch TV or read the newspaper in Spanish. This "isolated" group tends to skew older than the Latino average and will always constitute an important part of the

Latino community because of the constant flow of Spanish-speaking immigrants to the United States.

In my opinion the most important group of Latinos in the United States is also, curiously, the most ignored. "Acculturated" Latinos are younger, more educated, and bicultural. Currently, they represent any-where between 30 percent and 60 percent of all Hispanics in the United States, depending on how you define "acculturated." Synovate has been tracking acculturation trends for decades, and as you can see on chart 7 these trends have changed over time. Acculturated Latinos are the fastest growing group among Hispanics, and they are distin-guished by their comfort in navigating between both English and Span-ish language and cultures. "Acculturated," or bilingual Latinos, also tend to be highly concentrated in urban areas. They definitely consume media in both languages, but in terms of reading and writing, if they are U.S. born, they tend to *prefer* English, their Spanish being more con-versational (and usually grammatically poor) than anything else.

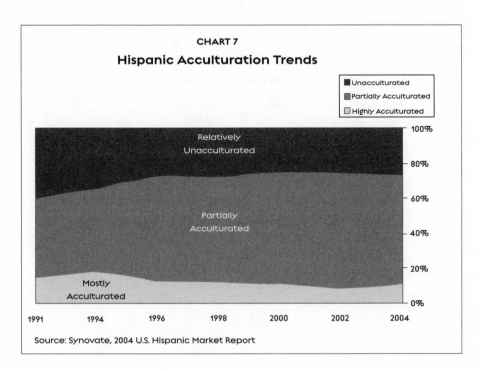

CHART 7
Hispanic Acculturation Trends

- Unacculturated
- Partially Acculturated
- Highly Acculturated

Relatively Unacculturated

Partially Acculturated

Mostly Acculturated

100%
80%
60%
40%
20%
0%

1991 1994 1996 1998 2000 2002 2004

Source: Synovate, 2004 U.S. Hispanic Market Report

The last group of Latinos, which accounts for the remaining 10 percent to 20 percent of the population, are the "assimilated" Latinos who have been here for generations but who may still have a Hispanic surname. Although they barely speak any Spanish at all, they are proud to identify themselves culturally as Hispanics. These are the Latinos who have assimilated into the mainstream and are as American as apple pie, even though they may still eat *arroz con pollo*.

FOREIGN-BORN VERSUS U.S.-BORN LATINOS

As you have already seen throughout this chapter, the differences between foreign-born Latinos and their U.S.-born brethren can be striking. In addition to those differences, many marketers would argue that people who are foreign born behave differently as consumers from those who are not. While this is definitely true of all immigrant groups, an important factor to keep in mind here is at what age did you emigrate? You can be a foreign-born Latino who emigrated at age five and, as the Pew Hispanic Center study finds, you are no different, as a con-

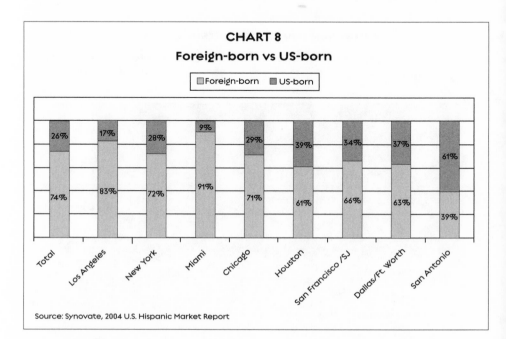

CHART 8
Foreign-born vs US-born

Foreign-born ■ US-born

	Total	Los Angeles	New York	Miami	Chicago	Houston	San Francisco /SJ	Dallas/Ft. Worth	San Antonio
Foreign-born	26%	17%	28%	9%	29%	39%	34%	37%	61%
US-born	74%	83%	72%	91%	71%	61%	66%	63%	39%

Source: Synovate, 2004 U.S. Hispanic Market Report

sumer, from any other U.S.-born Latino. But if you are a foreign-born Latino who emigrated at age 25, then you will definitely behave differently as a consumer here in the United States. The foreign-born incidence among Latinos varies widely from market to market. Here's a look at the top eight Hispanic markets.

According to chart 8 from Synovate, 91 percent of Latinos in Miami are foreign born versus only 39 percent of Latinos in San Antonio, so hard and fast rules don't apply nationwide. Because each product is different, you may have to make adjustments to your marketing campaigns, depending on your goals and your target market.

Does the fact that many Latinos are foreign born affect their knowledge of American brands? Yes and no. While some brands, like Coca-Cola and Levi's, have global recognition, it was not uncommon for big American companies to change their brand name abroad in order for their product to better penetrate certain markets. In Spain, for example, Pampers are called "Do-dots," but if you are Venezuelan, you know Pampers as "Arruchaditos." In the 1980s and 90s, a common practice for companies such as Procter & Gamble, Unilever, and Colgate-Palmolive, was to acquire the leading local packaged-goods company in each country they were penetrating and adopt the name of the leading brand in those countries. As a result, Tide is known as "Ace" in Mexico, but as "Ariel" in Venezuela and Spain. At the time it made sense to do this, but now that global communications have made our world smaller and global brands strong, that practice is changing.

How do you talk to specific demographic groups within the Hispanic market with one voice and one message? Is it possible? Absolutely. You just have to know your target market very well. My advice to you is to do your own research. Sure it costs a bit more, but it will give you the answers you need to address the specific needs of your specific product. Research is invaluable!

3

~~~~~

THE PERFECT MARKET

As a group, Hispanics are a marketer's dream come true. Latinos are highly concentrated in a few urban areas, which makes them easy to reach. They are much younger than their non-Hispanic counterparts. The median age of Hispanics is 25.9 years while the median age for the entire population is 35.3 years. Hispanics are also famous for being brand loyal and big spenders. The Hispanic market's buying power is currently estimated at more than $686 billion and is expected to more than double over the next ten years. The economic clout of the Hispanic market comes both from its larger households (Hispanics in the United States have an average of 3.63 persons per household versus 2.56 persons for non-Hispanic households) and its tendency to buy more of everything from groceries to fashion, accessories, and cars. The relative youthfulness of our population is another eye-opener. Again, according to recently released Census Bureau figures, 34.4 percent of all Hispanics are under 18 years of age, compared to only 22.8 percent of the U.S. population. When you compare the total number of adults 18–34, the so-called Generation X, you'll see that Hispanics within this group, known as Generation Ñ, are the second-largest group in terms of size, but the largest proportionately (chart 9).

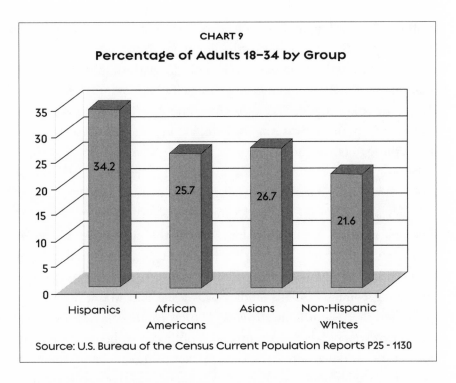

CHART 9

Percentage of Adults 18–34 by Group

Hispanics: 34.2
African Americans: 25.7
Asians: 26.7
Non-Hispanic Whites: 21.6

Source: U.S. Bureau of the Census Current Population Reports P25 - 1130

UNIFIERS AND DIFFERENTIATORS

The big question for corporate America is can the U.S. Hispanic population be treated as one group? Its power lies in its numbers, but does it have enough *in common* to be spoken to as one group? In its executive summary of the 2002 *National Survey of Latinos,* Roberto Suro, the director of the Pew Hispanic Center/Kaiser Family Foundation, says that the Hispanic community is "neither monolithic nor a hodge-podge of distinct national origin groups. Latinos share a range of attitudes and experiences that set them apart from the non-Hispanic population." The last chapter showed you how different Latinos are from their non-Hispanic counterparts. Now let's talk about what they share in common. Whether they are predominantly Spanish or English speaking, Latinos share a very defined culture, rich in family values, customs, and traditions that come from our "motherland," Spain, and the religious teachings of Roman Catholic Church. That rich cultural history dates back more than 500 years. That it remains alive and well in the United States of America should be no surprise to anyone.

Academics and researchers have come up with different "models" that demonstrate the cultural traits that unify Latinos and differentiate Hispanics from Anglos. The ideas and cultural beliefs of Hispanics are different from those most Anglos share, but in some cases may be similar to those of other minority groups. The emphasis on family life; their relationship to work, peer groups, extended family; and their expectations of government and religious institutions are markedly different for Hispanics than they are for Anglos (or as the Census refers to you, non-Hispanic whites). M. Isabel Valdés, one of the pioneering experts in marketing to Hispanics, was the first to highlight these broad cultural differences between Hispanics and Anglos based on numerous national marketing communications studies which she and Marta Seone first published in 1995 in their *Hispanic Market Handbook. The Hispanic Market Handbook* was Valdes' first book of three that became the bible for anyone working in the Hispanic market in the past ten years (see table 19). Valdes herself is the first to acknowledge that broad cultural generalizations do not address important issues of socio-economic classes among Hispanics and that these charts are only basic models, or the minimum set needed to facilitate comprehension of complex issues. These models were designed with corporate, not-for-profit, and marketing communications managers in mind to help them to move to action. Her early studies demonstrate that there are distinct cultural traits and attitudes that differentiate Latinos from Anglos. In fact, the *2002 National Survey of Latinos* conducted by the Pew Hispanic Center confirms that some of these broad cultural traits, such as pessimism and distrust of institutions, do exist.

In addition to these cultural traits, Latinos share a set of common experiences as immigrants to the United States, such as learning English, learning how the school system works, learning how to get around, becoming citizens, and sharing in the "American dream."

The importance of the shared Spanish language cannot be underestimated either. It has been, and will continue to be, one of the key unifying factors among Latinos in this hemisphere. Yes, there are many

TABLE 19

Broad Cultural Differences Between Hispanics and the American Middle Class

Hispanics	Anglos
Group oriented ("for my family")	Self oriented ("for me")
Larger families	Smaller families
Lean toward collectivism	Lean toward individualism
Success means family, group satisfaction	Success means personal possessions, individual satisfaction
Stress hierarchies, social class, social stratification, interdependence	Stress equality, "equal rights," democracy, authority symmetrical relationships, individual autonomy
Believe in fate: pessimists	Believe in self-determination: optimists
Accept delayed gratification	Look for immediate gratification
"High touch," physical closeness, hugging, affectionate	"High tech," more physically distant
Spontaneous	Planners
Overt emotions are part of culture	Hiding emotions is encouraged
Pay careful attention to clothing, appearance	Far more relaxed about clothing, appearance
Longer social protocols, indirect	Brief, to the point, direct
Adapt to environment	Change environment
Low reliance on institutions	High reliance on institutions
Value highly personal or personalized service	Value fast, efficient service at arm's length
Appreciate being given all the needed time (the more the better) when interacting with service providers	Appreciate efficiency, to the point
Tend to prefer prestige brands	Less likely to prefer prestige brands
Stress cooperation, participation, being part of a group	Stress competition, achievement, motivation, self-competence
Doctors and any established source of authority are respected and trusted and never questioned	Doctors and other established sources of authority may be respected and trusted but are often questioned
Relaxed about time	Adhere to schedules

Source: M. Isabel Valdes, 2000, "Marketing to American Latinos, A Guide to the In-Culture Approach." Part 1, Figure 4.2 (pg. 42) Paramount Market Publishing, Inc., Ithaca, NY.

different "kinds" of Spanish, but they all come from the mother tongue, the language of Spain and Cervantes. As a consultant I always tell my clients to be careful about the kind of Spanish they use in their marketing messages so as not to alienate any one particular group. You see, the differences between Mexican Spanish and Argentine Spanish are not unlike those between British English, Australian English, and American English. (And then there is *Spanglish,* the collision of Spanish with English that was born in this country and is now spreading around the world, but that's a whole other story I'll save for another time.) The question of whether there is a "universal" Spanish that can work with this market has already been answered and the answer is, yes, of course there is!

When we were launching the first issue of *People en Español,* the editorial team was comprised of Mexicans, Cubans, Puerto Ricans, and Spaniards. Now I can laugh about it, but it was such an important moment for the Spanish-language publishing industry that we practically drove ourselves crazy trying to find a common language that everyone agreed would work. With time, the task became easier and easier, but we used to have huge blow outs over what words or expressions to use in headlines for fear that they wouldn't be generally understood. The same is true with Spanish-language television. Although you will find TV personalities hailing from many different Latin American countries, (news anchor Jorge Ramos is from Mexico, game-show host Don Francisco is from Chile, and talk show host Cristina Saralegui is from Cuba), they all speak a neutral Spanish that all Hispanics understand. If you hire Latino professionals, they'll find the right language to use for your product and your target market.

Even though Latinos come from different countries, for different reasons (as we have seen, some come for social reasons, others for political or economic reasons), they are *all* treated in the same way once they get to the United States. That shared immigrant experience forms a very strong bond among U.S. Hispanics as well. Another unifier comes by simply living in America. As Spanish-speaking immigrants, Latinos are faced with the challenge of learning a new language and learning how to live in a different "culture." As a result, they become *bicultural* as well as *bilingual*. The more they acculturate, the more they straddle the two worlds: usually the American world for school and work; and the Spanish world and language for time at home with friends and family. These bicultural experiences are especially marked for the younger, first-generation kids, who are born, educated, and are coming of age in this country but who often live in households with Spanish-dominant, foreign-born parents. Often, these younger kids become the interpreters and negotiators for the rest of the family. In the end, however, like all the other immigrant groups that come to America, Latinos simply want to fulfill their American Dream. They want to work enough to be able to send money home, live in a good house, and send their children to schools that will provide them with the best possible education so that they can do better for themselves in their own lives.

It is *how* Latinos behave that distinguishes them as a unique consumer group. "In many ways they are distinctive from the general population and from other minority groups," says Bob Jordan, co-chairman of International Demographics. For example, he says, "They share the American love for the automobile, but there are variations in what they buy. They are more likely to buy vans, trucks, and sport-utility vehicles than cars." International Demographics produces comprehensive audience profiles in a publication called *The Media Audit*, which provides quantitative and qualitative data that has been used by media companies over the past thirty years.

THE HISPANIC CONSUMER MARKET

The Hispanic consumer market is one of the fastest-growing segments of the U.S. economy. Total consumption spending reached $531 billion in 2002—up more than 50 percent over the five prior years, according to a Global Insight study conducted for NBC/Telemundo in 2003. That study also states that the Hispanic population accounted for just under 8 percent of total consumer expenditures in the United States during

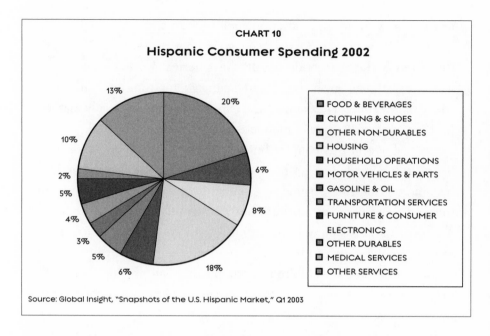

CHART 10

Hispanic Consumer Spending 2002

- FOOD & BEVERAGES
- CLOTHING & SHOES
- OTHER NON-DURABLES
- HOUSING
- HOUSEHOLD OPERATIONS
- MOTOR VEHICLES & PARTS
- GASOLINE & OIL
- TRANSPORTATION SERVICES
- FURNITURE & CONSUMER ELECTRONICS
- OTHER DURABLES
- MEDICAL SERVICES
- OTHER SERVICES

Source: Global Insight, "Snapshots of the U.S. Hispanic Market," Q1 2003

2002. The average disposable income per household was $56,431, or 77 percent of the average for all U.S. households. So, where and how do Hispanics spend their money? Chart 10 gives you a snapshot of Hispanic consumer spending for 2002.

Now, let's take a look at other snapshots Global Insight has prepared for specific industries to get a sense of how Hispanic consumer spending compares to that of the general market. It would be impossible to cover all the industries in this little book. So if you are interested in other industries that are not listed here, go to the resource guide where you will find all the research companies working in this market. Visit their websites and see if they may have some syndicated research that you could buy to help you out. There's more and more research on this market available every day!

Automotive Industry

Obviously, auto sales are a key driver of the U.S. economy—no pun intended. According to Global Insight, Hispanic consumers accounted for $18.7 billion or a 7.8 percent share of the $239 billion new car and light truck sales in 2002. "New car spending by the Hispanic population

TABLE 20 Overall Forecast of Automotive Market 1997–2012

	1997	2002	2007	2012
Total (Billions)	$155.6	$238.9	$249.6	$284.5
Hispanic (Billions)	$9.5	$18.7	$23.7	$31.6
% Hispanic	6.1	7.8	9.5	11.1

Source: Global Insight, "Snapshots of the U.S. Hispanic Market," Q1 2003

is supported by strong, fundamental demographic trends of particular importance to the automotive industry—household incomes that are growing faster than the national average and large household sizes. Larger families orient their purchases toward larger vehicles and are more frequent purchasers," says Global Insight.

Global Insight also found that Hispanic consumers are very loyal buyers. From 1998 to 2000, Hispanics ranked number one in brand loyalty, and were twice as likely to buy the same brand of vehicle for their next purchase as was the average consumer. In addition, Hispanics showed the second-highest percentage of dealer loyalty. Taken together, these statistics suggest that Hispanics could easily be buyers for life!

TABLE 21 Brand and Dealer Preferences

Ethnic Group	Brand Loyalty	Dealer Loyalty
Hispanic	**68.3% (1)**	**40.9% (2)**
African American	60.4% (3)	27.6% (4)
Asian	64.4% (2)	59.0% (1)
Caucasian	23.2% (4)	31.9% (3)
Average	34.4%	33.8%

Source: Global Insight, "Snapshots of the U.S. Hispanic Market," Q1 2003

Motion Picture Ticket Sales

According to the Motion Picture Association of America, the share of Hispanics in all motion picture admissions grew from 11 percent in 1998 to 15 percent in 1999 and remained at 15 percent through 2001. This is not surprising given the age profile of the Hispanic population, which is disproportionately young, making Hispanics a prime source of growth for this industry. Global Insight estimates that in 2002, Hispanic moviegoers accounted for $1.4 billion of the $9.5 billion in movie ticket sales.

TABLE 22 Overall Forecast of Motion Picture Market 1997–2012				
	1997	2002	2007	2012
Total (Billions)	$7.0	$9.5	$12.4	$16.1
Hispanic (Billions)	$0.7	$1.4	$2.0	$2.9
% Hispanic	10.7	15.0	16.0	18.0

Source: Global Insight, "Snapshots of the U.S. Hispanic Market"

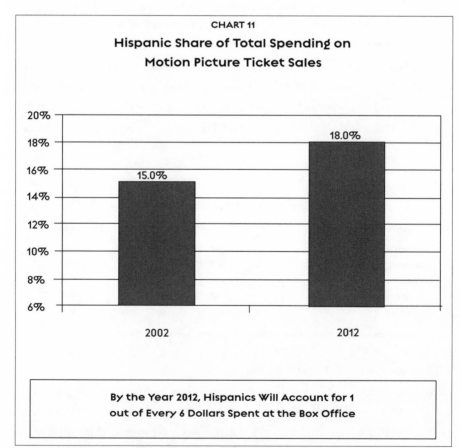

CHART 11

Hispanic Share of Total Spending on Motion Picture Ticket Sales

By the Year 2012, Hispanics Will Account for 1 out of Every 6 Dollars Spent at the Box Office

Source: Global Insight, "Snapshots of the U.S. Hispanic Market"

The Hispanic market will grow by 36 percent over the next ten years versus a 6 percent growth rate for the non-Hispanic population. As a result, Hispanic revenue at the box office will grow by $1.5 billion over the next ten years. Yet Hollywood studios continue to ignore the Hispanic market to a large degree, not only on-screen but also in its advertising. Exact figures to demonstrate how much money Hollywood studios are allocating to Spanish-language media are hard to come by, but anecdotally I can assure you that it was only in the past few years that Hollywood movie studios started advertising their movies on Spanish-language television and radio networks.

Consumer Electronics

"Even in the robust area of retailing like consumer electronics, sales to the Hispanic population lead the way," said Global Insight in 2003. "With spending propensities that lead Hispanics to spend more per household on audio equipment, telephones, and other core products of Consumer Electronics Stores, we estimate that Electronics Store sales to the Hispanic population grew 13.4% per year over the last five years (compared with 8.6% for non-Hispanic sales). Hispanic consumers spent $4.7 billion out of a total of $50.3 billion at Electronics Stores in 2002—accounting for 9.3% of total sales."

According to Global Insight, the Hispanic market will steadily outperform the non-Hispanic market over the next ten years with annual average growth rates of 10.6 percent versus 7.7 percent for non-Hispanics. By 2012, Global Insight calculates that the total share of Hispanic sales in consumer electronic stores will increase to 12 percent.

TABLE 23 Overall Forecast of Consumer Electronics Sales, 1997–2012

	1997	2002	2007	2012
Total (Billions)	$32.7	$50.3	$73.0	$108.5
Hispanic (Billions)	$2.5	$4.7	$7.9	$12.9
% Hispanic	7.7	9.3	10.8	11.9

Source: Global Insight, "Snapshots of the U.S. Hispanic Market"

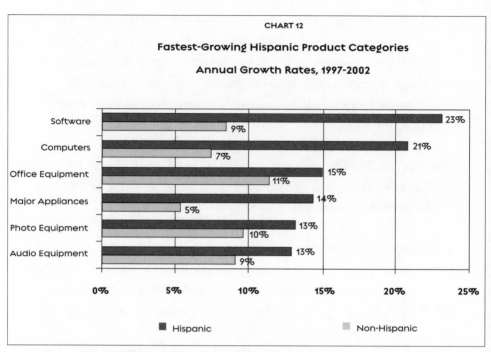

CHART 12

Fastest-Growing Hispanic Product Categories

Annual Growth Rates, 1997-2002

Source: Global Insight, "Snapshots of the U.S. Hispanic Market"

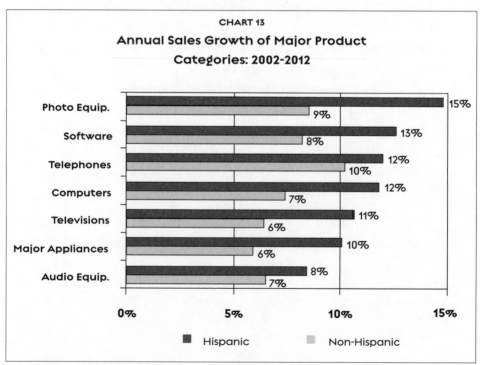

CHART 13

Annual Sales Growth of Major Product Categories: 2002-2012

Source: Global Insight, "Snapshots of the U.S. Hispanic Market"

These calculations are derived from trend projections of the relationship between spending per household for both Hispanic and non-Hispanic households in individual product categories. "Clearly Hispanic spending patterns will determine the success or failure of many youth-oriented products and services," says the Selig Center in its 2004 Third-Quarter Report.

Clothing and Shoe Stores

Given their relative youth and the larger family sizes, it is not surprising that Hispanics over-index in spending for many apparel items, especially children's clothing and footwear. According to Global Insight, purchases by Hispanic households in all types of clothing and shoe stores totaled $15 billion in 2002, which was 10.2 percent of these retailers' total sales. Purchases by non-Hispanics in all types of clothing and shoe stores totaled $132 billion in 2002.

"We expect growth in the combined sales of all Clothing and Shoe Stores to Hispanics to average 6.7% per year over the next ten years—nearly double the 3.5% annual rate for sales to the non-Hispanic popu-

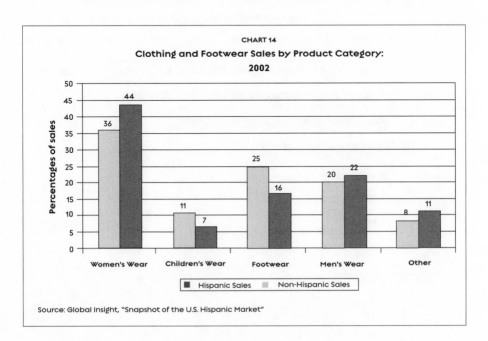

CHART 14

Clothing and Footwear Sales by Product Category:

2002

Percentages of sales

Women's Wear — 36 / 44
Children's Wear — 11 / 7
Footwear — 25 / 16
Men's Wear — 20 / 22
Other — 8 / 11

Hispanic Sales   Non-Hispanic Sales

Source: Global Insight, "Snapshot of the U.S. Hispanic Market"

lation," concludes Global Insight in its report for NBC/Telemundo. "As a result, the Hispanic share of Clothing and Shoe Store sales will rise to 13.2% in 2012, from 10.2% in 2002."

Home Improvement Stores

Hispanic households spend 30 percent more than the national average on hardware and tools, according to Global Insight's study of 2003. This study also indicates that Hispanics over-index on lumber and building materials as well, in spite of having lower home ownership rates. "We estimate that the combined sales of Home Improvements Stores to the Hispanic population totaled $9 billion, accounting for 9.4% of the total $95.8 billion in 2002. The do-it-yourself tendencies of the Hispanic population are the driving force behind a strong outlook for Home Center Sales over the next ten years. Hispanic spending will increase at a 10% annual rate while sales to the non-Hispanic population will average a 6.8% annual growth. The growth of sales to the

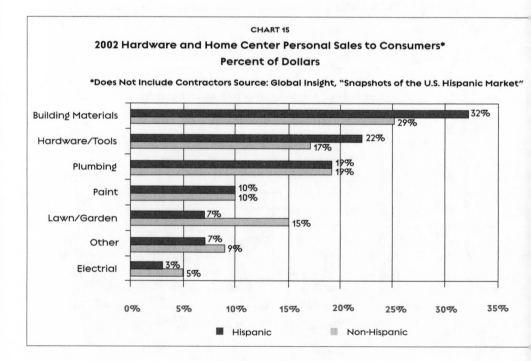

CHART 15
2002 Hardware and Home Center Personal Sales to Consumers*
Percent of Dollars

*Does Not Include Contractors Source: Global Insight, "Snapshots of the U.S. Hispanic Market"

Hispanic population will exceed non-Hispanic sales in all three components of Home Improvement Stores: Home Center sales, Hardware Stores and sales to professional contractors." Between 1995 and 2001, Latino households increased their spending on remodeling by 78 percent according to housing studies conducted by Harvard University in 2003.

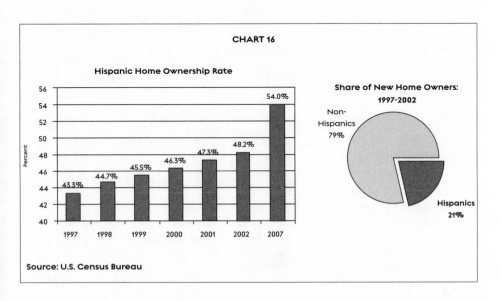

CHART 16

Hispanic Home Ownership Rate

Share of New Home Owners: 1997-2002

Source: U.S. Census Bureau

And according to the U.S. Census, from 1997 to 2002 Hispanics represented 21 percent of new home owners. By 2007 the Census Bureau projects that 54 percent of all Hispanics in the United States will be home owners, up from 48 percent in 2002 and 2004!

HOW DO WE COMPARE?

To give you a few more quick reference points as to how all this data on the Hispanic consumers compares to that of non-Hispanic whites and African Americans, here are a few charts that broadly compare some product usage and activities by group.

TABLE 24

Household Product	Hispanic	General Market	African American
Cable or Satellite/Digital TV	72%	85%	76%
DVD Player	52%	60%	60%
Video Game System	48%	37%	49%
PDA	10%	14%	11%
Computer at Home	49%	74%	59%
Internet Access at Home	36%	66%	47%
Cell Phone	61%	65%	68%

Source: Synovate, 2004 U.S. Hispanic Market Report

TABLE 25

Financial Services Use	Hispanic	General Market	African American
Savings or Checking Account	69%	97%	81%
Retirement Account	26%	66%	43%
Debit/Credit Card Ownership	57%	89%	61%
Insured	62%	91%	91%

Source: Synovate, 2004 U.S. Hispanic Market Report

TABLE 26

Activity Undertaken in the Past Month	Hispanic Males	General Market Males	African American Males
Movie at Theater	36%	28%	35%
Fast-Food Restaurant	69%	67%	71%
Home Improvement	64%	60%	54%
Read a Book	56%	54%	61%
Pizza Delivery	52%	31%	36%
Rented a Video/DVD	45%	36%	32%
Nat'l Department Store	61%	46%	52%
Shopped at a Mall	63%	50%	60%

Source: Synovate, 2004 U.S. Hispanic Market Report

TABLE 27

Activity Undertaken in the Past Month	Hispanic Females	General Market Females	African American Females
Movie at Theater	27%	27%	30%
Fast-Food Restaurant	67%	68%	69%
Discount Store	81%	87%	79%
Read a Book	62%	78%	69%
Nearby Store/Bodega	67%	70%	71%
Rented a Video/DVD	38%	42%	32%
Nat'l Department Store	52%	46%	55%
Shopped at a Mall	60%	58%	64%

Source: Synovate, 2004 U.S. Hispanic Market Report

4

MARKET-BY-MARKET OVERVIEW: THE TOP TEN HISPANIC MARKETS

Now, to give you better insight into this rapidly changing Latino market, let's take a closer look at each of the top ten Hispanic markets in the United States. I have culled data from several different sources to put together these "snapshots" of each market. The data are as current as possible, but will no doubt become outdated very quickly. Whenever possible, I will refer to Demographic Metropolitan Area data, since D.M.A.'s are larger and are widely used inside and outside of the media industry. D.M.A.'s are also used to determine advertising rates in print, radio, and television. But, as you will see, the top ten

TABLE 28 Top 10 Hispanic Markets in 2004				
Hispanic Market	Total Pop. (000)	Hispanic Pop. (000)	Total HH's (000)	Hispanic HH's (000)
Los Angeles	17,544.6	7,811.1	5,177.8	2,095.8
New York	21,055.0	4,316.4	7,356.5	1,334.8
Miami/Ft. Lauderdale	4,259.8	1,836.8	1,533.6	658.6
Houston	5,459.2	1,822.6	1,828.0	498.7
Chicago	9,654.2	1,838.0	3,405.3	476.3
San Antonio	2,144.8	1,293.7	733.6	407.8
Dallas/Ft. Worth	6,427.3	1,509.7	2,145.4	401.7
San Francisco/San Jose	7,013.3	1,491.8	2,574.6	381.3
Phoenix	4,443.3	1,208.0	1,482.2	318.8
Harlingen-McAllen/ Brownsville	1,206.4	1,142.0	330.9	313.6

Source: Synovate, 2004 U.S. Hispanic Market Report

Hispanic markets by D.M.A. vary slightly from the top Hispanic population that you saw earlier because D.M.A.'s are measured in terms of households and the average number of persons per household varies from market to market. Also, the "buying power" figures quoted in the following section are defined as after-tax personal income available to spend on goods and services, and those figures come from Synovate, not from the Selig Center, which only breaks down data by state.

1. LOS ANGELES, CALIFORNIA

Contrary to the general market, where the New York D.M.A. is king (with more than 20 million people), in the Hispanic market, Los Angeles is *número uno*. That's because more than 44 percent of the population in this city is Latino! According to the 2000 Census, seven states now have Hispanic populations of 1 million or more. California is leading the list with almost 11 million Hispanics officially living in the state, which accounts for 32.4 percent of the total Hispanic population in the United States!

Although Los Angeles is clearly a Mexican-dominant city, one must not think of L.A. as a monolithic market. Because of its proximity to the Mexican border, Los Angeles has always been a magnet for newly arrived Latinos, making it home to many Spanish-dominant immigrants from Mexico as well as Central America. But L.A. is also home to a large group of Mexicans whose roots go back many generations. These "Chicanos," as they like to call themselves, are proud of their cultural heritage, but may not speak Spanish anymore. Many Hispanics in L.A. are English-dominant, educated, and highly assimilated into the mainstream. In fact, according Synovate, 54 percent of all Latinos in the Los Angeles market are "partially acculturated," while only 37 percent are "unacculturated," or, as I refer to them, "isolated."

Los Angeles also has one of the lowest educational levels of the top ten markets, with only 57 percent of its population completing high school and 12 percent going on to college or technical school according to Synovate. Labor unions are still very strong, appealing to many of the Latinos who continue to work in large, unionized industries. Demographers predict that cities like Los Angeles and others in Southern California will soon have Hispanic majorities. I believe that cities like Los Angeles and San Francisco, which also have very large Asian communities, are more likely to become the trendsetters of the future. The rest of the country should follow closely how they handle the many issues that will arise in trying to understand the needs of their growing Hispanic and Asian populations and what impact these two different communities will have on the state's economy and government.

#1: Los Angeles, California

Counties included: Los Angeles, Orange, Ventura, Riverside, San Bernardino, and Inyo
Ranking: General Market #2   Hispanic: #1   African American: #6   Asian: #1
% of Total Population: 44.5%   8.5%   13.3%

	Total (000)	Hispanic	African American	Asian
Population:	17,544.6	7,811.8	1,497.1	2,300.5
Households:	5,177.8	2,095.8	510.7	653.4

Hispanic buying power in 2004: $105,047,500,000   Per capita: $13,543

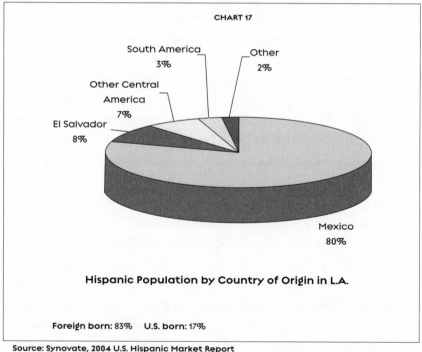

CHART 17

South America 3%
Other 2%
Other Central America 7%
El Salvador 8%
Mexico 80%

Hispanic Population by Country of Origin in L.A.

Foreign born: 83%   U.S. born: 17%

Source: Synovate, 2004 U.S. Hispanic Market Report

2. NEW YORK

New York is, by far, the most diverse Latino market in the United States. Because this D.M.A. is number one in the general market, comprising thirty-one counties from its four surrounding states, it is also one of the most expensive and difficult markets to enter. By its very nature, New York tends to attract not only Hispanics, but many other immigrants, and these tend to cluster not only as groups but also in certain areas. As a result, you can find large concentrations of Dominicans, for example, in Manhattan's Washington Heights. Large communities of Colombians and Peruvians live in Queens, and Cubans still predominate in Union City, New Jersey. Although Puerto Ricans still make up the largest percentage of the Hispanics in New York, they are no longer concentrated in one area—a reflection of their higher level of acculturation and economic power—although large groups of them still live in Manhattan's Spanish Harlem. Because of these very distinct "pockets," certain areas like Brooklyn will have high concentrations of Jews in certain neighborhoods and Mexicans in others. The changes in ethnic dominance can be felt almost block by block in New York City, which makes it a fun place to visit but a marketer's nightmare.

In terms of education, New York Latinos are better educated than most, but fall behind those living in Miami and San Antonio. According to Synovate, 68 percent have completed high school and 18 percent go on to college or do postgraduate work. In the year 2000, Latinos made up 33 percent of the student body at the City University of New York, which falls in line with the trends we talked about earlier: that younger, urban Latinos are getting better jobs because they are better educated. If you factor in high birth rates—an estimated 26 percent of all births in this area are to Hispanic mothers—I believe we will soon see an increase in educational levels for Hispanics in this market.

Because New York's economy is so strong, it attracts Latinos from all walks of life. Newly arrived, Spanish-dominant Mexicans can now be seen working as busboys in restaurants or as clerks in Korean grocery stores. Skilled Latino craftsmen can earn up to $30 an hour in construction. Many first- and second-generation Puerto Ricans or Dominicans can be found working for the government or as lawyers and doctors and, of course, many upper-class Latinos can also be found working in the banking, telecommunications, and media industries that dominate the New York economic landscape.

The main subgroups of Latinos are all well represented in this market. According to Synovate, 67 percent of all Hispanics in New York are "partially acculturated" while only 20 percent are unacculturated. The ethnic pockets I referred to earlier, which, by the way, exist in every Latino market, allow for Spanish-dominants to live comfortably without ever really "needing" to learn English. They can shop for all their needs in Spanish-speaking neighborhood stores, they can consume media in Spanish, and be informed about what's going on in their local neighborhoods as well as back home, and they can even vote in Spanish. In fact, Spanish-language radio formats have for years been more popular in this market than their English-language counterparts. WSKQ, one of the seven Spanish-language stations in this market, is so strong that it was the most listened to radio station in the country in the year 2000 (with a four-week cum number of listeners of 1.5 million) and WPAT ranks fourth nationwide, with 900,000 listeners.

#2: New York

Counties included: Monroe, Fairfield, Bergen, Essex, Hudson, Hunterdon, Middlesex, Monmouth, Morris, Ocean, Passaic, Somerset, Sussex, Union, Warren, Bronx, Dutchess, Kings, Nassau, New York, Orange, Putnam, Queens, Richmond, Rockland, Suffolk, Sullivan, Ulster, Westchester, and Pike

Ranking: General Market #1   Hispanic: #2   African American: #1   Asian #2
% of Total Population: 20.5%   18.1%   7.5%

	Total (000)	Hispanic	African American	Asian
Population:	21,055.0	4,316.4	3,808.1	1577.6
Households:	7,356.5	1,334.8	1,271.0	523.7

Hispanic buying power in 2004: $59,189,700,000   **Per capita:** $13,713

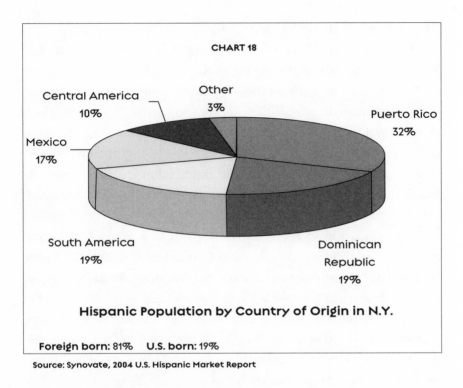

CHART 18

Central America
10%

Other
3%

Puerto Rico
32%

Mexico
17%

South America
19%

Dominican
Republic
19%

Hispanic Population by Country of Origin in N.Y.

Foreign born: 81%   U.S. born: 19%

Source: Synovate, 2004 U.S. Hispanic Market Report

3. MIAMI, FLORIDA

Miami has been called the "Hong Kong of the Americas" not only because it is the most affluent of all U.S. Hispanic markets, but also because it has become the business center for American corporations doing business in Latin America. Miami is also the epicenter of the Spanish-language media business. Both television broadcasters Univision and Telemundo are headquartered there, and almost all of the major cable networks (with the exception of Fox) with Spanish-language channels broadcast from there. On the radio front, the acquisition of H.B.C. by Univision in 2003 created Univision Radio, which is still headquartered in Dallas, Texas, but has growing offices in Miami. The second-largest Spanish-language network, Spanish Broadcasting Systems, is also headquartered in Miami.

Although the Cuban population is still the most dominant, the mix of Latinos in Miami has drastically changed over the past decade. In

1990, Miami was predominantly Cuban, today Cubans comprise slightly more than 40 percent of the total Hispanic population. The influx of South Americans fleeing their politically and economically unstable homelands (among them Brazil, Argentina, and Venezuela) has brought many more South Americans to Miami. With them come many more Central Americans looking to fill the service needs of the newly arrived, wealthier Latin Americans. Unlike the situation in most other markets, the waves of Latino immigration that have come to Miami have historically been of the more "well off." Cubans are largely responsible for transforming Miami into the thriving business metropolis it is today. The conservative bent of Miami's Latino exile communities, whether they be anti-Castro Cubans, anti-Sandinista Nicaraguans, or anti-Chavez Venezuelans, has made Miami's Hispanic community staunchly Republican. This is contrary to the norm for the rest of the state of Florida or, for that matter, the rest of the United States, where the Hispanic population is overwhelmingly Democratic. According to Synovate, nationwide 47 percent of Latinos are registered Democrats, 24 percent are Republican, and 29 percent are other, although, as we saw in the last presidential election, these percentages may be changing quickly.

Unfortunately, the extreme views of some Cubans have landed Miami in the news more than other cities, giving the false impression to many Americans that all Latinos are like Cubans. The handling of the Elián González case put Miami in the center of a heated national debate that pitted older Cubans against the younger Cuban generation. In 2001, the Recording Industry Association of America was forced to move its annual Latin Grammy Awards event to Los Angeles after threats of demonstrations by anti-Castro forces. The move cost the city of Miami millions in lost revenue.

In Miami, the Latino influence is felt in all aspects of life. I like to call Miami the "Wild, Wild East," but not all is bad. Miami has the best educated Hispanic population among the top ten Hispanic markets, with 73 percent completing high school and 25 percent completing college or post graduate studies according to Synovate. As a result, Miami's blockbuster Hispanic buying power is nearly $33 billion strong, making it the biggest market in terms of per capita buying power ($17,926). That buying power translates into an affluence that makes Miami unique. But bear in mind that the affluence of Miami's Hispanics is certainly not the norm for the rest of the Hispanic markets. Keep this in mind when picking test markets for your products because what works well in Miami may not work well elsewhere and, of course, vice versa!

#3: Miami

Counties included: Broward, Dade, and Monroe
Ranking: General Market: #15   Hispanic: #3   African American: #9   Asian: #22
% of Total Population: 43.1%   20%   2.4%

	Total (000)	Hispanic	African American	Asian
Population:	4,259.8	1,836.8	853.2	102.8
Households:	1,533.6	658.6	262.9	34.3

Buying power in 2004: $32,926,100,000   Per capita: $17,926

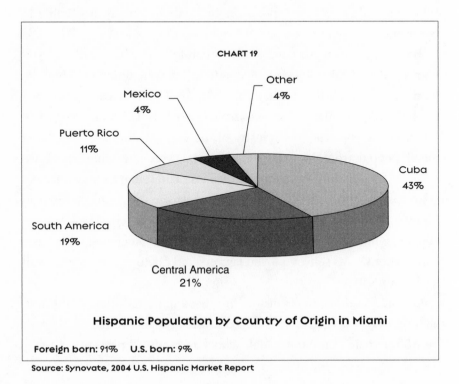

CHART 19

Mexico 4%

Other 4%

Puerto Rico 11%

Cuba 43%

South America 19%

Central America 21%

Hispanic Population by Country of Origin in Miami

Foreign born: 91%   U.S. born: 9%

Source: Synovate, 2004 U.S. Hispanic Market Report

4. HOUSTON, TEXAS

Houston is a booming market. It is one of the fastest-growing markets of the top ten Latino markets. In fact, Latinos in Houston today account for one-third of the total population and more than 50 percent of all students in the Houston Independent School System. This is a very interesting market because, contrary to most other Hispanic markets (with the exception of San Antonio), a large percentage (39 percent) of Latinos were born in the United States. If you look specifically at the Mexican American population, the number of U.S.-born Mexicans was a whopping 56 percent in 2000. This is very important to keep in mind because what you find in this market are two very distinct Hispanic groups: second- and third-generation bilingual *Tejanos* who are very acculturated, and, on the other hand, newly arrived, Spanish-dominant, unacculturated immigrants. This can be measured in terms of language usage at home. In Houston, 51 percent of Latinos speak Spanish only or mostly, while 25 percent are bilingual and 25 percent speak English only or mostly, according to Synovate.

Because they are so completely integrated into Texas culture, you tend to almost take *Tejanos* for granted, but you shouldn't. They are loud and proud of their heritage and culture. Houston also has the distinction of luring many Hispanics from other U.S. Latino markets. The boom in the construction industry of the late '90s, in fact, attracted a lot of people from Mexico, and the local Mexican Americans have exceeded themselves in many craft trades. The boom in new business start-ups has also fueled the need for services in the Houston area, an industry in which many local Hispanics are employed. There are, of course, some Latino professionals working in management for large corporations or as self-employed lawyers and doctors, but they are still in the minority.

Overall, Latinos in Houston are becoming more sophisticated, although according to Synovate educational levels remain low, with only 55 percent completing high school and only 13 percent completing college. But home ownership is above average at 71 percent, and the percentage of Hispanic households with Internet access is almost 53 percent. Another indicator of upward mobility is the political clout Latinos are gaining in this Texas metropolis.

#4: Houston

Counties included: Austin, Brazoria, Calhoun, Chambers, Colorado, Fort Bend, Galveston, Grimes, Harris, Jackson, Liberty, Matagorda, Montgomery, Polk, San Jacinto, Walker.

Ranking: General Market: #10   Hispanic: #4   African American: #8   Asian: #11
% of Total Population: 33.4%   17.7%   5.6%

	Total (000)	Hispanic	African American	Asian
Population:	5,459.2	1,822.6	966.6	306.5
Households:	1,828.0	498.7	337.8	97.5

Buying power in 2004: $25,072,700,000   Per capita: $13,757

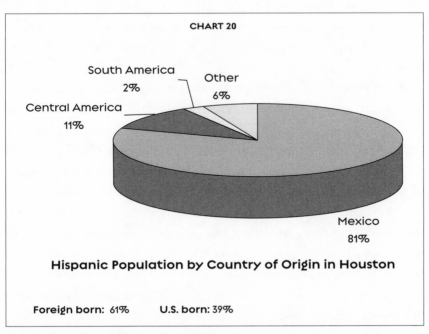

CHART 20

South America 2%

Central America 11%

Other 6%

Mexico 81%

Hispanic Population by Country of Origin in Houston

Foreign born: 61%   **U.S. born:** 39%

Source: Synovate, 2004 U.S. Hispanic Market Report

5. CHICAGO, ILLINOIS

This market has long been considered the best place to do test marketing of products geared toward the Latino community because its population mix closely represents the national averages for Hispanics in the United States. Demography, of course, is only one of the many criteria that should be used in determining appropriate test markets for your products! Surprisingly, Chicago ranks among the top in terms of comfort level of speaking English, with only 51 percent of Chicago Hispanics preferring Spanish and 31 percent claiming to speak both languages equally. Levels of education are relatively high, with 61 percent completing high school and 9 percent completing college or above. After San Francisco, Chicago is the market where most Hispanics are employed (75 percent) and today's Latino retail district, located on 26th Street, is second only to Michigan Avenue in terms of generating tax revenue for the Windy City. A quick breakdown of where Latinos are employed shows that most work in technical/clerical or sales jobs (35 percent) followed by 14 percent working as operators/fabricators, and 13 percent employed in the service industry. Only 6 percent hold managerial or professional jobs according to Synovate.

As for their media consumption habits, many Latinos in this market seem to be bilingual and bicultural, enjoying both English- and Spanish-language media equally. The important thing to understand here is preference. The high levels of bilingualism and education lead me to believe that Chicago Latinos are picky about what they choose to watch or listen to, and that language ability or usage is not necessarily the deciding factor. The issue in choosing one program over another on TV or listening to one radio station over another may now come down to which one has more appealing content and better production values. In fact, this is a trend I see developing in all of the Hispanic markets, especially as more and more U.S.-born or second-generation Latinos come into the workforce.

#5: Chicago

Counties included: Cook, De Kalb, Du Page, Grundy, Kane, Kankakee, Kendall, Lake (IL), La Sale, McHenry, Will, Jasper, La Porte, Lake (IN), Newton, Porter
Ranking: General Market #3   Hispanic: #5   African American: #2   Asian: #5
% of Total Population: 19%   18%   5.2%

	Total (000)	Hispanic	African American	Asian
Population:	9,654.2	1,838.0	1,738.0	504.8
Households:	3,405.3	476.3	577.3	145.3

Hispanic buying power in 2004: $24,235,200,000   Per capita: $13,448

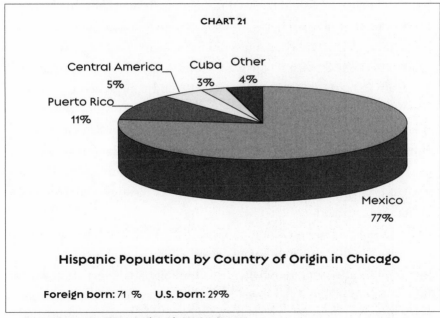

CHART 21

Central America 5%   Cuba 3%   Other 4%
Puerto Rico 11%
Mexico 77%

Hispanic Population by Country of Origin in Chicago

Foreign born: 71 %   **U.S. born:** 29%

Source: Synovate, 2004 U.S. Hispanic Market Report

6. SAN ANTONIO, TEXAS

The most striking statistic about this unique market is the percentage of "partially acculturated" Latinos it has, 83 percent, which goes against the trend for all the other top ten Latino markets. This is not that surprising when you take into consideration San Antonio's history. The home of the Alamo has seen many generations of Latinos establish roots there and, as a result, the majority of Latinos are U.S. born, with only 39 percent of all Latinos being foreign born. In recent years, in this highly acculturated, bilingual, and bicultural community, there has been a strong movement toward retro-acculturation, the process by which one tries to reconnect with his or her roots by relearning the language and traditions of his or her cultural heritage. In terms of educational achievement, San Antonio is second only to Miami, with 72 percent of its Latino students completing high school and a whopping 22 percent completing college, according to Synovate.

In Alamo City there were more than 21,000 Hispanic-owned businesses in 1999, with aggregate sales of more than $1.7 billion. Latinos here are well established in the middle class. In fact they are 29 percent more likely to earn between $50,000 and $75,000 a year than the national average. The consumption of English versus Spanish media is also very telling, with English TV viewing slightly beating Spanish-language television viewing. The same trend can be seen in newspaper and radio consumption. Not surprisingly, San Antonio ranks at the top of the list in terms of the percentage of Latinos who feel more comfortable speaking English, with 35 percent speaking English and Spanish equally at home and 31 percent speaking only or mostly English at home. Only 34 percent claim to speak mostly or only Spanish at home.

Because San Antonio is home to four U.S. Air Force bases and does not have a significant number of manufacturing or construction jobs that tend to attract more newly arrived immigrants, the Latino workforce is predominately employed by the government. While this is certainly not your "normal" Hispanic market, it could well be a different take on another "future" Hispanic market.

#6: San Antonio

Counties included: Atascosa, Bandera, Bexar, Comal, De Witt, Dimmit, Edwards, Frio, Gillespie, Goliad, Gonzales, Guadalupe, Karnes, Kendall, Kerr, Kinney, La Salle, Lavaca, McMullen, Maverick, Medina, Real, Uvalde, Val Verde, Wilson, Zavala
Ranking: General Market: #36   Hispanic: #6   African American: #71   Asian: #42
% of Total Population: 60.3%   6.9%   1.8%

	Total (000)	Hispanic	African American	Asian
Population:	2,144.8	1,293.7	147.7	37.4
Households:	733.6	407.8	49.7	10.2

Buying power in 2004: $17,869,100,000   Per capita: $13,812

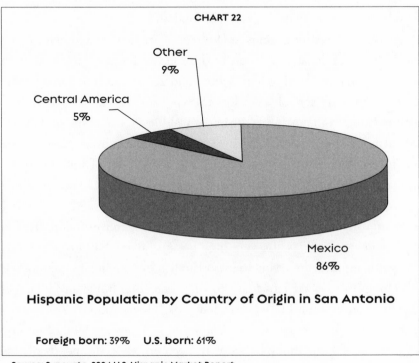

CHART 22

Other
9%

Central America
5%

Mexico
86%

Hispanic Population by Country of Origin in San Antonio

Foreign born: 39%   U.S. born: 61%

Source: Synovate, 2004 U.S. Hispanic Market Report

7. DALLAS/FORT WORTH, TEXAS

As is Houston, the Dallas/Fort Worth area is one of the fastest-growing Hispanic markets in the country. Over the next 15 years, the projected Hispanic growth rate for Dallas/Fort Worth is an astounding 48 percent (compared to a not so shabby 21 percent growth rate for non-Hispanics). Already the Latino community in Dallas/Forth Worth is 1.5 million strong and accounts for half of all the students in the Dallas

school district. Slightly more than 60 percent of the Hispanic population in this market is foreign born. The other 40 percent are second-
and third-generation bilingual *Tejanos* who are English-dominant and
highly acculturated. How can you tell one from the other? The bilingual *Tejanos* are the big football fans who can be found rooting for the
Dallas Cowboys while the more recent Latino arrivals are soccer fans
who will do anything to watch their home team play and usually prefer
baseball and basketball to American football.

As is the case with Latinos in Houston, Latinos in this area have one
of the lowest educational levels of the top ten Hispanic markets, with
only 57 percent finishing high school and 23 percent not even getting
through primary school according to Synovate. The bulk of the immigrants come from northern Mexico or California, and because they are
Spanish-dominant, they heavily depend on Spanish-language media
for information. According to Synovate, 55 percent of Latinos in the
Dallas/Fort Worth area speak Spanish mostly or only at home, while 24
percent speak Spanish and English equally at home and 21 percent
speak mostly or only English at home. However, consumption of English-language media is also very high because many Latinos, especially
the younger ones, are trying to learn English by listening to the radio or
watching TV. Skilled labor is a top job category, but many bilingual
Tejanos can be found in white-collar jobs. There are also lots of Hispanic-owned businesses, and their number will most certainly continue
to increase exponentially in order to accommodate the needs of this
booming economy.

People here like to think of themselves as living in the Silicon Valley
of the South and, in fact, the Dallas/Fort Worth area is home to many
important Internet and telecommunications companies. On the Spanish-language media front, Dallas is home to Univision Radio, formerly
known as the Hispanic Broadcasting Corporation, the largest Spanish-
language radio network in the country, as well as several of the important Hispanic advertising agencies, such as Dieste Harmel & Parterns
and Ornelas & Associates.

The buying power of Latinos in this area jumped from $17 billion
in 2000 to an estimated $25 billion in 2004, and the mean household

income is above average. Dallas/Fort Worth Hispanics spent an astounding $49 million on groceries each week in 2002 and made 15,000 visits to fast-food restaurants per day. Not surprisingly, according to Synovate 69 percent of Dallas/Fort Worth Latinos are "partially acculturated" while only 17 percent are "unacculturated."

#7: Dallas/Fort Worth

Counties included: Anderson, Bosque, Collin, Comanche, Cooke, Dallas, Delta, Denton, Ellis, Erath, Fannin, Freestone, Hamilton, Henderson, Hill, Hood, Hopkins, Hunt, Jack, Johnson, Kaufman, Lamar, Navarro, Palo Pinto, Parker, Rains, Rockwell, Somervell, Tarrant, Van Zandt, Wise.

Ranking: General Market: #6   Hispanic: #7   African American: #10 Asian: #13
% of Total Population: 23.5%   13.1%   4.1%

	Total (000)	Hispanic	African American	Asian
Population:	6,427.3	1,509.7	842.9	266.7
Households:	2,145.4	401.7	294.5	78.4

Buying power in 2004: $24,235,200,000   **Per capita:** $13,757

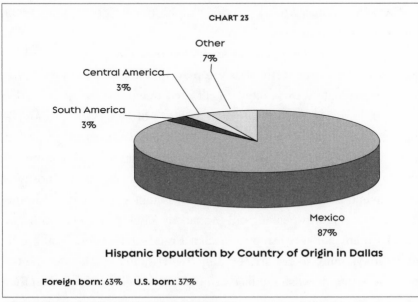

CHART 23

Other
7%

Central America
3%

South America
3%

Mexico
87%

Hispanic Population by Country of Origin in Dallas

Foreign born: 63%   **U.S. born:** 37%

Source: Synovate, 2004 U.S. Hispanic Market Report

8. SAN FRANCISCO/SAN JOSE, CALIFORNIA

This market is also made up of two very different kinds of Latino populations. The high-tech orientation of Silicon Valley makes San Francisco a magnet for sophisticated and well-educated Latinos. According to Synovate, 63 percent of all Latinos in this market are completing high school and an additional 18 percent are completing college or above. As a result, metropolitan San Francisco is home to a diverse group of Central and South Americans, with Mexicans representing only about 30 percent of the total Latino population. On the other hand, the city of San Jose is dominated by Mexican Americans, who mainly work in nonskilled jobs. Its large and expanding Hispanic population is often composed of assembly-line workers, but more and more Hispanics in the San Jose area are becoming small business owners and joining the ranks of the middle class. Because the market comprises equally large segments of Latinos and Asians, as mentioned before this is a market that could become a microcosm of the future Hispanic community in the United States, as well as one of the trendsetting cities of the United States. In 2002, *Hispanic Business* magazine ranked San Francisco as the best city for Latinos to live and work in. Its per capita buying power is $14,039, according to Synovate.

The Latino population in this area has grown 126 percent since 1980 and, again, Hispanic birth rates are playing a key role in that growth, with an estimated 28 percent of all area newborns being of Latino descent. Perhaps due to a larger percentage of U.S.-born Latinos (34 percent) and higher levels of educational attainment, language preference in this market tilts toward English. According to Synovate, only 47 percent of all Latinos in this market speak Spanish only or mostly at home while 21 percent are speaking both languages equally at home, and 29 percent are speaking only or mostly English. This is confirmed also by their media consumption. San Francisco/San Jose, California, and San Antonio, Texas, are the only two Hispanic markets in the top ten where total English media consumption is slightly *higher* than total Spanish media consumption.

#8: San Francisco/San Jose, California

Counties included: Alameda, Contra Costa, Lake, Marin, Mendocino, Napa, San Francisco, San Mateo, Santa Clara, Sonoma.

Ranking: General Market: #5   Hispanic: #8   African American: #14 Asian: #3
% of Total Population: 21.3%   8.9%   21.5%

	Total (000)	Hispanic	African American	Asian
Population:	7,013.3	1,491.8	623.7	1,510.7
Households:	2,574.6	381.3	228.0	437.7

Hispanic buying power in 2004: $20,942,700,000   Per capita: $14,039

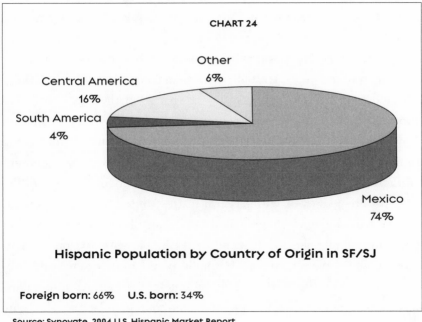

CHART 24

Other
6%

Central America
16%

South America
4%

Mexico
74%

Hispanic Population by Country of Origin in SF/SJ

Foreign born: 66%   **U.S. born:** 34%

Source: Synovate, 2004 U.S. Hispanic Market Report

9. PHOENIX, ARIZONA

The presence of Hispanics in the Phoenix area dates back to the sixteenth century when Spanish conquistador Álvar Nuñez Cabeza de Vaca came looking for gold. After being shipwrecked in the Gulf of Mexico in 1528, Cabeza de Vaca heard stories of the great riches of the cities of Cíbola, but never found them. Phoenix has always been a magnet for Latinos. Up until the 1980s, however, Phoenix mainly attracted second- or third-generation Latinos who were primarily bilingual, and who wanted to get back to their Spanish roots in their older age. A look at the Census data for 1980 indicates that 256,300 Hispanics accounted for 14 percent of the total population of Phoenix. Fueled by a strong economy and a growing number of younger Latinos with large families in the late '90s, Phoenix propelled itself onto the top ten list of Hispanic markets. By 1999 it ranked eleventh in terms of cities with the largest U.S. Hispanic population. After making *Hispanic Magazine*'s "Top 10 Cities for Hispanics" for several years in a row, by 2000 this market had attracted more than 783,000 Latinos, which grew to 893,195 by 2002, and is now slightly more than 1 million strong.

The Hispanic composition of this market has also been changing over the past few years. In 1999, more than 90 percent of Latinos there claimed to have roots in Mexico. By the year 2002, that percentage had dropped to 81 percent, while the percentage of Central and South American Latinos had shot up from 5 percent to 17 percent during the same period. The strong job market has also turned this retirement community into a thriving metropolis. In fact, Phoenix has one of the largest percentages of Latinos born in the United States, 37 percent (surpassed only by Harlingen/Weslaco, Texas). Tourism and construction rank among the top five industries in Phoenix, Arizona, where more than 73 percent of the Hispanic population is employed full-time, with about half of those holding blue-collar jobs. Although Latinos comprise more than 25 percent of the total population today, only 10 percent of the student population of Arizona State University is Hispanic.

#9: Phoenix

Counties included: Coconino, Gila, Graham, Greenlee, La Paz, Maricopa, Mohave, Navajo, Pinal, Yavapai

Ranking: General Market: #13   Hispanic: #9   African American: #57   Asian: #20

% of Total Population:	27.2%	4.2%	2.6%

	Total (000)	Hispanic	African American	Asian
Population:	4,443.3	1,208.0	186.2	117.1
Households:	1,482.2	318.8	64.7	33.9

Hispanic buying power in 2004: $16,686,900,000   Per capita: $13,814

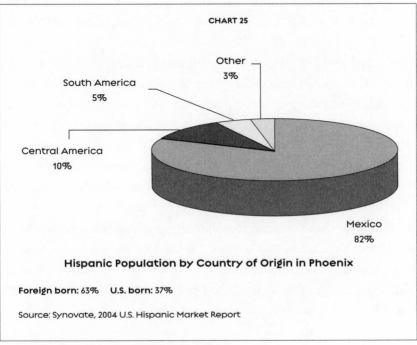

CHART 25

Other
3%

South America
5%

Central America
10%

Mexico
82%

Hispanic Population by Country of Origin in Phoenix

Foreign born: 63%   **U.S. born:** 37%

Source: Synovate, 2004 U.S. Hispanic Market Report

Source: Synovate, 2004 U.S. Hispanic Market Report

10. HARLINGEN/WESLACO/BROWNSVILLE/ MCALLEN, TEXAS

With Hispanics making up 94.8 percent of the total population of the Harlingen/Weslaco/Brownsville/McAllen D.M.A., the tortilla is completely flipped in this border town that barely registers on most people's radar. Here Hispanics *are* the general market. "El Valle," as this area of the Lower Rio Grande Valley is known, is famous for being the birthplace of

Tejano music and culture, which is now popular everywhere in the Southwest. But that's not the only thing this area is famous for. With more than a million Mexicans living across the border in the cities of Reynosa and Matamoros in Mexico, this area has, over the past decade, become home to many electronics assembly factories as well as many textile sewing and manufacturing plants, known as *maquiladoras,* that employ many low-wage workers, many of whom who live across the border. In fact, border patrol records indicate that more than 4 million people cross this border each year.

The valley is also famous for being one of the world's leading producers of aloe and citrus fruits. Other important agricultural crops are cotton, grains, and vegetables. After manufacturing, the agriculture industry is the second largest employer in town, followed by construction and tourism. Although the Harlingen/Weslaco area ranks forty-ninth in terms of overall per capita purchasing power, it comes in at eleventh in terms of Hispanic buying power. The Hispanic middle class of this area has been hard hit by the recent economic recession. As a result, the median household income dropped from $45,965 in 1999 to $40,114 in 2002, according to Synovate, and the area dropped in overall Hispanic ranking from number nine in 2000 to number ten in 2004.

This market has one of the highest percentages of Latinos born in the United States: 42 percent. Older area residents are bilingual, with almost 26 percent saying that English is the language they feel most comfortable speaking and another 16 percent saying they speak comfortably in both English and Spanish. Not surprisingly, the Latino community here strongly supports bilingual education, many Anglo residents speak Spanish, and intermarriage is common. Although Harlingen/Weslaco has the lowest number of Latinos completing high school, the University of Texas-Pan American, in Edinburg, has the highest number and percentage of Latino students of any U.S. college. Many of these students are actually Mexican nationals attending school in the United States. In an area where Hispanics are so dominant, it is not surprising that the mayors of McAllen, Brownsville, Edinburg, Hidalgo and Rio Grande City are all Latino.

#10: Harlingen/Weslaco/Brownsville/McAllen

Counties included: Cameron, Hidalgo, Starr, Willacy
Ranking: General Market: #66 Hispanic: #10 African American: #186 Asian: #156
% of Total Population: 94.82%   0.3%   0.3%

	Total (000)	Hispanic	African American	Asian
Population:	1,206.4	1,142.0	3.2	4.2
Households:	330.9	313.6	1.0	1.4

Hispanic buying power in 2004: $11,004,500,000   Per capita: $9,636

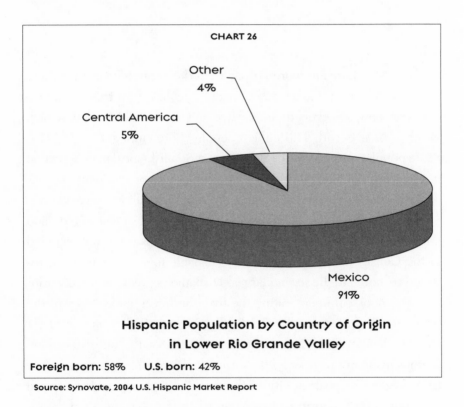

CHART 26

Other
4%

Central America
5%

Mexico
91%

**Hispanic Population by Country of Origin
in Lower Rio Grande Valley**

Foreign born: 58%   U.S. born: 42%

Source: Synovate, 2004 U.S. Hispanic Market Report

5

HISPANIC NATION AND IDENTITY

There are more Hispanics in the United States than there are Canadians in Canada! This has been true for almost five years now, and every time I say it, people are dumbfounded. In fact, in terms of size, with 41.3 million people and counting, the U.S. Hispanic population ranks as the third largest Spanish-speaking population in the world, behind Mexico with 104 million people, Colombia with 42.9 million people, but ahead of Spain with 40.3 million, and Argentina with slightly more than 39 million people. However, if you were to add the 3.8 million Puerto Ricans counted by the Census but not included in the Census figures as part of the Hispanic total, the United States would be home to the *second* largest Hispanic population in the world!

In his book commemorating the five hundredth anniversary of the discovery of the Americas, *The Buried Mirror: Reflections on Spain and the New World,* Carlos Fuentes says that with almost 8 million Latinos living in Los Angeles, this American city is already the second-largest Spanish-speaking city in the world! (It places behind Mexico City, but before Madrid or Barcelona.) The fact that the Spanish language can be heard from coast to coast on the radio and on TV, and in the streets of any major city of America has "breathtaking implications for corporate America," as the economist Louis E.V. Nevaer so eloquently puts it: "It creates *parallel* consumer markets separated by *language.*" In this chapter we will examine how the immigration trends of

Latinos in the United States are changing. We will explore the question of Hispanic "identity" and how it is formed inside and outside of the United States, and we will discuss how Latinos use the Spanish language as a way of differentiating themselves in this country. Finally, we will talk about how Latinos are forced to deal with the question of race, the fragmentation of markets it creates, and how Latinos defy the traditional racial paradigm of America.

CHANGING IMMIGRATION PATTERNS

During the 1970s and 1980s, the growth of the Latino population was felt mainly in large urban areas. Mexicans crossing the border through California or Texas gravitated toward Los Angeles, San Diego, Houston, El Paso, and Phoenix, big cities where they knew they could survive and quickly be absorbed by the large and economically vibrant Latino communities there. This has also been the immigration pattern of Puerto Ricans, who traditionally flocked to New York or Chicago, and Cubans who fled Cuba knowing that they had family in Miami or New Jersey that could claim them and help them secure citizenship in the United States. In the 1990s, however, that pattern began to change.

Although the exact number of illegal aliens is unknown and perhaps unknowable, experts estimate that the number ranges somewhere between 4 million and 10 million persons. Of course, not all of them are Latino, but certainly a large percentage of them do come from Spanish-speaking countries. As a result of the growing unease with "illegal aliens," especially after 9/11, the U.S. Border Patrol and other government agencies of the United States' Immigration and Naturalization Service have been cracking down on the flow of immigrants. Their focus, of course, has been on these magnet cities mentioned above. But some say the crackdown on illegal aliens in big cities has simply diverted the flow of illegal immigration to nontraditional areas, where vigilance is more relaxed and there was, and still is, a growing demand for laborers. For example in North Carolina, the total number of Hispanics *quadrupled* in the last decade from 76,726, or 1.2 percent, of the total population in 1990, to 378,963, or 4.7 percent, of the total population in 2000.

GROWTH OF HISPANICS IN
NONTRADITIONAL AREAS

"Hispanic, that is our puzzle," claimed the assistant chief of population estimates for the Census Bureau, Signe Wetrogan, in an *Advertising Age* article about the impact of the 2000 Census. "We have started to see growth of Hispanic populations in nontraditional counties," she added, referring to the remarkable increase in the number of Latinos in the decade from 1990 to 2000. The new "magnets" became states like Georgia and North Carolina, where the textile manufacturing and meat-processing industries concentrate. New England has also become a magnet for new immigrants working in the manufacturing and service industries. Many Dominicans now live in Massachusetts and Rhode Island where, one family at a time, entire towns from the Dominican Republic have made their way to cities north of Boston. Preparations for the 2002 Winter Olympics made Salt Lake City, Utah, another magnet for Latino immigrants in the late 1990s. These Latino workers who came for the Olympics stayed and were very quickly absorbed into the service industries of Nevada. Between 1990 and 2000, the Latino population in Utah more than doubled, from 84,597, or 4.9 percent of the state's total population, in 1990, to 201,559, or 9 percent, in 2000. And, finally, in New York City, where Latinos already represent 21 percent of the city's total population, Mexicans are now the third largest Latino population of the Big Apple—which has been traditionally a haven for Latinos from the Caribbean (Puerto Rico, the Dominican Republic, and Cuba)!

Although the reasons for the unprecedented growth in the number of Latinos in nontraditional areas have not been studied yet by demographers, it can be attributed somewhat to trends in the manufacturing and service industries. For example, I have seen how textile plants in Georgia are attracting large numbers of Hispanic workers. Through informal conversations with immigrant workers in these areas, and with busboys or delivery boys in New York City, I have learned that if the working conditions are good, entire families will relocate to the same area over time. Obviously my experiences are anecdotal, but it is not uncommon, especially among Mexican immigrants, to discover that someone in their family came first and then, often one at a time, many families from a certain town or area in Mexico followed, forming miniclusters in certain neighborhoods, counties, or cities. For example, many of the recent Mexican immigrants to New York City are from the state of Puebla, in southern Mexico. This may also help explain the unprecedented growth of Latinos in the Midwest where, according to the 2002 Census update, 7.7 percent of the total Hispanic population lives, up from 5 percent in the 2000 Census.

	Hispanic Population 1990	Hispanic Population 2000	% Difference
TABLE 29 Growth of Hispanics in the Midwest			
Minnesota	53,884	143,382	166%
Nebraska	36,969	94,425	155%
Iowa	32,647	82,473	153%
Indiana	98,788	214,536	117%
South Dakota	5,252	10,903	108%
Wisconsin	93,194	192,921	107%
Kansas	93,670	188,252	101%
Missouri	61,702	118,592	92%
Illinois	904,446	1,530,262	69%
North Dakota	4,665	7,786	67%
Michigan	201,596	323,877	61%
Ohio	139,696	217,123	55%

Source: U.S. Census Bureau, Forecast Analysis; American Demographics FORECAST, April 21, 2001

The fact that Latino immigration patterns have changed is important to keep in mind. Whereas before Hispanic immigrants were naturally drawn to larger cities where they mixed with Latinos from other countries, now they tend to go to smaller cities and don't necessarily mix with other Latinos. They will still congregate in their own neighborhoods or *barrios* but now, because they are made up primarily of people from the same country or area, the ties back home, and with one another, are stronger.

IN SEARCH OF A HISPANIC IDENTITY

The fact that 75 percent of all Hispanics living in the United States come mainly from Mexico and Central America has been an important unifier for this market too. People from these countries have a lot more in common than they do with Latinos from other countries in South America or the Caribbean. People from Mexico and Central America have similar tastes in music (norteña, ranchera, cumbia, etc.) and in food. They also often share the same religious and cultural values. Likewise, Hispanics from Caribbean nations, who tend to congregate in larger cities along the Eastern Seaboard of the United States, also have similar tastes in music (salsa, merengue, and bachata) and food, and they also share many of the religious and cultural values more typically associated with the Caribbean or South America.

Although Spanish is the official language of all of these countries, variations can be striking from country to country. It is also important to note that in Mexico alone there are 60 native languages still spoken, and that many Mexican and Central American immigrants may be more fluent in their native languages than in Spanish! That said, Spanish *is* the language that all Latinos share, and it has become the "glue" that helps create part of the Hispanic identity here in the United States.

Roberto Suro, M.S., the director of research at the Pew Hispanic Center, delves into the question of Hispanic identity in his 2002 *National Survey of Latinos.* "The terms people use to describe themselves are an important measure of how they see themselves and of how they relate to the society they inhabit. Terms such as white, African American, Hispanic or Latino are especially important in the United States, where individuals are routinely categorized into racial and ethnic groups as a matter of social convention and government policy," he says.

This Pew Hispanic Center/Kaiser Family Foundation study found that when it comes to identity, "Hispanics demonstrate a very strong association with their countries of origin, whether it be their birthplace or their parents' or the land that their ancestors hailed from generations ago." But when asked about racial identity, "Hispanics indicated that they do not fit into one of the racial categories typically used by the U.S. government." This was clearly demonstrated when the Census Bureau revealed its data on race from the 2000 Census.

In an effort to improve their system of tracking race and ethnicity, in 2000 the Census Bureau announced that it would change its form in

TABLE 30 Population by Race for the United States: 2000

Race	Number	Not Hispanic or Latino	
		Percent of Hispanic Population	Percent of Total Population
Total	246,116,088	100	87.5
One Race	241,513,942	98.1	85.8
White	194,552,774	79.1	69.1
Black or African American	33,947,837	13.8	12.1
American Indian or Alaskan Native	2,068,883	0.8	0.7
Asian	10,123,169	4.1	3.6
Native Hawaiian or Other Pacific Islander	353,509	0.1	0.1
Some Other Race	467,770	0.2	0.2
Two or more races	4,602,146	1.9	1.6

Source: U.S. Census Bureau, Census 2000 Redistricting Summary file, Tables PL1 and PL2

order to allow all Americans to identify themselves as belonging to more than one race. As a result, almost half a million people (0.2 percent of the U.S. total—table 30) identified themselves as "some other race" in Census 2000. The six racial categories tracked by the Census Bureau are: white, black, Asian, American Indian or Alaska Native, Native Hawaiian or Other Pacific Islander, or "some other race." Contrary to what most people think, Hispanic is not a race, it is an ethnicity.

TABLE 31 Population by Race for the United States: 2000

Race	Number	Hispanic or Latino	
		Percent of Hispanic Population	Percent of Total Population
Total	35,305,818	100	12.5
One Race	33,081,736	93.7	11.8
White	16,907,852	47.9	6
Black or African American	710,353	2	0.3
American Indian or Alaskan Native	407,073	1.2	0.1
Asian	119,829	0.3	—
Native Hawaiian or Other Pacific Islander	45,326	0.1	—
Some Other Race	14,891,303	42.2	5.3
Two or more races	2,224,082	6.3	0.8

Source: U.S. Census Bureau, Census 2000 Redistricting Summary file, Tables PL1 and PL2

Interestingly, while only 0.2 percent of all Americans identified themselves as being of "some other race," almost half of all Latinos, 42 percent, indicated that they belonged to "some other race" (table 31).

Why this huge discrepancy? Either Latinos didn't understand the question correctly because of the way it was phrased, or they simply didn't feel comfortable with the choices they were given!

According to Suro, the 42 percent of Hispanics who chose "some other race" in the 2000 Census probably prefer to be identified as "Latino" or "Hispanic." In order to understand their identity preference, the Pew Hispanic Center survey substantially replicated the Census question on race, but then offered respondents the opportunity to volunteer other options. "Almost half (47 percent) of Latino respondents volunteered Hispanic or Latino when asked to pick among the standard racial categories, and an additional 9 percent indicated that they would prefer that Latino or Hispanic be one of their options," says Suro in his report (chart 27).

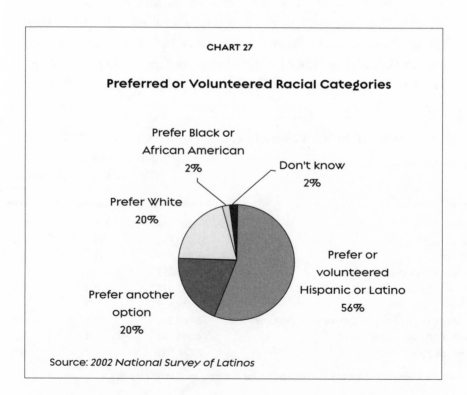

CHART 27

Preferred or Volunteered Racial Categories

Prefer Black or African American 2%

Don't know 2%

Prefer White 20%

Prefer or volunteered Hispanic or Latino 56%

Prefer another option 20%

Source: *2002 National Survey of Latinos*

"What Latinos seem to be indicating is that it is important to them that they be considered a distinct group from Non-Hispanic Whites and African Americans. And at the same time they acknowledge that there is considerable diversity within the Latino population as well," Suro adds. According to Hispanic market expert and consultant Louis E.V. Nevaer, Hispanics defy the "racial boxes" America tries to put them in, and they use language as a way of self-segregating. "Hispanics use Spanish both to resist Americanization and as a defense mechanism against racism," he says. "Hispanics thus choose not to think inside the racial box that otherwise dominates American life. This is infuriating and problematic for corporate managers, for it challenges the assumptions upon which the consumer marketplace in the United States is understood."

BILINGUAL NATION

Louis E.V. Nevaer has written several books examining the U.S. Hispanic and Mexican marketplaces. In his latest work, *The Rise of the Hispanic Market in the United States,* Nevaer espouses the idea that Hispanics in the United States keep the Spanish language alive not only as a key building block to their identity but also as a means to keep in check mainstream American social values that come with assimilation. "For Hispanics to speak Spanish is a repudiation of assimilation into mainstream society, a direct challenge to the historic social contract of American life: the 'huddled masses' who wash up on these shores are welcome, provided they embrace an 'American' identity in due course."

He goes on to credit the Cubans of Miami in the 1960s as the first Hispanic group in the United States to openly embrace the Spanish language as a way of not "losing their soul" and becoming Americanized. "Cubans, in essence, decided to protect the integrity of their community by self-segregating through the act of speaking Spanish *in public.* Never before had a Hispanic group, whether Mexicans in Los Angeles or Puerto Ricans in New York, decided to take such a radical move," he says. As a result, Spanish started being publicly spoken and therefore *heard* in the United States. I'm not sure that all the credit for that can go to the Cubans since at the same time U.S.-born Mexicans in Los Angeles and Chicago were also embracing a renewed sense of Hispanic identity through the Chicano movement, while writers in Puerto Rico were exploring their relationship to the United States and how it affected their identity through seminal literary novels like *Spiks* and *USMail*, by Pedro Juan Soto or the later works of Piri Thomas, such as *Down These Mean Streets.*

When the 1980 Census was released, it showed for the first time the rapid growth of the Hispanic community, and suddenly the eighties were being heralded as the "decade of the Hispanic." The Spanish-language media industry jumped on this Census data and set out to demonstrate how the Hispanic market was different from other minority markets and could effectively be reached by advertising in Spanish. Advertising agencies started to create specialized shops that could cater to this "newly identified" group that distinguished itself by the use and consumption of Spanish-language media. Their sales pitch to American companies was that to properly advertise products to Hispanics, these companies needed to communicate with Hispanics in their own language: Spanish. Luckily for the Hispanic advertising agencies, there was already a vibrant Spanish-language media industry with viable television stations, radio, and print vehicles to reach this growing "in-language" market. "Regardless of their language skills, Hispanics feel more comfortable in Spanish," says Nevaer, "almost as if their emotional needs are better satisfied living life in Spanish than in English. Time and time again, Hispanic consumers indicate that they 'thought in English' and 'felt in Spanish,'" continues Nevaer. Twenty years later, corporate America readily acknowledges that in order to conduct business with Hispanic consumers, you must give them the option to do it *en español.*

But the linguistic revolution this country is going through is very different from that of our neighbor to the north, Canada. As Nevaer points out, "in Canada, bilingualism is the result of a *political* compromise between the Québécois and their English-speaking compatriots, while in the United States the spread of Spanish is the result not of legislation but of *economics.* Whereas French is mandated by federal authorities in Canada, in the United States the use of Spanish in public is the result of corporate America (and local governments) trying to meet the needs of consumers (and constituents) driven by the marketplace." This is why the word "bilingual" used in just about any context is often so politically charged and controversial in this country. But let's face it. Spanish is here to stay. "Hispanics will learn English, to be sure, but out of self-respect, they cannot abandon Spanish," concludes Nevaer. "The United States in the twenty-first century will mature as a bilingual society, one in which these two languages will exist side by side, at times in conflict, but more often seeking an accommodation."

In her book, *Latinos Inc.*, professor Arlene Dávila warns us of the danger of defining this market purely by the use of the Spanish language, a view that has been perpetuated for the past two decades. "Convinced that Latinos who are English-dominant or bilingual are already being reached through mainstream media, corporations almost always approach Hispanic marketing agencies already having decided to limit their marketing efforts to Latino customers who are Spanish-speaking. Faced with these pressures, all advertising presentations include a statement explaining that Spanish is the preferred language of all Hispanics, some being more emphatic about Hispanics' use of or proficiency in this language, but all stressing that Hispanics *speak* Spanish and they will continue to do so and that the best way to reach them is through 'their language.' Even if they don't speak it, Latinos are hence deemed to be symbolically moved and touched by Spanish, reproducing essentialist equations of Latinos with their language. The irony that remains unstated is that such language purity is an unattainable goal in the world of advertising, where U.S. products are being advertised and where product names—all in English—necessarily fill the airwaves with English names and Spanglish phrases."

So while language is one of the key traits that helps define the Hispanic market in the United States, there are other cultural traits and characteristics that also help define the Latino identity, regardless of language preference or usage. Broad generalizations, however, are not "absolutes," because, as you have already seen, Hispanics are not a homogeneous or monolithic group. In an attempt to further understand the Hispanic or Latino identity in the United States, the Pew Hispanic Center's *2002 National Survey of Latinos* explored how Latinos viewed life in the United States, and its research revealed that there are also striking cultural differences between Latinos and their white and African-American counterparts. The research also revealed that there are some "nuanced yet notable cultural differences" among foreign-born Latinos, native-born Latinos, and non-Latinos as well.

"When it comes to social values, Latinos have social values that are somewhat more conservative than Whites, but that are often similar to those of African Americans. Some of those differences in values may be explained by religion," says Suro in his *2002 National Survey of Latinos*. While the vast majority of Latinos describe themselves as Catholic and very religious, sometimes their conservative social values also are derived from their country of origin. "In general, Mexicans and Central Americans tend to be slightly more socially conservative than Latinos from other countries," he adds. Here are some interesting charts (tables 32 and 33) comparing views on key social issues, family, religion, and government.

Again, while this research helps you get a sense of how Latinos think and feel about certain issues, it is important to note that there are also striking differences *among* Latinos, depending on their age, country of origin, religious orientation, and, especially, between foreign-born and U.S.-born Hispanics. For those interested in delving more into these

TABLE 32 Importance of Religion

How important is religion in your everyday life?	The most important thing	Very important	Somewhat important	Not at all important
Latinos	21%	47%	25%	6%
Whites	20%	41%	28%	11%
African-Americans	37%	37%	20%	6%

Trust in Government	Just about always	Most of the time	Some of the time	Never
Latinos	14%	29%	47%	4%
Whites	8%	38%	48%	4%
African-Americans	7%	24%	62%	7%

Source: *2002 National Survey of Latinos*

TABLE 33 Views on Some Social Issues

Percent who say each is in general acceptable/unacceptable...

Divorce	Acceptable	Not acceptable
Latinos	56%	40%
Whites	74%	24%
African Americans	59%	40%

Abortion	Acceptable	Not acceptable
Latinos	20%	77%
Whites	43%	53%
African Americans	28%	70%

Gay Sex	Acceptable	Not acceptable
Latinos	25%	72%
Whites	38%	59%
African Americans	14%	84%

Source: *2002 National Survey of Latinos*

fascinating issues, I highly recommend getting a copy of the Pew Hispanic Center's report.

CENSUS 2000 AND ITS IMPACT ON CORPORATE AMERICA

While Census officials are still trying to figure out what caused their population estimates to be so far off in the 1990s—some say there was better counting in the 2000 Census; others claim that there was severe undercounting in the 1990 Census; and yet others point toward a possible underestimate of immigration as the problem—whatever the reason, the new Census numbers have already started to have an impact on corporate America. And, for the first time, the media are starting to tune in, covering the exploding Hispanic market like never before. Doing business with this market has become the corporate mantra of the past couple years because, simply put, to fail to do so will put any company at a competitive disadvantage. This is why all the companies that make up the Fortune 500 realize they must do business with this market to stay on top.

"It's pretty clear that it is a huge shift taking place," Randy Melville, vice president of urban marketing at Pepsi-Cola Co., told *Advertising Age* in 2001. "You don't even need a lot of interpretation. It's like one and one is two." The numbers may be there, but the advertising budgets certainly are not. In the year 2000, only about 2 percent of total advertising dollars were devoted to Spanish-language advertising, which is far below the estimated 8 percent the Hispanic consumers are spending every year in the United States. For years, studies have shown that Hispanic consumption is far greater than that of any other minority group within certain product categories, among them groceries, cosmetics, clothing and footwear, home improvement, long distance telephone, travel, and automobiles. Some companies, Procter & Gamble, Sears, Toyota, GM, Pepsi, and McDonald's, realized this a long time ago and have been leading advertisers in the Hispanic market for decades, but many corporations still don't get it. In the spring of 2003, the Association of Hispanic Advertising Agencies conducted a follow-up to their 2002 "Right Spend" study and found that even among the top 50 Hispanic marketers, on average only 3.2 percent of their national advertising budgets was being allocated to the Hispanic market!

Companies such as Nielsen Media Research, which monitors television viewing, or Arbitron, which tracks radio listening among other things, have already started to acknowledge that they need to make changes to their ratings systems to more accurately measure Spanish-dominant household viewing and listening patterns. These new ratings will, in turn, have a ripple effect throughout corporate America, but especially in the advertising community. And the question of language is front and center in the ratings debate. As I write this book in December of 2004, Nielsen Media Research, the company that produces the Nielsen television ratings, is still defending its Local People Meters (LPM) and asserting that its new methodology includes Spanish-dominant viewers. As you can imagine, in large Hispanic markets, such as Los Angeles or Miami, English-language programming is expected to lose a significant share of the total viewing as measured by Nielsen, since the new methodology will in theory "proportion Spanish-dominant viewers according to their ratio of the Hispanic population living in the local area." The first report with a balanced language sample will be released by Nielsen in 2005, but the fireworks have already begun partly because of how Nielsen has chosen to define language usage in the Hispanic market. The real problem is that in the Hispanic market, everyone defines "language usage" or "language preference" and "Spanish-dominant" differently, and *until we all agree* on how to define these terms, we will not hear the end of it. We are talking about hundreds of millions of dollars in advertising dollars and trust me, blood will flow down Madison Avenue before it's all over. According to Nielsen Media Research, the breakdown of Hispanic households by language usage in 2003 in table 34.

TABLE 34 2003 Language Use in Hispanic TV Households

TV Households	Adults 18+		Persons 2+	
	(000)	% of Total	(000)	% of Total
Only Spanish	2,110	21.70%	1,580	16.20%
Mostly Spanish	2,880	29.60%	2,680	27.50%
Spanish/English	1,300	13.40%	1,990	20.50%
Mostly English	2,290	23.50%	2,340	24%
Only English	1,150	11.80%	1,140	11.70%
Total Hispanic	**9,730**	**100%**	**9,730**	**100%**

Source: Nielsen Media Research

As mentioned in chapter 2, the Census also breaks down Latinos by self-identified "language ability." According to the Census Bureau, 89% of all Hispanics (ages 5+), or about 28 million persons in the United States, speak Spanish (at least some of the time) at home. As you can see in table 35 on self-reported *speaking* ability, Spanish speakers in the United States are almost evenly divided between foreign born and

TABLE 35 Language Ability by Place of Birth

Language ability	Native Born		Foreign Born	
Speak Spanish	14,760,788	100%	13,340,264	100%
Speak English "very well"	10,598,734	72%	3,751,062	28%
Speak English "well"	2,631,784	18%	3,187,624	24%
Speak English "not well"	1,313,595	9%	3,816,895	29%
Speak English "not at all"	216,765	1%	2,584,683	19%

Source: U.S. Census Bureau ST4, July 2003

native born. The big differences in this table lie in the speakers' English proficiency, which should correlate somewhat with what Nielsen Media Research reports, but it doesn't. You see why this is frustrating?

And finally the 2002 *National Survey of Latinos* gives us one more perspective on this issue. According to the Pew Hispanic Center, a slight majority of Hispanics (53 percent) report they predominantly speak Spanish at home. Nineteen percent say they speak both English and Spanish equally and 28 percent say they predominantly speak in English at home. The key here, is *at home.* When you look at the various other situations in which language comes into play, these percentages vary quite significantly (table 36).

TABLE 36 Language Spoken in Various Situations

What language do you...	Predominantly Spanish	Both Equally	Predominantly English
Speak at home	53%	19%	28%
Speak at work	26%	26%	48%
Watch TV or listen to the radio	38%	26%	36%
What language do your children...	**Predominantly Spanish**	**Both Equally**	**Predominantly English**
Speak with their friends	17%	26%	58%

Source: *2002 National Survey of Latinos*

While bilingualism is probably the most defining characteristic of the U.S. Hispanic identity, it is clear to me that as a community we need to start agreeing on how to define language usage so that we can compare apples with apples. Results will still vary from one research report to another because language is so closely tied to level of acculturation and education, but still there ought to be some uniformity to these numbers or else we will all go crazy!

IN THE TWENTY-FIRST CENTURY, NICHE MARKETING IS KING

In the eighties and nineties, as the cable television industry made inroads into the established media landscape dominated by the big three networks, marketing managers started taking market segmentation to a whole new level. Cable networks that could consistently deliver certain demographics—the teen market (MTV) or the women's market (Lifetime), for example—started attracting major advertising dollars, and suddenly niche marketing was born. But not all niches are equal or desirable, and somewhere along the way minority communities got lost in the shuffle. Unfortunately the one-size-fits-all mentality of the "general market" did not go away either. As a result, the African-American market was put under the same multicultural banner as the Hispanic and Asian markets. While this move toward "multiculturalism" made people working in corporate America feel better about themselves on their political-correctness meters, these individual markets were still not given the proper attention or budgets and, of course, their performance suffered. A common mistake is to think that these markets simply aren't profitable. Unfortunately, this racist attitude and corporate prejudice are still alive and well. Trust me. The reason why some of these minority markets don't "perform" as well as the general market is because they are different, but many companies still try to measure their performance against the general market, and that's just not right. Using the one-size-fits-all mentality doesn't work anymore!

When I worked at Columbia House, our own research indicated that Hispanic members were considered "better" members because they bought more CDs with each order and they bought more frequently than other club members did, yet they were leaving the Latin music club at slightly higher rates than members of other clubs did. This puzzled us, so we dug into the issue and discovered that many Latino members simply didn't understand how the club worked. The quick (and racist) assumption would be to say that Latino club members were either stupid or trying to beat the system, but in fact what we had on our hands was a translation problem. The materials we were sending to our Latin members simply translated what had existed before in English. Well, this didn't work because the English text was written with the assumption that you know what you are getting into when you join Columbia House. Latinos come from countries where music and video clubs do not exist, much less "negative option" clubs, where you must send a reply card in order *not* to get something sent to you. Being a Hispanic marketing expert, I also knew that our members were not accustomed to transacting business through the mail. Latinos come from countries where the mail system does not work very well, so they are used to paying their bills in person with cash. So we were asking a lot of our members without properly explaining to them what they were getting into when they joined. As a result, they felt "tricked" and were leaving the club. Once we knew what the problem was, we reviewed all of our communication touch points with our members and made sure people understood what they had to do in order to keep their membership in good standing. Guess what? It worked!

When dealing with minority markets, you need to make sure your business model works for them, and if it doesn't work as is, you need to be willing to change it. Corporate America has been too quick to write off minority markets and say they can't make money with blacks or Latinos. But black and Latino entrepreneurs are proving corporate America wrong, as is demonstrated by the success of Black Entertainment Television, Phat Farm, and Goya Foods, to name but a few examples of minority businesses that successfully cater to niche markets and make loads of money. There is plenty of money to be made in these markets. You just need to be open-minded to understand how to do business in slightly different ways.

LACK OF DIVERSITY IN THE MEDIA

Another sector of corporate America that still does not understand the Hispanic market is Hollywood and network television. It is disturbing to see how underrepresented Latinos still are on network television. While we represented more than 13.4 percent of the total population in 2002, according to a 2003 study conducted by the University of California in Los Angeles, only 4.1 percent of all characters on prime-time television were Latino (and half of them are bad guys). The issue of diversity on the small screen is not new in Hollywood. It reared its ugly head in 1998, when the big three television networks released their fall schedules and *not one* of more than thirty new shows included a black or Latino character. A boycott of network television by Hispanic and African-American groups in the year 2000 led network executives to promise to do better, both in front of and behind the cameras. But all they did was sprinkle their shows with a few minority characters and later went on to cancel most of those shows in 2001.

I do believe network executives see the upside potential for this market. If not, NBC would not have purchased Telemundo in 2001 for $2.7 billion. The problem with Hollywood, as it is with everybody else, is that they don't know how to change what they do best and still make money. How do they start putting together a creative team that can deliver programs that will attract Latinos without alienating the rest of the nation? What story lines will resonate with these new American audiences? Do they allow their characters to use some Spanish? Will that turn off the so-called general market viewers? These are all valid questions.

The problem with diversity in the media is further complicated by the "whiteness" of entertainment companies, where minorities are woefully absent from positions of power. Add to that the fact that very few network executives are actually willing to try anything new, and what you get is one huge brick wall. Media executives would rather stick to the few mainstream formulas that have worked for them in the past than try something new. How quickly they forget that their most successful shows—*Cosby, Designing Women, Friends, Law & Order,* and *The Simpsons* to name just a few—were the ones that broke that formula.

When FOX, UPN, and the WB channels launched in the mid-'90s, the only way to compete with the established broadcasters was to attract minority viewers who had so often been ignored by the big three networks. The result was an onslaught of creative new ideas and programs directed to minority viewers, especially African-Americans, thus opening up the television industry to an important segment of the population that had been clamoring to get in for decades. It worked. Those stations got ratings, and advertisers soon followed. Once they achieved some degree of success, however, FOX and WB quickly changed their programming slates in order to attract *younger and whiter* audiences that were more appealing to general market advertisers. UPN is the only one that has kept true to its minority programming orientation. Nevertheless, thanks to that initial push ten years ago, today African-American writers, directors, actors, and producers have been able to find success not only with black audiences but with mainstream audiences as well. I believe the same thing will happen with Latinos. Unlike the African-American community, however, the U.S. Hispanic community is bilingual and bicultural, so in order to successfully reach them, corporations are going to have to learn how to talk to them in *both* languages.

ARE YOU TALKING TO ME?

I have made a career of working in Spanish-language media, and I certainly want to see Spanish media get their fair share of the advertising pie. But I also believe—and I say this at the risk of becoming a pariah in my own community—that we need to see more reaching out to Hispanics in English-language media. Why? For several reasons. For one, we have already seen a marked increase (from none to very little) of Hispanic-themed programming on English-language networks that have successfully attracted audiences and advertising dollars. (Yes, I am talking about the *George Lopez* show on ABC, *Dora the Explorer* and *The Brothers Garcia* on Nickelodeon.) Second, let us not forget that Hispanics consume just as much English-language TV as they do Spanish. In fact, as huge numbers of Latino kids grow up watching TV in English and being educated in American schools, I'm convinced that their language of choice will not be Spanish only. According to a telephone survey conducted by Sapo Communications in conjunction with the Cultural Access Group in June of 2002, the Latino youth (ages 14–24) of Los Angeles overwhelmingly favor English language media. This finding is not surprising, since two-thirds of those interviewed were born in the United States and more than half of those who were born elsewhere have spent most of their lives in this country!

Finally, I think the Spanish language itself has always been a kind of psychological "barrier" that has scared corporate America away from this market. I truly believe that creating English-language programs and media products in which corporate executives can promote their products and services to Hispanics will actually foster corporate America's desire to get into this market in a more serious way. In the television arena, some English-language ventures have already started to pay off. Nickelodeon's series *The Brothers Garcia* and *Dora the Explorer,* which debuted during the 1999–2000 season, are still among their biggest hits. Other cable networks have also won accolades and Emmy nominations for their Hispanic-themed programming: HBO's original movie, *For Love or Country: the Arturo Sandoval Story,* and Showtime's series, *Resurrection Boulevard,* are two prime examples. When I was executive editor of *TV Guide en Español,* my advertising director and I were pleasantly surprised to see how many English-language networks came to us wanting to reach out to Hispanic viewers with tune-in ads for their English-language programs. Television executives should realize that attracting Hispanic viewers to their programs could help stop the hemorrhaging of audiences the networks have been suffering now for years. Supporting Hispanic-themed television in any language is the right thing to do!

THE BLIND LEADING THE BLIND

Whatever you do, when you start working in this market, make sure you hire the right person with the right experience. I'm appalled at how quickly executives will assume a new hire knows everything about the Hispanic market simply because he or she has a Hispanic surname. Of course many people have taken advantage of this situation and have allowed their bosses to believe they *can* do the job, when they really *can't.* Believe it or not, there are many corporate executives who right now are responsible for Hispanic products and services and who don't have a clue about what they are doing. The numbers will eventually catch up to them, but in the meantime they are collecting fat paychecks and delivering nothing. Who's going to check on them? Their bosses can't read or write Spanish properly and are unable to give much needed direction or feedback. Often, these Latino executives themselves can't read or write Spanish well enough to give those who work for them proper direction on how best to sell their products in Spanish. So it's a vicious cycle that ends when someone pulls the plug or the right person gets hired. In some cases, even when the right person is in charge, corporations don't want to change the way they do business. It is no wonder the failure rate in this market has been so high! The smallest bump in the road makes these executives want to pull the plug because they feel they are blindly going forward.

The president of one of the largest Hispanic advertising agencies once told me: "It used to be that people who were not necessarily professional got the job by virtue of being Hispanic, thus creating a generation of 'professional Hispanics.' Now, people need to first be professionals in their field and then have knowledge of the Hispanic market in order to get the job, thus creating a new breed of Hispanic professionals." The only way for corporate America to get comfortable with the Hispanic market is by hiring senior level Hispanic executives who know what they are doing and trusting them to do the job right!

6

~~~

THE SPANISH-LANGUAGE
MEDIA LANDSCAPE

I n this chapter you will get a general overview of the Hispanic media market in the United States. This review by
industry will give you enough background to understand who the major
players in this market are and will outline the challenges and opportunities you may face when entering this exciting and growing marketplace. Please keep in mind that the data presented here becomes dated
the moment it is published, so you might need to get updated information before you move forward with any project of your own. The industries covered in this chapter will be television (broadcast and cable),
radio, print (magazines and newspapers), Internet, and finally, direct
marketing. But first, a few words on the role Hispanic media have
played in keeping the Spanish language and Hispanic identity alive in
the United States.

As have all immigrant groups, Hispanics in the United States created media outlets to communicate important information in their own
language to their people. The Spanish-language newspaper of Los
Angeles, *La Opinion,* and its New York counterpart, *El Diario/La
Prensa,* have each been serving the Spanish-speaking populations of
those cities for more than seventy-five years now! The first Spanish-
language radio station, KCOR in San Antonio, began transmitting in
Spanish in 1945! But as the decades have passed, the Spanish-language
media landscape has grown and become stronger, inadvertently play-

ing a critical role in keeping Hispanics from completely assimilating into the great American melting pot. By covering news and transmitting programs from back home, Hispanic media have been able to establish a direct line of communication that keeps the Spanish language alive in this country. As a result, Hispanic culture has remained strong and, more important, Spanish has become a viable consumer language in the United States. Research studies indicate that the usage of English in Latino households was at an all-time high in the late '60s and early '70s. That trend toward English usage should have continued in the Hispanic market, but it did not. In fact, it has gone in reverse! Why? Several reasons: An awakening of the Hispanic identity was partly sparked by the civil rights struggles of the '60s and '70s, making Latinos more proud of their heritage. Second, the United States experienced a significant influx of Hispanic immigrants fleeing political and economic instability in Latin America during the '80s and '90s. This phenomenon coincided with the development of national (as opposed to only local) Spanish-language media, which, in turn, spurred the growth of the His-panic advertising industry in the United States. As a result, the use of Spanish at home and at work has been steadily *increasing* over the past ten to fifteen years. When Nielsen Media Research started tracking Spanish-language media in 1992, ten of the top twenty-five programs viewed by Latinos were in Spanish. Today, all of the top twenty-five programs viewed by Hispanic adults are in Spanish!

CHANGING MEDIA HABITS

In previous chapters you have seen some data regarding media con-sumption by Hispanics. Although different companies measure His-panic media consumption differently, it is fair to say that Hispanics are heavy media consumers. Table 37 taken from *Hispanics and Entertain-ment: Insights for Culturally Relevant Marketing,* the study published in July 2003 by Cheskin Research and *People en español,* shows that overall Latino media consumption skews slightly toward Spanish in tel-evision and radio and slightly toward English in print media and the Internet.

	TABLE 37 Hispanic Media Consumption by Language		
Medium	English Avg. hours per week	Spanish Avg. hours per week	% Spanish
TV	4.54	7.14	61%
Radio	4.16	5.88	59%
Magazines	0.8	0.72	47%
Books	1.39	1.16	45%
Newspapers	1.11	0.72	39%
Internet	1.71	0.46	21%

Source: *Hispanics and Entertainment: Insights for Culturally Relevant Marketing.* Cheskin 2003

A more recent study conducted by Westhill Partners for *Poder* magazine and published in January of 2004 gave similar results.

TABLE 38 Media sources and language preference		
	Spanish	English
Television	57%	43%
Radio	56%	44%
Newspaper	53%	47%
Magazines	54%	46%
Books	55%	45%
Internet	45%	55%

Source: *What Hispanics Think, Poder*/Westhill Survey, December/January 2004

Instead of disappearing over time, as have most other immigrant media outlets, Spanish-language media have grown. In fact, during the last five years the growth of Spanish-language media has outpaced the growth of general market media! The reality is that the constant flow of Spanish-speaking immigrants and a growing Hispanic identity are going to keep fueling the growth of Spanish-language media consumption in the United States for years to come. According to Census 2000, 45 percent, or roughly 13 million people of the total foreign-born population (28.4 million) in the United States, are Hispanic. We must also keep in mind that a significant portion of the Hispanic population is also on the verge of entering the middle class, which will undoubtedly take Spanish-language consumerism to new heights in the United States. Ladies and gentlemen, you are about to experience a media revolution. Do not attempt to adjust your radio or TV. Just adjust your attitude slightly and you'll do fine.

A BRIEF HISTORY OF
SPANISH-LANGUAGE TELEVISION

Since its launch in 1956, Spanish-language television has become the largest and most profitable segment of Hispanic media. For thirty years, Univision was the only choice for Spanish-dominant television viewers in the United States. A second Spanish-language broadcast network, Telemundo, was launched in 1987. The first Spanish-language cable network, Galavision, was launched in 1979 following the boom of cable television in the United States. However, it would take twenty more years for Galavision to have any competition at all in the cable market. It wasn't until the early nineties, when cable channels were expanding their footprints in Latin America, that a second Spanish-language cable network, GEMSTV, was created. The third Spanish-language cable network, Fox Sports en Español, was launched in 1996, when the News Corporation joined forces with Liberty Media to further diversify Hispanic cable-television offerings. Today, there are dozens of Spanish-language cable channels available in the United States, most of them Spanish-language versions of well-known cable channels, among them MTV en Español, CNN en Español, and Discovery en Español, as well as some strong, new competition from cable channels from Spain and Latin America, such as RTVE or Antena 3, Casa Club TV, and Canal Sur.

However, the true explosion of Spanish- and English-language programming geared toward U.S. Hispanics occurred in the year 2000. Since then, the number of Spanish-language broadcasters in the United States has doubled: Univision and Telemundo now share airwaves with Telefutura and Azteca América, while the number of Spanish-language cable networks has increased tenfold, from three in 1999 to the more than thirty channels available on most cable systems today. On the English-language front the number of Hispanic-oriented, English-language television shows on mainstream network and cable TV has increased from zero to five since 2000. In 2004 the first English-language cable network oriented toward Hispanics, SiTV, was launched after a four-year incubation period!

For any company seriously looking to get into the Hispanic market, it is important to understand who the key media players are and how the television landscape has evolved over time. Here is a brief chronology cobbled together by using information from *Hispanic Market Weekly*'s Special Reports and *Multichannel News* magazine.

CHRONOLOGY OF SPANISH-LANGUAGE TELEVISION IN THE UNITED STATES

1955 In response to the growing number of Mexican workers living in the southwestern United States (and almost ten years after the first Spanish-language radio stations appeared in the United States), Hispanic media pioneer Raoul A. Cortéz inaugurates the first Spanish-language TV station in San Antonio, Texas. KCOR-TV, Channel 41, broadcast seven hours of live programming a day, supplemented with Mexican programming supplied by Emilio Azcárraga Vidaurreta, then chairman of Grupo Televisa, the largest Spanish-language media company in Mexico. Shortly after the launch of KCOR-TV, Cortéz launched KMEX, Channel 34, in Los Angeles, this time in partnership with Azcárraga Vidaurreta. In 1961, KCOR was acquired and changed its call letters to KWEX, when the son of Azcárraga Vidaurreta, "El Tigre," Emilio Azcárraga Milmo, joined forces with Emilio Nicolas Sr. and two other media pioneers, René Anselmo and Frank Fouce, to form the first group of Spanish-language TV stations in the United States. Together these men would play a critical role in the development of Spanish-language TV in the United States.

1961 "El Tigre" Azcárraga Milmo, Anselmo, and Fouce creates Spanish International Network (SIN), the precursor to Univision, with the launch of New York's WXTV, Channel 41, and two other TV stations. Over the next decade SIN would continue to acquire television stations and station affiliates in key Hispanic markets in order to create a national footprint, but until then, by and large the stations acted independently from one another.

1976   In an attempt to centralize its network of station affiliates, SIN starts distributing its television programming via domestic satellite, thus creating, for the first time, a national Spanish-language television footprint.

1979   Emilio Azcárraga Milmo's Grupo Televisa launches Galavision as the first Spanish-language cable network in the United States.

1986   The FCC forces SIN to sell its network and station affiliates after an investigation concludes that a majority of the company is controlled by foreign investors. Hallmark steps in and buys SIN, and one year later changes the network's name to Univision.

1987   Seeing an opportunity to enter the Spanish-language broadcast market in the United States, several former Univision executives create Telemundo by combining the strongest television station in Puerto Rico, WKAQ-TV, Channel 2, with the oldest Spanish-language station in New York, WNJU, Channel 47, and launching WSCV, Channel 51, in Miami. Picking up affiliates and buying stations whenever it could, Telemundo quickly challenged the leadership of Univision by pioneering a slate of Hispanic programming that was "made in the U.S.A." and could be much more relevant to U.S. Hispanics than the imported programming that Univision offered. By 1993, Telemundo had effectively challenged Univision's dominance, capturing a 43 percent share of the Spanish-language viewing audience.

1992   Hallmark sells Univision to a group of investors led by boxing promoter Jerrold Perenchio. Perenchio's acquisition of Univision is supported by Azcárraga Milmo's Grupo Televisa and Venezuelan media mogul Gustavo Cisnero's Venevision (the two media powerhouses of Latin America, which still today account for 80 percent of all Spanish-language TV production in the world). The deal is seen as a coup because Univision got first right of refusal to *all* of Televisa's and Venevision's television programming in exchange for 15 percent of Univision's advertising revenue. The deal was renewed under new terms in 2002, and is currently valid through 2017.

1993   Former Telemundo executive Gary McBride creates GEMS TV, the first Spanish-language cable network for women in the United

States. A secondary strategy for this new cable network was to sell its programming to the growing Latin American cable market.

1996 In order to consolidate Univision's Spanish-language offerings so that advertisers could buy across both broadcast and cable platforms in one stop, Univision acquires the largest Spanish-language cable network, Galavision, from its partner Grupo Televisa. In addition, Univision hoped to attract the younger generation of bilingual Latinos with distinctive, original programming. The bilingual programming strategy was launched in 1999 by then General Manager Lucia Ballas-Traynor, and though it gained momentum with advertisers, the strategy was abandoned abruptly in 2002 with the launch of Univision's second broadcast network, Telefutura.

1996 News Corporation and Liberty Media acquire Prime Deportiva and convert it into Fox Sports en Español, the first regional cable network dedicated to Latin sports in the United States.

1998 Sony Corporation and Liberty Media lead a small consortium of investors in the acquisition of the Telemundo network.

2001 TV Azteca, Grupo Televisa's biggest rival in Mexico, decides to enter the U.S. broadcast market by launching Azteca América in partnership with Pappas Telecasting, which owned a series of independent stations in key Hispanic markets across the United States. In Mexico, TV Azteca, which was launched originally in 1994, had successfully counterprogrammed Televisa by producing hipper *telenovelas* (Spanish soap operas) that delved into modern themes that affected Mexicans, and reality shows that captured the youth market (for example, *La Academia,* a Mexican version of *American Idol*). With thirty-eight affiliate stations, Azteca América currently reaches 78 percent of U.S. Hispanic households and has become a real contender in this space.

2001 Telemundo rebrands its women-oriented channel GEMS TV and creates MUN2, a new cable channel with programming geared toward younger, bilingual Hispanics. After being acquired by Sony in 2000, Telemundo began heavily betting on the growing Hispanic youth segment (18 to 25-year-olds). Under the leadership of Telemundo CEO Jim McNamara, and thanks to keen programming insight from its then president of entertainment, Manuel Martinez, Telemundo once again gained ground on Univision's share of the market. MUN2 was also helped by Galavision's exit from the youth-oriented, bilingual space that same year. Since NBC acquired Telemundo and MUN2 in 2002, both networks have been infused with even more English or bilingual programming, reflecting the network's ongoing bet on this growing segment of the Hispanic population. Telemundo's current programming strategy is to produce 100 percent of its prime time shows, which will undoubtedly increase the network's programming costs. What remains to be seen now is how quickly this new strategy will pay off.

2002 In order to prevent TV Azteca from acquiring a ready-made, full-power distribution network throughout the United States, Univision created a second broadcast network using the thirteen TV stations it acquired from Barry Diller in 2000 and launched a sister broadcast network, Telefutura. The effort was aimed at combating the gains made recently by Telemundo in the younger Hispanic demographic, and it clearly worked. Today, Telefutura's schedule is filled with ESPN-like sports programs as well as dubbed Hollywood movies and variety shows that appeal to younger, Spanish-dominant viewers. Since its launch, Telefutura has successfully taken audience away from Telemundo.

2004 ESPN Deportes launches in January into a relatively crowded Spanish-language sports space dominated by Univision, Telemundo, and Fox Sports en Español. But this twenty-four-hour sports channel is betting that there is room for more sports programming that appeals to the coveted adult male demographic. It also has a corporate parent with deep pockets behind it.

On the English-language cable front, SiTV, a twenty-four-hour cable network for Latinos, launched nationwide in February 2004 with an innovative slate of shows that shows off the programming expertise of founder and CEO Jeff Valdez, who has toiled long enough in Hollywood to know what's going to work with younger, bilingual Hispanics. This channel is one to watch for sure!

2004 and beyond . . . The landscape of television programming that appeals to Latinos in the United States continues to grow and evolve. Viacom has already announced the launch of several extentions of their

MTV and VH1 brands for the U.S. Hispanic market toward the end of 2005 and so has Discovery Networks! On the Spanish-language front, just about every major cable operator has started offering Spanish-language packages with its digital services, and more cable operators are expected to follow. We will also continue to see more new Latino-oriented shows on mainstream network TV, following the success of ABC's *George Lopez Show,* and a second English-language cable network for Latinos, VOY, is expected to debut sometime in 2006.

OVERVIEW OF MEDIA LANDSCAPE BY INDUSTRY

In the world of Spanish-language media, Univision is king. Its media empire is composed of two broadcast networks, Univision and Telefutura, as well as the largest Spanish-language cable network, Galavision. It also controls the largest Spanish-language radio network, Univision Radio, the largest Latin music record label, Fonovisa, and it owns 50 percent of the second largest Latin music record label, Disa. Univision also owns the Spanish-language Internet portal, Univision.com, which according to ComScore Media Metrix's January 2005 report is the most visited Spanish-language website by Hispanics in the United States. Expect to hear a lot about Univision in this chapter.

SPANISH-LANGUAGE TV

Focusing now on TV, according to the Nielsen Hispanic Television Index, the share of total Hispanic adults watching Spanish-language programs during prime time Monday through Sunday has steadily increased from 37 percent during the 1992–1993 season, when they started tracking it, to 51 percent during the 2003–2004 season (chart 28).

Univision network regularly dominates all television demos and day parts, delivering more Hispanic eyeballs than anyone else. In fact, if you look at Nielsen's list of the top twenty-five Spanish-language shows during the 2003–2004 season (table 39), Univision reigns supreme.

In major media markets such as Los Angeles or Miami, Univision network easily beats all the English-language networks as well as its

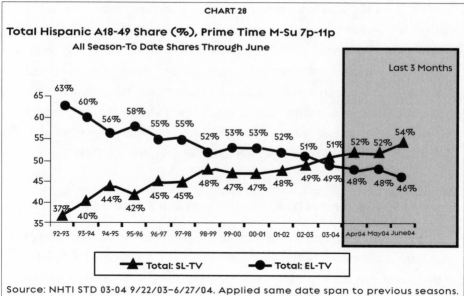

CHART 28

Total Hispanic A18-49 Share (%), Prime Time M-Su 7p-11p
All Season-To Date Shares Through June

Last 3 Months

Total: SL-TV   Total: EL-TV

Source: NHTI STD 03-04 9/22/03–6/27/04. Applied same date span to previous seasons. Monday–Sunday 7:00–11:00pm (includes only advertiser-supported networks, cable, and independents; excludes, pay cable, pay-per-view and PBS). The Spanish-Language TV category includes viewing to all TF, TEL and UNI affiliates (including network cable outlets), plus any viewing to the following: Spanish-language stations originating in Mexico, Spanish-language independent stations (i.e., those stations that are not affiliated with either TF, TEL or UNI) and viewing to Spanish-language cable networks.

main competitor, Telemundo. In fact, it is the number-one station from sign on to sign off in L.A. and Miami among adults ages 18–34, adults ages 18–49, and adults ages 25–54! To give you a sense of the power of Univision, according to data from Nielsen research for November of 2004, Univision novelas *Rubi* and *Amor Real* averaged more total adult viewers ages 18–49 (Hispanic *and* non-Hispanic) than *Rebel Million-aire* on Fox, *LAX* on NBC, *JAG* on CBS, *One Tree Hill* on the WB, and *Extreme Makeover* on ABC, to name but a few of the English-language shows Univision beat during the 2004 November sweeps period.

In terms of advertising, Univision is King Kong, raking in $1.3 billion of the estimated $1.8 billion advertisers spent on Spanish-language TV in 2003, according to TNS Media Intelligence/CMR. Experts are now predicting that Univision's share of the national Spanish-language advertising pie is going to get even bigger, since the FCC gave Univision permission to buy the largest Spanish-language radio network in the

TABLE 39

TOP 25 PROGRAMS (May 03–May '04)	NETWORK	HHLD	HISPANIC ADULTS 15–49	TELEVISA NOVELA
PREMIO LO NUESTRO 2004	Univision	27.4	15.9	
NOCHE DE ESTRELLAS 2004	Univision	24.9	13.0	
ENTRE EL AMOR Y ODIO	Univision	25.2	11.8	X
NINA AMADA MIA	Univision	24.1	11.8	X
SELENA...ULTIMO ADIOS	Univision	21.8	11.7	
MARIANA DE LA NOCHE	Univision	21.1	10.8	X
NOTICIERO UNIVISION PRESENTA	Univision	19.9	11.3	
VELO DE NOVIA	Univision	21.8	10.0	X
FINAL: COPA DE ORO 2003	Univision	14.8	10.4	
PREMIOS TV Y NOVELAS 2003	Univision	18.8	10.1	
SELENA...INOLVIDABLE	Univision	18.2	10.0	
BAJO LA MISMA PIEL	Univision	19.1	9.0	X
CINE ESPECIAL	Univision	18.0	9.8	
PREMIOS FURIA MUSICAL 2004	Univision	17.4	9.5	
NOCHE DE ESTRELLAS 2003	Univision	15.9	9.4	
VIAS DEL AMOR	Univision	19.6	9.3	X
MANANTIAL	Univision	20.3	9.0	X
MARIANA DE LA NOCHE	Univision	18.4	9.2	X
AMAR OTRA VEZ	Univision	18.7	8.4	X
CINE ESPECIAL	Univision	13.5	9.0	
CINE ESPECIAL	Univision	18.9	8.9	
CINE ESPECIAL	Univision	17.4	8.9	
REBECA	Univision	17.2	8.3	
CRISTINA	Univision	17.5	8.7	
DON FRANCISCO PRESENTA	Univision	17.8	8.6	

Source: Nielsen Hispanic Television Index

country, Hispanic Broadcasting Corporation, in September of 2003. The $3.2 billion merger—the largest in Spanish-language media history— allowed Univision to become the dominant player in the radio space overnight, but its position did not come without controversy. The FCC spent over a year analyzing the deal before giving it its blessing. During that time, Univision executives, who are strictly forbidden to speak to the press by corporate mandate, were forced to publicly defend their position. Univision's argument was that the only way for it to compete with English-language networks in the general market was by becoming a one-stop shop for their advertisers. This cross-platform strategy would give

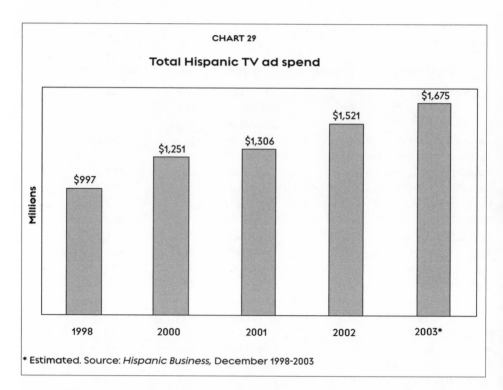

CHART 29

Total Hispanic TV ad spend

Millions

$997	$1,251	$1,306	$1,521	$1,675
1998	2000	2001	2002	2003*

* Estimated. Source: *Hispanic Business,* December 1998-2003

Univision the ability to attract mainstream advertisers who have never ventured into the Hispanic market before. Those who favored the merger said that a one-stop shop for advertisers would allow Spanish-language media to finally compete on the same playing field as English-language television networks for a larger slice of the more than $200 billion national advertising pie. But critics of the merger said that Univision was becoming a monopoly, with too much control over the total Hispanic media pie, both in terms of content and in terms of advertising clout.

According to a HispanTelligence report published in December of 2004, ad revenues in Spanish-language TV have increased 73 percent since 1999, experiencing double-digit growth every year, except for 2001. The reason behind that jump can be found in the demos and ratings Spanish-language television is drawing. According to Nielsen's Hispanic Television Audience Report for March 2003, which covered the February sweeps period, from Monday to Sunday during prime time, Univision had a 10.9 average rating with Hispanic viewers 21 years of age and older. Telemundo came in second, with a 2.8 average rating, and Telefutura garnered a 1.6 average rating—not bad for a one-year-old network! By comparison, the average rating for non-Hispanic broadcast networks was 8.7 and for ad-supported cable networks, 8.2.

Univision's main rival, Telemundo, is not down and out, however. Although the network's ratings slipped a little (perhaps due to transition issues arising from its merger with NBC and the important gains registered by Telefutura) since being acquired by NBC in 2002, Telemundo has recently been bouncing back. From February 2003 to February 2004, Telemundo saw a 59 percent jump in impressions and a 41 percent boost in its share of Spanish-language TV in the 18–49 demo, according to a special report published by *Broadcasting & Cable* in March 2004. Telemundo's mantra has always been to produce Spanish-language television *made in the U.S.A. for the Hispanic market,* and now that it has the help (and deeper pockets) of NBC, 100 percent of its prime time slate is original programming.

Meanwhile, 80 percent of Univision's prime time slate is still made up of Mexican *telenovelas* from its main programming supplier, Grupo Televisa, a programming strategy that continues to work effortlessly. Some people think that since the majority of Hispanics in the United States are Mexican, they remain faithful to shows from their homeland, and while that is true, it is not the only reason why *telenovelas* garner such great ratings for Univision. The *telenovela* has become a world-wide phenomenon and these Mexican soaps are successfully capturing audiences around the world! Unlike American soaps, however, these *telenovelas* do not go on forever. The ones on Univision air first in Mexico and Puerto Rico and usually come to an end after about only six months, so if they are good, there will be a built-in buzz about them even before they air here in the United States! As do American soaps, they air Monday through Friday, with a major cliff-hanger in the plot every day to keep people "hooked." But unlike American soaps, which dominate daytime programming, *telenovelas* dominate Spanish-language television's *prime time* schedule because they draw such huge ratings. So, during weekdays, the only choice from 7 P.M. until 11 P.M. on both Univision and Telemundo are *telenovelas.* If you want to watch something else, you have to go somewhere else. This is something unique about the Spanish-language TV industry in the United States and, in fact, in many Latin American countries. To the surprise of many in the television industry, the *telenovela* format has turned into an incredibly successful, multibillion-dollar industry, with Mexico's Grupo Televisa leading the way in terms of global sales. Because of their universal content and messages, *telenovelas* "travel well," as I mentioned earlier. They have become popular all over the world, from Russia to the Ivory Coast in Africa. Now, let's get back to our review of the major TV players in the United States today.

Televisa's main rival in Mexico, TV Azteca, decided to enter the U.S. Hispanic market in 2001 by launching a broadcast network in partnership with Los Angeles-based Pappas Telecasting, which owned a number of independent television stations in several of the key Hispanic markets in the United States. The new U.S.-based network, Azteca América, features programming produced in Mexico for a younger and hipper audience. It also fills its prime time slate with *telenovelas*, but their themes are geared to younger Mexican audiences and they deal with provocative issues, such as homosexuality and drug abuse, subjects that rarely surface in the more traditional Cinderella stories that Televisa is famous for. They also have exclusive rights to certain key Mexican soccer league matches, which is a big plus for attracting male viewers.

As a result of some initial difficulties with its U.S. partner, TV Azteca signed a programming deal with Echostar's Dish Latino, which allowed Dish to carry the TV Azteca signal on its satellite network, diluting the power of its new American venture. Over the past couple of years, however, TV Azteca has been able to restructure its partnership, with Pappas Telecasting taking over control of all of its affiliates across the country and expanding its signal to thirty-eight affiliates which reach 78 percent of the Hispanic market. In March of 2005, TV Azteca's deal with Echostar's Dish Latino was set to expire, which I believe will definitely help drive loyal satellite viewers to the broadcast network. In addition, Azteca América executives announced some very aggressive and interesting programming changes during their 2005 upfront presentation, like airing the same episode of the same popular *telenovela* on the same day and time in Mexico and here in the United States.

In summary, the dominant player in the Spanish-language TV market is Univision, whose three networks combined garner an 80 percent share of the national Spanish-language TV viewing audience (18–49). Individually, Univision network's share is roughly 60 percent of the national Spanish-language TV viewing audience (18–49). Telemundo, a distant second, garners about a 20 percent share of the market, while Univision's sister network, Telefutura, has a 13 percent share. Univision's sister on cable, Galavision, gets about a 3 percent share of the national Spanish-language TV viewing audience (18–49). Azteca América is still not measured nationally but has been making significant gains since it launched in 2001.

CABLE TV

Twenty years ago, very few believed in the idea of creating new channels of entertainment tailor-made for niche segments of the television viewing audience. Certainly, nobody—except cable industry executives—ever expected cable TV to eventually attract *more* viewers than broadcast networks, which occurred for the first time in 2002 and continues to be the case today! Nevertheless, today 83 percent of U.S. households are cable subscribers, and the number of ad-supported networks increases every year, generating more than $19 billion in revenues annually, according to the Cabletelevision Advertising Bureau (CAB). According to Nielsen Media Research, the total number of Hispanic TV households in the United States has increased 9 percent, from 8.94 million in 2001 to 9.73 million in 2003. According to the CAB, cable penetration among the total Hispanic population was at 72 percent in 2004, which is only 10 percent below the average for the U.S. population.

With the exception of Galavision, the development of Spanish-language cable channels did not occur until the decade of the '90s, when general market cable networks such as CNN and the Discovery Channel were looking to expand into new markets. The logical first step was to go south of the border, where they already had satellite footprints, so the cable industry first developed Spanish-language networks for the growing cable markets of Latin America. Expansion to Europe followed, and now, of course, everyone is trying to get into India and

China. After an initial successful run in Latin America, Spanish-language cable channels stopped growing due to the limitations of the existing Latin American advertising market and to the various economic crises that have rocked key markets, among them Mexico, Argentina, and more recently Venezuela. As a result, these Latin American cable channels have had to look for more stable markets for growth, and their eyes are definitely fixed on the U.S. Hispanic market.

"Although in its infancy still, the outlook is great for Hispanic cable," says the Hispanic Marketer's Guide to Cable, a special guide developed in 2002 by the CAB in conjunction with the Association of Hispanic Advertising Agencies (AHAA). "Rising in the shadows of a progressive general-market cable industry, Hispanic cable subscribers increased 98% from 1994 to 2002, the number of viewers increased 72% and the total day viewing share increased 40% from 2000 to 2002. And finally, the number of advertisers using Hispanic cable has increased 142% from 1998 to 2002."

The cable industry is finally waking up to this underserved market, especially since satellite providers DirecTV and Dish Latino have experienced significant growth over the past five years by specifically catering to the Latino market. Time Warner cable was the leader of the pack in 2002, when it used New York as a testing ground for a package of Spanish-language channels called *DTV en español*. The test was successful, and now the package is being rolled out nationwide. In 2003, Charter Communications and Comcast jumped on the Hispanic cable bandwagon, introducing their own Spanish-language packages fortified by television channels from all over the Hispanic world, from Spain to Argentina. By picking up ready-made channels from other parts of the Spanish-speaking world, cable operators now hope to attract more Hispanic subscribers to their services.

In order to compete with the Spanish-language broadcasters, Hispanic cable television is touting its ability to target specific segments of the Hispanic market that are underserved by the Spanish-language broadcasters. The Hispanic Marketer's Guide to Cable identifies those underserved Hispanic segments as (1) Hispanic males, (2) the "New Latina," (3) the elusive youth market, and, of course, (4) Hispanic kids. Since Hispanics are fueling most of the growth in the 18–34 demographic and in the youth and children's market, it is only logical that the cable industry would focus on them. Table 40 illustrates the impressive population growth that can be attributed to Latinos within those key demographic groups.

Nobody can argue with the fact that television is the medium of choice among Hispanics. According to Synovate's 2004 U.S. Hispanic Market Report, on average Hispanics spend 43.5 percent of their media time watching television, versus 36.6 percent for African-Americans and 33.9 percent for the general population, so advertising on television is a must for anyone entering this market. As cable offerings grow, the share of advertising dollars allocated to cable will also increase. According to Synovate's study, Hispanic males divide their TV viewing time more evenly between English TV (54 percent) and Spanish TV (45 percent) than do Hispanic females, who watch Spanish-language TV 58 percent of the time they spend watching television. According to CAB's upfront 04/05 Multicultural Marketing Guide, already in the year 2004:

- Hispanic kids, youth, and men (in that order) view substantially more cable TV than Hispanic women.
- Cable viewing among Hispanics increases significantly on weekends, when English and Spanish cable combined capture a 91 percent share of viewing against total Hispanic cable households.
- English-language cable captures higher percentages of Hispanic TV viewing than English-language broadcast TV.

TABLE 40 Hispanic population growth 2001–2002

		HHs	Persons 2+	M 18–34	F 18–34	Persons 2–17
Total U.S.	2001	102,200	261,780	30,410	30,450	62,510
	2002	105,500	269,880	31,080	31,110	64,250
	Growth	3,300	8,100	670	660	1,740
Hispanics	2001	8,940	30,382	4,302	4,057	10,056
	2002	10,200	34,405	4,917	4,519	11,353
	Growth	1,260	4,023	615	462	1,297
	% of U.S. growth	**38.20%**	**49.70%**	**91.80%**	**70.00%**	**74.50%**

Source: 2001–2002 Nielsen Media Research Universal Estimates

TABLE 41

Network	U.S. Subscribers	Network	U.S. Subscribers
Canal 24 Horas	100,000	La Familia	400,000
Canal Sur	1,800,000	Latin TV (LTV)	1,500,000
Caracol TV Internacional	500,000	LATV	3,500,000
Casa Club TV	1,200,000	Mas Musica Teve	12,500,000
Cine Latino	1,600,000	MTV español	13,000,000
CNN Español	2,600,000	Mun2	6,000,000
Discovery Español	7,300,000	SiTV	7,700,000
ESPN Deportes	2,500,000	Sorpresa	500,000
Fox Sports en Español	6,600,000	TBN Enlace USA	1,500,000
Galavision	5,900,000	Telefe Internacional	200,000
Gol TV	5,000,000	Telehit	7,000,000
Grandes Documentales	500,000	TV Chile	1,300,000
HBO Latino	NA	TVE Internacional	1,600,000
HITN	13,700,000	Utilisima	800,000
HTV	1,300,000	VHUno	4,300,000
Infinito	200,000		

Source: *Multichannel News* Hispanic Television Summit, December 6, 2004

The strongest barriers for Hispanic cable channels to overcome are the limited bandwidth of analog television, and, more important, whether they are located in English- or Spanish-language tiers. Now, with digital technology, the bandwidth available for new channels has grown exponentially, and cable providers will soon be able to offer hundreds more channels. To give you a sense of who are some of the key players in Spanish- and English-language cable today, table 41 lists the current national distribution levels for each of the Hispanic cable networks. Keep in mind that the subscriber base in Hispanic households is *significantly* lower.

As mentioned at the very beginning of this chapter, Hispanics watch both English- and Spanish-language television, but not too much attention has ever been paid to how much TV Hispanics are watching in English. The following list, which comes from the *Hispanics and Entertainment: Insights for Culturally Relevant Marketing* study, will give you an idea of what English-language channels Hispanics are tuning in to:

TABLE 42 Most Watched English-Language Channels

Disney	ESPN
HBO	ABC
CNN	Cinemax
FOX	NBC
PBS	Showtime
CBS	Starz

Source: *Hispanics and Entertainment: Insights for Culturally Relevant Marketing,* Cheskin

Of course, the English-language channels Hispanic households will be watching varies every season, if not every day, but table 43 gives you a glimpse of the most popular shows Hispanics were watching on broadcast television in December 2004.

SPANISH-LANGUAGE RADIO

Radio is the pioneer media of Spanish-language media. It predates Spanish-language television by ten to fifteen years, and like broadcast

TABLE 43 Top 15 Prime Time Programs—English-Language Broadcast

HH Ranking	Program name	Network	Rating	Hispanic HH's	Hispanic Viewers 2+
1	CSI	CBS	7.4	810,000	1,075,000
2	Monday Night Football	ABC	7.1	771,000	1,074,000
3	Lost	ABC	6.6	723,000	1,078,000
4	CSI: Miami	CBS	6.2	676,000	887,000
5	Without a Trace	CBS	5.9	643,000	846,000
6	NFL Monday Showcase	ABC	5.5	600,000	774,000
7	Extreme Makeover	ABC	5.4	589,000	847,000
8	Will & Grace	NBC	5.2	569,000	1,096,000
8	E.R.	NBC	5.2	566,000	857,000
8	Fear Factor	NBC	5.2	563,000	948,000
11	CSI: N.Y.	CBS	4.9	532,000	717,000
12	My Wife and Kids	ABC	4.5	492,000	686,000
12	Law & Order	NBC	4.5	489,000	764,000
14	Joey	NBC	4.4	484,000	736,000
15	Smallville	WB	4.4	484,000	684,000

Source: Nielsen Media Research

television is growing stronger today than general-market radio. When talking about pioneers in the Spanish-language radio industry, one must talk about the legacy of the Tichenor family from Texas. The Tichenors were the first to broadcast Spanish-language programming on their English-language stations as early as 1949. You see, McHenry Tichenor was a radio entrepreneur who had acquired the license to KGBS in Harlingen, Texas. Shortly after buying this station, he realized that the ratings were very low. So, in order to improve his ratings, Tichenor started broadcasting Spanish-language programs at night, figuring that the proximity to Mexico would help. The strategy worked, and the Tichenor family continued to acquire radio stations in Texas. Prompted by the success of his nighttime programs, in 1962 Tichenor converted KGBS into a full-time Spanish-language radio station. After that the Tichenor radio empire was literally built on the power of Spanish-language formats, and the rest, as they say, is history.

Another pioneer in Spanish-language radio is Eduardo Caballero, who, in 1973, started the first and largest rep firm for Spanish-language radio, Caballero Spanish Media, which he sold to Interep in 1995. Legendary for his advocacy of a united Hispanic market, Caballero was inducted into the Broadcasting & Cable Hall of Fame in the fall of 2004 not only for his work in radio and TV early on, but for continuing to set the pace for many in the Hispanic media world. In 1998 he launched a new venture, Más Música TeVe, a Spanish-language music and video network, and in 2004 he launched Caballero TV and Cable Sales, a rep firm for independent Hispanic stations!

According to Arbitron's 2003 edition of *Hispanic Radio Today: How America Listens to Radio,* in 1980 there were sixty-seven Spanish-language radio stations, whereas today there are about 700. Although that sounds like a lot, keep in mind that that figure represents only 5.7 percent of all the radio stations in the United States. Most of the growth in Spanish-language radio, however, has occurred over the last decade via consolidation.

Up until the late '90s, Spanish-language radio industry was growing organically. Small independents started buying up more and more stations and converting them to Spanish-language formats, but there was no real "national" presence until 1997. The 1997 merger of Tichenor Media Systems and Heftel Broadcasting allowed the new station group to have a presence for the first time in all of the top ten U.S. Hispanic markets, giving the newly formed network a national advertising footprint and changing the Spanish-language radio landscape forever. With thirty-eight stations under its control, the merged company kept on growing, and then changed its name to Hispanic Broadcasting Corporation in 1999. With the help of Spanish-language mergers and acquisitions expert Julio Rumbaut, by 2002, H.B.C. had become the leading Spanish-language radio broadcaster in the United States. In 2002, of course, Univision announced it was buying H.B.C. and changed its name to Univision Radio. Univision Radio is based in Dallas, Texas, and has sixty-eight stations under its control in seventeen of the twenty-five top Spanish-language radio markets.

The second largest national Spanish-language radio network in the United States is Spanish Broadcasting Systems (SBS), which was launched in 1983 by Raúl Alarcón Sr., a Cuban media entrepreneur who began his radio career by acquiring a single AM station in New York City. During the 1990s the company grew tremendously by appealing to younger Latinos, who also were predominantly from the Caribbean. SBS is credited with creating some of the most interesting and successful Spanish-language radio formats, and its New York station has been one of the most listened to stations in any language in that market since 1999. Now run by Alarcón's son and headquartered in Miami, SBS owns twenty-seven stations in seven of the top ten U.S. Hispanic markets: Chicago, Los Angeles, Miami, New York, San Antonio, San Francisco, and Puerto Rico. When the H.B.C.-Univision merger was first announced in July of 2002, Raúl Alarcón, Jr., became its most vocal opponent. Initially, Alarcón was fighting against the merger alone, claiming that the union of the two dominant players in Spanish-language television and radio would result in a monopoly that would give Univision control over 70 percent of the total Hispanic advertising pie. During the fifteen months it took for the FCC to review the proposed merger, opposition gained momentum as Alarcón was joined by other important groups and media players. But, in the end, the FCC allowed the merger to go through on two conditions:

1. That Univision divest itself of at least two H.B.C. radio stations in order to comply with the new media ownership regulations, and
2. That Univision reduce its 27 percent investment in Entravision, the third major player in the Spanish-language radio industry, to 10 percent by May of 2009.

Established in 1996 with its corporate headquarters based in Santa Monica, California, Entravision Communications Corporation is a diversified Spanish-language media company with interests spread across television, radio, and outdoor advertising. Entravision owns and operates television stations in twenty of the top fifty U.S. Hispanic markets and two television stations in Hispanic markets that are ranked between 50 and 75 in the United States. Its television stations consist primarily of affiliates of the two broadcast networks of Univision Communications Inc., making it the largest Univision-affiliated television group in the United States. It also owns and operates fifty-three radio stations in twenty-one markets, fifty-two of which are located in the top fifty Hispanic markets in the United States, making Entravision one of the nation's largest Spanish-language radio broadcasters.

These are the main players in the Hispanic radio space today, although in the fall of 2004, all the major players in the English-language radio market indicated that they too were seriously considering getting into the Spanish-language radio game. Clear Channel is the one that has taken the biggest steps toward that goal when it announced that it was converting twenty-five of its English-language stations to Spanish-language formats and had developed a new "hurban" format (Hispanic + urban) that is currently being tested in Texas. ABC Radio also got in the game in 2005 by syndicating several top-rated Spanish-language radio shows on its network of radio stations. Viacom and Infinity broadcasting also took baby steps in this market, which clearly indicates to me that the conga beat is going to be heard loud and clear for years to come!

Listening Preferences

In its 2003 edition of *Hispanic Radio Today: How America Listens to Radio* Arbitron combined for the first time consumer data from Scarborough Research to additionally provide detailed information on the consumer habits of Hispanic radio listeners in 2002. The results are startling. According to Arbitron, Hispanics listen to radio more than their non-Hispanic counterparts, averaging about nineteen hours per week versus sixteen hours per week for non-Hispanics. When listening to Spanish-language stations only, the average number of hours Hispanics listen jumps to almost twenty-two hours per week.

In addition, Spanish-language radio's total "average quarter-hour persons" share, which measures the number of people listening to a particular station for more than five minutes at a time, has risen to 8.1 percent of the nation's total in 2002, up 1.1 percent from 2001.

When it comes to Spanish-language music formats, regional Mexican music is king, just as it is in record sales. The format accounts for 17.7 percent of all Hispanic listening, up 3.1 percent from 2001. But among Hispanic listeners in general, the second-most favored format is English-language Top 40, with a 14.6 percent share of the total Hispanic audience. These data clearly reflect and reinforce the bilingual nature of the Hispanic population. Spanish contemporary radio ranks third, with 13.4 percent of the Hispanic listening audience—up 2.5 percent from 2001—while another English-language format, adult contemporary, follows it with 8.2 percent of the Hispanic listening audience. Tropical music formats trail on the list of Spanish-language formats, with just 6.1 percent of the total Hispanic radio audience, and Tejano is at the bottom of the list with a mere 1.4 percent, probably because the format is mostly confined to southwestern states.

"The key here is that people who are young prefer the latest stuff, and they will turn to [top 40] as well as Hispanic radio [for it]," Thom Mocarsky, Arbitron's vice president of communications, told *Billboard*'s Leila Cobo in an interview in June of 2003. But, he cautions, "just because they listen to [top 40] radio doesn't mean they don't listen to Spanish-language radio." The issue of language again rears its ugly head in the Spanish-language radio industry as well, since Arbitron does not factor in language preference in its market reports. According to Mocarsky, Hispanic households are defined as specified by the household members. And although Spanish preference is tracked, it will likely not be used in market reports until 2006.

Show Me the Money!

Although there are no reliable, industrywide figures, it is estimated that 26 percent of all Hispanic advertising budgets go to local and national radio, which in 2004 was worth roughly $664 million. The good news is that Hispanic radio gets a larger percent of share than general-market radio buys, which usually captures only a 9 percent share of the total advertising spend.

While Spanish-language television is clearly the dominant player in terms of Hispanic advertising share, I think Spanish-language radio comes in second because it delivers both reach and frequency. Usually radio is considered only a frequency vehicle because it delivers the same message to the same audience over and over. But as you have already seen, Spanish-language radio is different, mainly because music formats are more popular than talk radio and because of the nature of

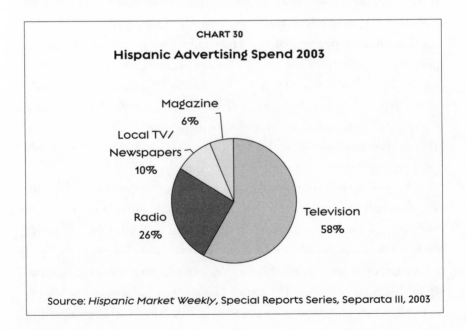

CHART 30

Hispanic Advertising Spend 2003

Magazine 6%

Local TV/ Newspapers 10%

Radio 26%

Television 58%

Source: *Hispanic Market Weekly*, Special Reports Series, Separata III, 2003

Spanish-language *television* programming. Remember *telenovelas* dominate the prime time schedule of the two largest Spanish-language networks, and since they are on at the same time every day, they tend to draw the same people at the same time night after night. So, smart media buyers use Hispanic radio as a cost-effective "reach" vehicle because of Spanish radio's ability to offer different music programming in different markets at the same time. Unlike English-language radio, which is dominated by the talk/news format, music is the leading Spanish-language radio format for Hispanics in the United States. Since the various music formats that exist today in Spanish-language radio also closely reflect different segments of the Latino population across the United States (regional Mexican = Mexicans; tropical = Puerto Ricans, Cubans, and Dominicans; Top 40 and Spanish contemporary = Latino youth), media buyers can specifically target those segments of the Hispanic community they are most interested in reaching. Finally, another very important thing to note about the Spanish-language radio industry is that unlike the Spanish-language television networks, radio networks have been much more flexible with advertisers about what language to run spots in. So it is not uncommon to be listening to a Spanish-language radio station with bilingual radio hosts that not only use both languages on air, but also mix in English-language commercials in their commercial lineup, inadvertently creating another platform for bilingualism in this country.

SPANISH-LANGUAGE PRINT

Another common myth about the Latino market is that Hispanics don't read. Nothing gets my goat more than this misconception because it denies the historical love affair Hispanic countries have always had with the written word. I am happy to report that the Spanish-language publishing industry is alive and well all over the Spanish-speaking world! All you have to do is go to Mexico City or Buenos Aires or Barcelona, and you will find people everywhere you look, young and old, consuming all sorts of print products, especially books, newspapers, and magazines! Growing up in Spain—a country that is the size of Texas—I vividly remember that everybody in Madrid read at least *three* newspapers a day. (There are about half a dozen national newspapers in Spain!) In fact, going to the corner kiosk to buy your newspapers or magazines was, and still is, a sacrosanct tradition, a way of communing with your neighbors and partaking of life on the streets.

I'm not even sure how this myth came about here in the United States, but I can tell you that it is definitely not true. Perhaps the misconception began because it is hard as hell to find a good bookstore that sells modern Spanish-language literature. What you usually find in bookstores are classic works of Spanish literature or books that are "required reading" at the local university. In New York City, for crying out loud, there are only a handful of Spanish-language bookstores! Honestly, as do most of my friends, I buy most of my Spanish-language literature when I'm traveling abroad. The other common way of getting books is by having someone send you stuff from abroad. I cherish the lovely packages my aunt Carmelina (another avid reader) sends me every Christmas from Spain. Ask anyone you know who is Latino where they buy their Spanish-language books and I bet you most of them will tell you they get stuff sent from back home, wherever that may be. Thankfully, that is changing now that the book publishing and bookselling giants have realized there is a huge untapped market of Hispanic readers in the United States.

In terms of newspapers and magazines, it wasn't until very recently—maybe in the past five to ten years—that some of the major newsstand chains started carrying Spanish-language newspapers and magazines. As long as I've been in this country, which is more than twenty years now, the place to get your Spanish-language newspapers or magazines was at the local *bodega,* or grocery store. In the barrio, of course, there always were one or two independent newsstand owners who carried Spanish-language materials, but you have to know where to go. Contrary to publications in the general market, many Spanish-language newspapers and magazines don't even offer subscription services! (But that is another story.) And finally, the magazine offering is very limited. In a country where there are thousands of magazine titles for every imaginable niche or interest in English, there are only about seventy-five magazines servicing the entire Hispanic magazine-reading population. And of those, only *six* are actually made for the U.S. Hispanic audience. One-third of the magazines available to Hispanics in this country are actually produced in Mexico, overprinted and sold in this country. The other third are translations of English publications written with an American reader in mind, and more often than not they are also poorly translated. (How many times have you read the instructions that come with an electronics product and not understood a thing, even though it is written in English? Well, believe it or not, sometimes that's what it feels like reading some of these so-called "Hispanic" magazines.) So I wonder if the perception that Latinos don't read perhaps comes from the fact that *they don't have anything good to read!*

Spanish-language Newspapers

I have spent half of my career working in Spanish-language television and the other half in Spanish-language print, which is why this subject is near and dear to my heart. Although I haven't worked in the newspaper business for a while now, it is exciting to know that the Spanish-language newspaper industry is growing, something the English-language newspaper industry cannot claim. In fact, 2004 began with a virtual declaration of war between the established old guard *La Opinión* and the new kid on the block, *Hoy.* The war had been festering for a year before it broke in January, but when all was said and done, it looks like Latinos may soon have not one, but two national newspapers to choose from! Let me give you some history.

It all began in 2000 when the Tribune Company purchased the Times Mirror Company (owners of the *Los Angeles Times*), which had a 50 percent equity stake in the largest Spanish-language newspaper, *La Opinión.* In 1990 Times Mirror had purchased its share of *La Opinión,* which was owned and operated by the Lozano family, in the hope of expanding its reach into the coveted Hispanic market of Los Angeles. Tribune's foray into the Hispanic market began in 1998, when it decided to launch *Hoy,* a new Spanish-language daily, in New York City, to compete with the oldest Spanish-language newspaper in the United States and the largest metropolitan newspaper servicing Hispanics in the New York area, *El Diario La Prensa*. By 2003, *Hoy* was a huge success. It had doubled its circulation over *El Diario La Prensa*'s daily circulation and in September of that year, the company was announcing the launch of another *Hoy* newspaper, this time in Chicago. Once Tribune had completed its purchase of the Times Mirror Company, the Lozano family suspected that Tribune might want to launch another *Hoy* in Los Angeles, which it did in March of 2004. So, the Lozano family decided to buy back their 50 percent share from Tribune and then teamed up with the new owners of *El Diario La Prensa*, CPK Media, to create a new company in early 2004. The new company, Impremedia LLC, has been pursuing an aggressive plan to expand to other markets and develop a "national footprint." In the fall of 2004, Impremedia acquired *La Raza*, Chicago's largest Spanish-language newspaper. But in order to have a viable "national footprint," Impremedia will have to have a presence in most, if not all, of the top ten Hispanic markets, and that won't be easy.

However, Tribune's Cinderella story with *Hoy* was rocked by scandal in the summer and fall of 2004, when it was disclosed that the company had overstated its circulation of *Hoy* in New York by 46.4 percent in 2003. As a result, both *Newsday*'s and *Hoy*'s publishers suddenly announced their retirements, and the Chicago and Los Angeles editions of *Hoy* moved from a paid circulation model to a controlled distribution model in January 2005. But the circulation scandal has not shaken the faith in the growing Spanish-language newspaper industry as other players continue to launch products in this market. In 2003 *The Dallas Morning News* launched *Al Día*, a Spanish-language daily intended to service the 1.5 million Latinos living in the Dallas/Fort Worth area. *Al Día* will have to compete, however, with a healthy stable of a dozen weekly, fortnightly, and monthly Latino publications that already exist in north Texas. In 2004, Pearson acquired a majority stake in Meximerica Media Inc., announcing plans to launch at least four more regional newspapers under the Rumbo name in the south Texas area. In addition, several other companies have announced plans to launch Spanish-language newspapers everywhere from Long Island, New York, to Boston, Massachusetts, adding to the more than

634 Hispanic newspapers that already exist in the United States, according to the National Association of Hispanic Publications.

The National Association of Hispanic Publications, Inc. (NAHP, Inc.), is a nonprofit trade advocacy organization representing more than 200 Hispanic publications (both in English and in Spanish) serving more than fifty-five markets in twenty-eight states and Puerto Rico with a combined circulation of more than 14 million. Its members are weekly newspapers distributed all over the United States. Since March of 2004, all of its member newspapers have been required to be audited, something that has hindered the growth of many Spanish-language publications in the past, since big advertisers will not place advertising in publications that are not audited. So, in an effort to help more publications be audited, Verizon Communications gave NAHP a $185,000 grant in 2003 to develop an "Audit as Growth Initiative." Nevertheless, the NAHP reported a 32 percent increase in newspaper ad revenues from 1990 to 2000 and a 12 percent increase from 2000 to 2001. The drivers of much of that growth, however, are the big four newspapers that dominate the U.S. Hispanic market:

- *La Opinión* had a daily circulation of 125,862 copies and a Sunday circulation of 68,363 in 2004. With more than 7 million Latinos living in the Los Angeles D.M.A., representing 44 percent of the total population, *La Opinión* is still the largest Spanish-language newspaper in the country.

- *El Nuevo Herald* had a daily circulation of 88,291 copies and a Sunday circulation of 95,575 in 2004. This Spanish-language sister of *The Miami Herald* has grown in leaps and bounds since it relaunched in 1987. That is no surprise given the fact that 1.8 million Hispanics live in the Miami area and represent over 40 percent of the total population.

- *El Diario La Prensa*—the nation's oldest Spanish-language daily—in January of 2005 was selling 50,040 copies from Monday through Friday, 49,908 copies on Saturday, and 35,740 copies on Sunday. Unlike other dailies in Miami or Los Angeles, *El Diario La Prensa's* circulation is mainly based on newsstand sales, since it only recently began offering subscription services.

- **Hoy,** *Newsday's* Spanish-language sister in New York, which debuted in 1998 with 25,000 copies, had reached a circulation of 49,681 during the twelve-month period ending September 30, 2003 according to its revised audit released in 2005. Although it does not produce a Saturday paper, *Hoy's* Sunday circulation was 25,465, which is small for a city where 20 percent of the population (more than 2 million people) are Latinos.

There are also a good number of English-language publications of varying frequencies that are available throughout the U.S. Hispanic markets. However, I do want to note one growing trend in this market and that is newspaper inserts, both in English and in Spanish. The granddaddy of them all is *Vista,* an English-language newspaper insert with a national circulation of 1 million which is distributed nationwide in twenty-seven newspapers. It's similar to a Hispanic version of *Parade,* and has been around already for twenty years! The most recent addition to this trend is *Sobre Ruedas,* a Spanish-language automotive insert that debuted in February 2004. Launched by Miami-based Megazines Publications, *Sobre Ruedas* is distributed by leading Spanish-language newspapers in the six largest U.S. Hispanic markets: New York, Miami, Houston, San Jose, Chicago, and Los Angeles. But *Sobre Ruedas* is only the first of three titles the company plans on launching and distributing this way, each targeting different and important segments of the Hispanic population: women 18–34, youth under the age of 21, and Hispanic families. Another important player coming into the market is Hogar Latino, LLC, which is launching a shelter magazine-insert called *Casa y Hogar* in 2005. What is interesting about this kind of publication is that it can offer highly targeted demographics with high-end production values and a larger circulation for advertisers than what you normally get through a Hispanic magazine. And this kind of publication allows you to target by language preference as well. This is one of the most interesting developments in the Hispanic print industry that I see happening in the near future!

Hispanic Magazines

The biggest problem with Hispanic magazines in the United States is circulation. Even with the power of Time Inc. distribution behind it, *People en Español* has not been able to break the 500,000 circulation mark after seven years in the market. That fact has many in the magazine industry scratching their heads, and perpetuates the myth that Hispanics don't read! Not only is that not true, but when you look at what those numbers really mean, you'll be surprised to know that *People en Español* actually has a higher penetration than *People* magazine. That's right, according to the latest Census Bureau projections and circulation figures for both titles, about two out of every 100 people over the age of 18 read *People* magazine, while three out of every 100 Hispanics over the age of 18 read *People en Español* and that is assuming that only two-thirds of Hispanics are Spanish-dominant or bilingual!

According to the Hispanic Market Profile report published in 2003 by the Magazine Publishers of America, nearly 75 percent of all adult Hispanics actually *do* read magazines—about nine issues per month. That is about the same number of magazines read on average in the United States. So, why don't Hispanic magazines explode? I think the answer to that question is complex. First, Latinos come from countries where mail subscriptions are not customary. General market magazines usually get 70 percent of their circulation from subscriptions, so Hispanic magazines have an uphill battle on this front. As I mentioned earlier, Hispanics like to buy their newspapers and magazines on the street, so perhaps another culprit in the low circulation figures is the lack of representation on the newsstands—or, better said, the lack of a national magazine distribution system for Spanish-language publications. But also part of the blame has to go to the current selection of magazines available to Hispanics in the United States. Very few are actually *made for this market.* So availability, quality, and relevance are huge factors to take into consideration. Finally, the lack of Spanish-language magazines with large circulations means that advertisers often have to pay premium prices to place ads in these magazines. When advertising budgets are small and you are trying to reach a broad audience, you can see why Spanish-language magazines are a hard sell. It's the classic chicken and egg story. In order to compete with TV or radio, where CPMs (cost per thousand) are in the $8–$15 range, Spanish-language magazines need to grow their circulation and bring down their CPMs from $30 to $50 to something more competitive. But do not be mistaken. Latinos love to read magazines.

Key Players

Editorial Televisa, the publishing arm of the multimedia conglomerate Grupo Televisa, is the undisputed king of the Spanish-language magazine industry in the United States and in Mexico, of course. Editorial Televisa is also a dominant player in many other Latin American countries with the exception, perhaps, of Argentina and Brazil. (In both of those countries there are other important media companies, Grupo Clarin, Globo, and Grupo Abril, respectively, with large publishing units.) This is one of the few media industries where Univision does not have a presence, although they did publish a family magazine in the 1990s called *Más*, but that's another story for another time. The fact is that Univision has steered clear of the Spanish-language publishing world, so far.

In the United States, Editorial Televisa publishes twenty-three Spanish-language magazines, including some of the largest titles, like *Vanidades, Cristina La Revista,* and *Cosmopolitan en Español.* With control over one-third of the Spanish-language magazines available in the United States, Editorial Televisa, with men's titles, women's titles, teen titles, and general interest magazines, is the only company that offers advertisers a one-stop shop where they can hit targeted segments within the Hispanic market. However, Televisa's magazines have very low circulations. *Vanidades* is its largest title, with sales of 125,000 copies a month, and up until 2004 not all of Televisa's titles were audited, something it is in the process of changing.

Editorial Televisa could be in a much stronger position today had it not abandoned this market ten years ago. Grupo Televisa is a family-run business in Mexico, where its magazine division is enormously successful. In the late '80s the family headed by "El Tigre" Emilio

Azcárraga Milmo (remember him—the same guy who started the Spanish-language TV group Univision?) decided to buy the largest Spanish-language magazine group in the United States, Miami-based Grupo de Armas. With the acquisition of the de Armas group, Editorial Televisa put a stake in the ground in the U.S. print market. After acquiring Grupo de Armas, however, Editorial Televisa used its U.S.-based operation to simply maintain the titles it had acquired and, over time, the U.S.-based operation simply became a selling arm for its Mexican magazines here in the United States. That strategy worked for a while, but by the mid-1990s Editorial Televisa realized that to sell more magazines here, it was going to have to change the way it did business in the United States. It tried producing more U.S.-based magazines, but costs got out of hand at the same time that the Mexican economy took a dive, so Editorial Televisa decided to move everything back to Mexico, from where it continued to produce its United States and Latin American titles until a couple of years ago.

After a long period of neglect, in 2002 Editorial Televisa announced its plans to make a comeback in the United States. In 2003, it hired a new business director, David Taggart, who launched three new titles: *Maxim en Español, Ocean Drive en Español,* and a Spanish version of *Travel & Leisure.* In 2004 the young heir to the Televisa throne, Emilio Azcárraga Jean, moved to Miami to set up new headquarters for his Mexico-based operations and announced that one of his company's goals was to double the size of Editorial Televisa within the next five years. According to *Hispanic Market Weekly,* in 2003 sales of Editorial Televisa products in the United States totaled $160 million and the company ranked twenty-eighth among the top fifty audited newsstand publishers by retail sales in the United States.

Although Time Inc. owns the largest Spanish-language magazine in the market, *People en Español,* with more than 425,000 in circulation, this is the only Spanish-language title in the stable of this venerated magazine conglomerate. The granddaddy of Spanish-language publishing is, of course, Reader's Digest's *Selecciones,* which comes in second place today in terms of circulation figures, with 325,000 copies a month. To its credit, *Selecciones* has been around since the seventies and is still among the top five players in the country! Other players with several Spanish-language titles in their mix are American Media, with *Mira,* a Spanish-language version of *The National Enquirer,* and Zoom Media Group, which publishes *Poder* and *Loft* magazines.

In the English-language magazine landscape you also have a few successful "Hispanic" titles, which are mostly independently owned. They are: *Latina, Hispanic Business,* and *Vista,* which, as I mentioned earlier, is a newspaper magazine "insert." According to Synovate, Hispanic men read more magazines in English than in Spanish. In fact, 65 percent of the time Hispanics spend reading magazines, they are reading in English!

The competition for advertising pages is fierce between English and Spanish publications, as you can see from table 44. Like the Synovate study mentioned earlier, the MPA found that current Hispanic consumption of magazines skews slightly toward English; 63 percent of the time Latinos spend reading, they are reading English-language magazines, and 53 percent of the time is spent reading Spanish-language magazines. Table 45 with the top ten titles taken from the Cheskin/*People en Español* study indicates that, contrary to the appeal of general market magazines, the most popular Spanish-language magazines skew female. You'll also notice that the English titles on this list

Magazine	Ad pages in 2003	Estimated Billings* (*based on rate cards)
TABLE 44 Top 10 Hispanic Magazines (ranked by estimated dollars)		
1. People en Español	774.57	$29,080,800
2. Latina (ENG)	890.10	$18,025,194
3. Selecciones	481.00	$12,472,675
4. Hispanic Business (ENG)	443.92	$8,282,974
5. Vanidades	610.95	$7,278,948
6. Vista (ENG)	171.13	$6,268,230
7. Hispanic Magazine (ENG)	365.23	$6,096,945
8. Ser Padres	147.15	$5,945,200
9. TV y Novelas	468.12	$5,627,402
10. Glamour en Español	403.23	$3,788,688

Source: Hispanic Monitor Magazine.com

are more mass market, with only certain titles skewing either male or female. (Not to mention the differences in circulation, which for the English language titles are all in the millions, not in the hundreds of thousands!)

Nevertheless, according to the MPA, from 1999 to 2002, the total paid circulation for ABC-measured Hispanic titles grew 21.4 percent while total subscriptions jumped 60 percent. According to a recently released study, *The U.S. Hispanic Media Market 2000–2007*, published by HispanTelligence in December 2004, advertising expenditures in Hispanic magazines were projected to grow 68 percent, from $55 million in 2000 to $92.8 million in 2007! These figures seem a bit conservative, because MPA was estimating that Hispanic advertising expenditures had already reached $98 million in 2002 (table 48), but they do indicate the future growth expected in this sector.

Here's another interesting table that shows you which general market publications have the highest index of readers of Spanish/Hispanic origin.

Once again, the Hispanic population proves to be complex in terms of its reading habits, choosing to read newspapers and magazines in both English and Spanish, which is not surprising given what we know about this market. And again, the fact that Hispanics tend to read more in English is probably a reflection of the lack of Spanish reading skills among the younger generations and the limited choice of magazines that interest them in Spanish. I always tell clients to think of this mar-

TABLE 45 Top 10 magazines: Total U.S. vs. Spanish-language

Top U.S. Titles (000)	Top Spanish-language Circulation (000)
Reader's Digest (11,045)	Ser Padres (510.0)
TV Guide (9,010)	People en Español (410.8)
Better Homes & Gardens (7,607)	Reader's Digest Selecciones (279.3)
National Geographic (6,603)	Latina (243.7)
Women's Day (4,280)	Vanidades (109.7)
Time (4,112)	TV y Novelas (102.8)
People Weekly (3,603)	Cristina la revista (86.0)
Sports Illustrated (3,210)	Cosmopolitan en Español (55.9)
Newsweek (3,122)	Newsweek en Español (46.7)
Cosmopolitan (2,918)	Furia Musical (22.4)

Source: MPA 2003 Demographic Profile on the Hispanic Market

TABLE 46 English-language Publications with Highest Index of Hispanic Readers

	Spanish/Hispanic Origin	Total U.S. Adults	
	U.S. Coverage %	Coverage %	Index
Harper's Bazaar	3.4	1.6	212
Fit Pregnancy	1.9	0.9	207
Teen People	8.1	3.9	206
Los Angeles Times (Sunday)	3.5	1.7	204
CosmoGIRL!	3.0	1.6	183
Super Chevy	2.8	1.5	181
Elle	3.5	2.0	180
Baby Talk	4.4	2.5	175
WWE Magazine	4.2	2.4	174
Muscle & Fitness	6.0	3.5	172
Sport Truck	1.9	1.1	167
New York Magazine	1.3	0.8	165
Child	3.8	2.3	164
Discover	4.6	2.8	163
Scholastic Parent & Child	5.7	3.5	162
Cosmopolitan	13.1	8.1	162
Nick Jr.	4.5	2.8	161
Continental	1.4	0.9	159
Vogue	7.6	4.8	158
Photographic	1.1	0.7	157
Spin	2.0	1.3	156
Vanity Fair	3.7	2.4	156

Source: Fall 2003 Mediamark Research Inc. (MRI) Study

ket in terms of the American market back in the '60s. Back then, there were three broadcast networks and a handful of magazines to choose from. Now think of the potential growth that lies ahead for the Hispanic market!

How do Hispanic magazine readers compare to general market magazine readers? Well, as you can see from table 47 from the MPA's *Hispanic Market Profile,* Hispanic magazine readers tend to be younger and less educated than the general market magazine-reading population of the United States. The mean Hispanic magazine reader's household income, however, is significantly higher than the average for the U.S. Hispanic population, as is the level of education.

TABLE 47 Comparison of Hispanic Magazine Readers vs. Total Population		
	Hispanic Adults Read Magazines	Total United States Read Magazines
Mean Age	38	45
18–49	77%	63%
Mean HHI	$52,785	$73,938
Education		
Attended high school +	59%	85%
Attended some college +	31%	51%
Marital Status		
Married	55%	57%
Single/Divorced	37%	35%
One or more children <18 at home	60%	37%

Source: MPA 2003 *Hispanic Market Profile*

By the way, the MPA published two other Market Profiles, one for African Americans and another for Asians, which are all available as free downloads on its website at www.magazine.org.

TABLE 48 Top 10 Hispanic Magazine Advertisers (Total Expenditures in Millions)	
	2002
1. Procter & Gamble	$8.4
2. Ford Motor Co.	$4.7
3. L'Oreal	$3.3
4. General Motors	$2.6
5. Toyota Motor Co.	$2.6
6. Colgate-Palmolive	$1.3
7. Sears Roebuck & Co.	$1.3
8. Kraft Food Holdings	$1.3
9. Brown & Williamson	$1.2
10. Kimberly Clark	$1.2
TOTAL	$98MM

Source: MPA 2003 *Hispanic Market Profile*

And finally, when analyzing younger magazine readers, the MPA found that seven in ten Hispanic teens are bilingual or English-dominant, and that 59 percent of them are magazine readers. I believe that quality, choice, and *relevance* are the main reasons why Latinos are reading more magazines in English than they are in Spanish. There are huge gaps in the magazine categories available in Spanish. For example, there are no sports magazines or shelter magazines in Spanish. Can you imagine not having the equivalent of *Sports Illustrated* or *This Old House*? Well, that is the current state of Spanish-language magazine publishing, and until someone breaks the 500,000 mark with one title, everyone else is going to be reluctant to enter the space. So, who is the leader in this space? *People en Español* is the largest single title, but Editorial Televisa is certainly the largest magazine publisher and has recently made some bold moves, announcing in the fall of 2004 that it had purchased a 51 percent stake in *Hispanic* magazine, their first English-language title. Could there be more down the line? Are they finally acknowledging the growing importance of bilingual Latinos? Another established magazine publisher, Meredith Corporation, made a bold move in 2005 announcing the launch of a new women's title, *Siempre Mujer.* As Editorial Televisa and other American magazine companies grow their presence in this space, I predict that the consumption of Spanish-language magazines will grow by leaps and bounds. But you have to get in the game to win it, and so far the big magazine publishers are only watching from the sidelines.

HISPANICS ONLINE

U.S. Hispanics are relatively new arrivals to cyberspace. While their computer ownership still lags behind that of the general market, they are the group most likely to be purchasing a computer in the next year. ComScore Media Metrix reports that more than 50 percent of Hispanic adults were online as of June 2003. But growth, as you have already seen, is not a problem with this market. According to the 2004 AOL/ Roper ASW study, 17 percent of off-line Latinos expect to get access to the Internet at home in the next six months, and a whopping 53 percent expect to do so in the next couple of years! According to the second annual America Online/Roper ASW study released in May of 2004, 20 percent of Hispanics who are online at home have been online for fewer than six months versus 6 percent of the general at home online population. "Forty-two percent of Hispanic online consumers have had an Internet connection at home for less than two years, compared with just 15 percent of the general at home online population," says the AOL/Roper ASW study.

How many Latinos are online, then? 13.8 million as reported by ComScore Media Metrix's U.S. Hispanic Service in January of 2005. Now to put that in perspective for you, take into consideration this: Using ComScore's figure of 13.8 million active users, the total U.S. Hispanic online population is 5 percent smaller than the total online population of Mexico (a country of 100+ million people) and 11 percent larger than the total online population of Spain (a country of 40+ million people). In fact, Hispanic Internet penetration is increasing exponentially as word of mouth and access to cheaper services and computers are making the Hispanic population one of the fastest growing segments online.

As would be expected, Hispanics online are different from the general online population. According to both ComScore and the AOL/ Roper ASW online study, Hispanics are slightly younger (47 percent are between the ages of 18 and 34 compared to 36 percent of the general online population) and skew slightly more female (53 percent female versus 49 percent male) for now. Like their general market counterparts, online Hispanics are more educated and more upscale than Hispanics off-line.

Hispanics also spend more time online: on average ten hours a week versus eight for the general population. According to Synovate, within the Hispanic market the two groups that use the Internet most are South Americans and Puerto Ricans. And not surprisingly, computer usage rises with level of acculturation, so that those Hispanics who are acculturated use the computer more than those who are isolated, although that may be changing with more options available in Spanish. In terms of online behavior, Hispanic online consumers tend to have embraced some Internet tools and features more than the general population (table 49). For example, nearly two-thirds of online Hispanics (64 percent) regularly or occasionally use the Internet to instant mes-

TABLE 49		
Online Activity 2003	Hispanic Adult	U.S. Adult
Communicating with friends and family	80%	90%
Make travel arrangements	52%	40%
Online instant messages	64%	48%
Listening to music like you do on the radio	54%	30%
Download music files	39%	27%
Watching video clips	34%	23%

Source: AOL/Roper ASW Hispanic Cyberstudy 2004

sage, compared with less than half (48 percent) of the general online population. And 34 percent of Hispanic online cell phone users use their phones for instant messaging versus only 9 percent of those in the general online population. "When compared to other online consumers, several trends in Hispanic online usage emerge," says the AOL/Roper ASW study. "Perhaps in part because Hispanics are also younger overall, they emerge as more avid consumers of entertainment-related online features and activities."

As with other media, language usage and preference is again the most controversial issue when talking about U.S. Hispanics online. The Internet is by and large a nascent industry, and because, when it started, English was the dominant language, it is not surprising to note that Hispanic Internet usage skews more toward English than toward Spanish. According to ComScore's Media Metrix January 2005 Key Measure reports, 56 percent of current Hispanic online users are English preferred.

In the first annual AOL/Roper ASW Hispanic Cyberstudy on Hispanics conducted in 2002, 75 percent of those Hispanics interviewed opted to speak in English and 83 percent said having English-language content online was very or somewhat important to them. However, at that time, 58 percent considered Spanish-language content also very important. The truth is that Spanish content online was hard to find in the beginning of the Internet boom and was only starting to develop when the bubble burst. So finding good Spanish-language content on the Net has always been a bit of a challenge. In their 2004 Hispanic

TABLE 50		
	Total Unique Visitors	% of Unique Visitors
US Hispanic Internet Population	13,880,000	100.0%
Males		
2–17	2,235,000	16.1%
18–34	2,420,000	17.4%
35–49	1,532,000	11.0%
50+	633	4.6%
Females		
2–17	1,828,000	13.2%
18–34	3,027,000	21.8%
35–49	1,653,000	11.9%
50+	557,000	4.0%
By Language Preference		
Spanish Preferred	2,166,000	15.0%
Bilingual	3,962,000	29.0%
English Preferred	7,758,000	56.0%

Source: *ComScore Media Metrix US Hispanic Service—January 2005*

Cyberstudy, however, AOL/Roper ASW delves much deeper into the language issue, perhaps motivated by the launch of their AOL Latino service in 2002. As a result, in their May 2004 study, 71 percent of Hispanics who were *not* online said that online Spanish content was important to them and 56 percent cited "lack of Spanish content" as a reason for not going online at home. Of those Hispanics who were already online, 67 percent said they "wish there were more websites that offered information of interest to Hispanic Americans." Again, coming to a consensus about how to define Hispanics by their language preference or usage is going to be key going forward, as this market grows both in the short and the long term.

In terms of shopping, the AOL/Roper ASW study found that the average amount spent by Hispanics online during a three-month period increased to $480 in 2003 from $439 in 2002, but is still about $100 behind the average for the general online population, which was $577. In 2003, 43 percent of online Hispanics said they regularly or occasionally shopped online. Online researchers have seen trends in the general online population that indicate that the longer people are online, the more comfortable they feel carrying out transactions over the Internet, so this figure is likely to increase. But another important barrier to shopping online for Hispanics is access to credit cards, especially for the more recent arrivals who may not have a credit record (because access to credit cards in Latin America is much less common than here). But we will get more into that issue in chapter 10. Now let's look at the dominant players in this space.

The Big Nine

At least nine portals that specialize in the U.S. Hispanic market have managed to survive the boom-turned-bust known as the Internet "bubble." Those who are in the U.S. Hispanic online space now are confident of their future growth, given the overall population projections in this market and the fact that more advertising dollars are being allocated to this space. Hispanics already represent a large chunk of two key Internet demographics: the youth market 12–24 and the young adult market 18–34. Hispanics online are also more affluent than the U.S. Hispanic market in general, so this is an important market for everyone in the online space. And while the industry is still trying to figure out if they are going to be advertising driven or user driven, the reality is that overall a larger percentage of advertising budgets are going to be allocated to this space. In 2003 only 2 percent of general market advertising spending went to the Internet. In the U.S. Hispanic market that figure is only 0.6 percent (which was worth about $50 million in 2003). Some advertisers are already jumping on the Hispanic Internet bandwagon, especially in the automotive, banking, and travel industries. Why? Because the Internet is one of the few media that easily allows marketers to measure their return on investment.

AOL Latino

The most recent addition to the Latino Internet space comes from the company that pioneered access to the Internet, America Online. After launching Spanish- and Portuguese-language portals all around the world, AOL finally realized that it was neglecting its own backyard. So in 2002, it launched AOL Latino to service the needs of the U.S. Hispanic community. AOL studies show that its service had already captured the largest share of Latinos in the United States, but clearly those Latinos who were signed up through AOL were navigating the Net in English. So in order to better service and grow their Hispanic market share, they decided to launch a Spanish-language service. Access to Time Warner's content without a doubt makes AOL Latino a big player to watch out for in this arena.

Univision.com

Another big player that got into the game late was Univision.com. To its great fortune, its timing couldn't have been better! High-flying Internet portal Star Media, the pioneer in the Spanish-language Internet space, was in the throes of a worldwide expansion when the Internet bubble burst. The company then quickly faded away after the resignation of its founder Fernando Espuelas, and an accounting scandal in 2002. Thanks to Univision's power in the Spanish-language media and its deep relationships with corporate America, Univision.com quickly became the center of the redefined Spanish-language Internet space. Thanks to its parent company, Univision.com is able to offer clients key benefits no other Hispanic website can claim: major brand recognition within the U.S. Hispanic market, television commercials to promote its online products, and access to the most popular stars, news, and events on an exclusive basis.

MSN Latino (formerly known as Yupi MSN)

Launched in 1997 as a pure start-up, Yupi was acquired in 2001 by Microsoft, which allowed this start-up to survive the bust. Its longevity has also made this site very popular among Latinos for the past seven years. With features such as hotmail and a truly bilingual service, Yupi MSN is now able to deliver any and all segments of the Hispanic population online, although their numbers are not huge. Yupi MSN's content is smart and hip and its managers are always one step ahead of the market, which makes the portal a viable player in the future.

Terra Networks

One of the keys to Terra's success is its focus on entertainment, which, as you saw earlier, is a major driver of Latinos online. Its management has been able to strike unique, user-friendly partnerships with important media players, and their gambles have paid off. With solid backing from its corporate parent, Spain's giant media and telecommunications conglomerate Telefónica S.A., Terra is not going anywhere but up.

Star Media

In March of 2003, this pioneering portal relaunched in the United States with a renovated site powered by Wanadoo, part of the French conglomerate that bought the assets of Star Media in 2002. With more than 8 million users in the United States and Latin America, this Internet portal continues to offer a large variety of online features, (e-mail, chat, and classifieds) and enough news and information channels to satisfy any Hispanic need online. Its biggest obstacle will be overcoming the bad press it got.

Yahoo en Español

The first of the "established" Internet portals to go all Spanish in the United States, Yahoo en Español deserves a lot of credit. It gets even more kudos in my book for hanging in there and making a commitment to this market, which is very unusual in corporate America. These guys are smart and they know they will reap the benefits of what they sowed. Yahoo en Español is already very popular among Latinos, and with increased access to Yahoo.com's network of services, this team is really worth taking seriously.

ClickDiario.com

With over 4 million unique subscribers in March of 2005 and 7.2 million unique visitors a month, this privately owned company has quickly become a contender in the Spanish-language online space. Since it began two years ago, ClickDiario.com has cobbled together a network of more than thirty vertical portals and has gained traction first in Mexico and most recently in the United States by the power of its content, which is very user friendly and appealing. The other very important key to its success has been its strong promotion and marketing programs that have delivered proven results for its advertisers.

MiGente.com

Launched in October of 2000 as part of Community Connect, Inc., a company that creates and maintains online communities for ethnic markets in the United States, MiGente.com targets second- and third-generation Latinos who are either bilingual or English-dominant. The other websites operated by Community Connect, Inc. are BlackPlanet.com and AsianAvenue.com. Combined, all three websites have more than 8 million registered members who can network with one another and have access to culturally relevant content, services, and information that is hard to find otherwise. According to ComScore Media Metrix, they are certainly up and coming, ranking at number 8 in terms of Spanish-language sites for active unique visitors.

Telemundo.com

Although it took Telemundo a long time to develop a solid online presence, it is not surprising to see this website round off the top nine Spanish language sites for active unique visitors in the United States. The website is easy to navigate, technologically advanced, yet user friendly which, over the past couple years, has made it a favorite among Latinos since it provides news and other important information for the Hispanic community. Kudos to the small and dedicated online team that makes this site great everyday!

In addition to these Spanish-language portals, Latinos are delving into the internet world in English. The following chart shows you which are the top 15 Internet properties visited by Hispanics in January of 2005.

TABLE 51 Top 15 Internet Properties Audience: US Hispanics

Rank		Total Unique Visitors (000)	% Reach
1	Yahoo! Sites	10,320	74.3
2	Time Warner Network	10,214	73.6
3	MSN-Microsoft Sites	9,556	68.8
4	Google Sites	6,043	43.5
5	eBay	5,226	37.6
6	Ask Jeeves	3,475	25
7	Viacom Online	3,257	23.5
8	Amazon Sites	3,193	23
9	About/Primedia	2,983	21.5
10	CNET Networks	2,560	18.4
11	Monster Worldwide	2,551	18.4
12	Walt Disney Internet Group (WDIG)	2,501	18
13	Lycos, Inc.	2,441	17.6
14	Intermix Media	2,264	16.3
15	Symantec	2,162	15.6

Source: ComScore Media Metrix, US Hispanic Service—January 2005

Who's Keeping Track

In terms of measurements and tracking tools, believe it or not it wasn't until 2002 that the major online research companies started really tracking Hispanics online. In addition to the AOL/Roper ASW study mentioned throughout this section, which is a proprietary study paid for by AOL, the only place to get data on Hispanics online is ComScore Media Metrix Networks, who was the first to launch a Hispanic service in 2002. Its service monitors the surfing and purchasing behaviors of Hispanics online on a continuing basis. It is by far the largest sample in the market, tracking 50,000 Hispanic users, and it updates its data for subscribers every month. The service tracks what sites Hispanics visit most, what they purchase, and where. Its newest features allow you to view behavior by language segmentation as well, which, as you have seen, is very important.

Following the lead of ComScore Media Metrix, in 2003 Nielsen/Net Ratings developed a new Hispanic panel, composed of 3,600 Hispanic individuals, to provide it with demographic data on Hispanic Internet users in the United States. This new Hispanic panel was created to serve the needs of media buyers and marketers interested in advertising to the

U.S. Hispanic online community, but in January of 2005 Nielsen/Net Ratings announced that it had cancelled its NetView Hispanic Service.

A FEW WORDS ABOUT DIRECT MARKETING TO LATINOS

It would be remiss of me not to mention the direct marketing industry in this chapter. Although direct mail, direct-response television, and direct marketing companies have been around forever in the United States, in the Hispanic market they are all relatively new. The grand-daddy of this industry in the Hispanic market was, of course, Columbia House, which had a Latin music club, Club Música Latina, since 1992. Its only competition in the United States was Bertelsmann, which recently acquired Columbia House and has had its Latin music club, Ritmo Y Passión, since 1997. And the most recent addition to the club world is a Spanish-language book club called Mosaico, which is owned and operated by Bookspan.

In the direct marketing world, there are several barriers to entry one must keep in mind. As I mentioned earlier, Latinos are unfamiliar with these kinds of marketing tools or how they work, because direct market-ing like this is very limited in Latin America. So one must take the time to clearly explain exactly what people are signing up for or run the risk of having people feel "tricked" into something they don't want. Second, Latinos are not used to conducting transactions through the mail, so you have to give them time to get used to doing business this way or give them options to do business in other ways. Third, be ready to get many money orders and cash in the mail, as many Latinos don't have bank accounts and are used to paying their bills in cash or via money orders.

On the bright side, Hispanics are much more receptive to direct marketing solicitations than the general market and usually have much higher response rates, something the telecommunications industry has been capitalizing on lately. In addition, you can always count on word of mouth to get your message out. If Hispanics like your product, believe me, they will tell all of their friends and family about it. And if you treat your customers well—by which I mean provide them with good customer service, they will come back to buy over and over again. Customer loyalty is one of the attractive things about this market, and some companies know that. For example, companies that offer long distance telephone service have been very successful in this market by offering good customer service and using direct mail as an acquisition tool. But as the number and quality of Hispanic lists grow over the next five years, the number of direct mail solicitations will too. Another area that is growing is direct-response TV. But you have to make sure your company is ready to handle a new and different kind of customer. The Gateway case study is truly an eye-opener.

GATEWAY CASE STUDY
By Roberto Ruiz, Partner Consumer Contacts

Do you want to be in the business of saying "No" to Hispanic customers? I hope the answer is no. Then make sure that before you start advertising, you have conducted a 360-degree audit of all the touch points between your product or service and Latino consumers. When Gateway started selling PCs to Hispanics who called their 800 number, the first step was to prequalify them for a line of credit. It is well known that many PC manufacturers make more money on interest on credit sales and peripherals than on actual PC sales. The issue was that Latinos were handled the same way a general market consumer was. Despite the fact that they wanted the advertised $899 PC, the representative on the phone submitted a request for a higher credit line to be able to add peripherals to the order. Unfortunately, many Hispanics did not qualify because they either had what is called "thin credit," meaning only a few lines in their credit report, or their credit score could not support the higher credit line requested. Suddenly, Gateway was in the business of saying "No." When they realized what was going on, they quickly moved to find a lender with the tools and experience to support the Latino market.

This is what we mean by a full 360-degree audit of touch points: Think about every instance when the brand touches the consumer, from the TV spot to the cash register. And if you really want to conduct business with Hispanics, be prepared to be paid in cash!

7

~~~

THE HISPANIC
ADVERTISING INDUSTRY

The Hispanic advertising industry is undergoing a major transformation. On the one hand the explosive growth of the Hispanic population has more and more businesses knocking on its doors. On the other, the agencies themselves are grappling with important issues unique to the Hispanic market, such as which language to use to properly deliver brand messages to different Hispanic consumers. Hispanic agencies are, in fact, working with a moving target: the Hispanic consumer, who is constantly *redefined* not only by country of origin, but by level of acculturation and whether he or she is foreign born or U.S. born. Add to that a veritable explosion of media outlets in which to advertise products, and you can see why the Hispanic advertising industry is in flux. In this chapter I will try to give you a sense of how big the Hispanic advertising industry is today, how fast it is growing, who the key players are, and which are the leading agencies.

Although the birth of the Spanish-language advertising industry in the United States dates back to the 1960s, its focus early on was only on Latin America. The first Hispanic advertising agency, Interamericas, was founded in New York by Luis Diaz Albertini. Interamericas was the Hispanic agency for Goya Foods, but thanks to Albertini's persistence his agency, which would become famous under the moniker SAMS (Spanish Advertising and Marketing Services), would soon count among its clients Columbia Pictures, Azteca Films, and Kent cigarettes. In spite of Albertini's amazing business savvy, it really wasn't until the '70s and early '80s that major national brands started to focus on the Latino market in the United States. Among those early advertisers in the Hispanic market were Colgate-Palmolive, McDonald's, and Coca-Cola, which are brands that continue to lead in this market today! The 1980s and '90s were decades of tremendous growth both for the Hispanic population and for Hispanic agencies who developed the expertise to service this growing market. With the exception of Y&R's The Bravo Group, large multinational agencies were not interested in the Hispanic market. Now, however, after two decades of virtually ignoring the Hispanic market, general market agencies are finally starting to realize that they lack the necessary expertise and resources to tap into the fastest growing consumer segment in the United States!

A DECADE OF GROWTH

The late 1990s, in particular, saw a flurry of merger activity, as some of the more established independent Hispanic agencies were gobbled up by large multinationals. In fact, according to *Hispanic Market Weekly*, the number of Hispanic advertising agencies has actually doubled over the past six years! Today you will find more than seventy-two specialized agencies in the directory of the Association of Hispanic Advertising Agencies, an organization that was founded in 1997. And while the Hispanic agencies that belong to huge multinationals dominate the industry in terms of annual billings, the majority of Hispanic advertising agencies are still independently owned. Growth is definitely the word that best describes the future of this industry. And the best is yet to come. Every day there are new companies getting into the Hispanic market, and industry experts agree that those that are already in the market have not yet realized their full potential.

According to "Snapshots of the U.S. Hispanic Market," a study conducted for NBC/Telemundo by Global Insight in 2003, the number of Hispanic households is expected to double in the next fifteen years to about 20 million in 2020, and Hispanic consumer spending will triple

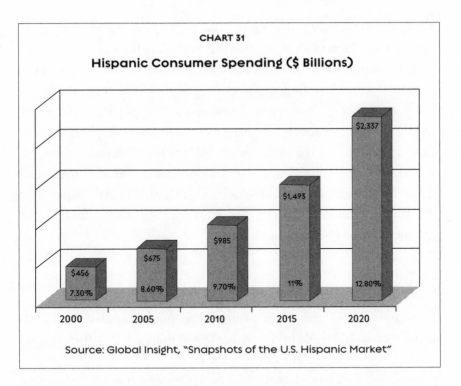

CHART 31

Hispanic Consumer Spending ($ Billions)

Source: Global Insight, "Snapshots of the U.S. Hispanic Market"

from $675 billion in 2005 to more than $2 *trillion* in 2020. In light of the tremendous growth we have experienced in consumer spending since 2000, advertising expenditures should have also increased, but they haven't. Table 52 tracks the growth of the Hispanic market as a percentage of the U.S. market between 2000 and 2004.

Advertising Budget Alignment, Maximizing Impact in the Hispanic

TABLE 52

Year	Advertising Expenditures ($M)	% of U.S. Total	Purchasing Power	% of U.S. Total	Population (Thousands)	% of U.S. Total
2000	$2,129.88	2.1%	$564.28	7.3%	35,622	12.6%
2001	$2,220.46	2.3	$584.61	7.5	36,850	12.9
2002	$2,463.39	2.6	$626.56	7.8	38,091	13.3
2003	$2,790.13	2.2	$668.51	8.1	39,335	13.4
2004	$3,091.15	2.2	$699.78	8.5	40,572	13.5
Growth 00–04	41.80%		24%		13.90%	

Source: *The U.S Hispanic Media Market 2000-2007.* HispanTelligence December 2004

Market, a 2003 study by the Association of Hispanic Advertising Agencies (AHAA) found that even companies who are the top 250 National advertisers in the Hispanic market spend on average only 5 percent of their total advertising budgets in the Hispanic TV and print media, way below the existing market size (14 percent of the population) and still well below the 8 percent attributed to Hispanic consumption in 2003. Through a series of research studies, AHAA has designed a "straight-forward and systematic way to calculate recommended advertising allocation levels for targeting Spanish-dominant and bilingual Hispanics in the United States." Those studies are very enlightening and can be downloaded for free at www.ahaa.org.

HOW BIG IS THE PIE?

In March of 2004, the Census Bureau was predicting that the Latino population would triple in size, rising to 103 million by 2050 and representing nearly one-fourth of the total U.S. population. Those projections, coupled with the fact that the Selig Center is now projecting that the buying power of U.S. Hispanics will slightly surpass the buying

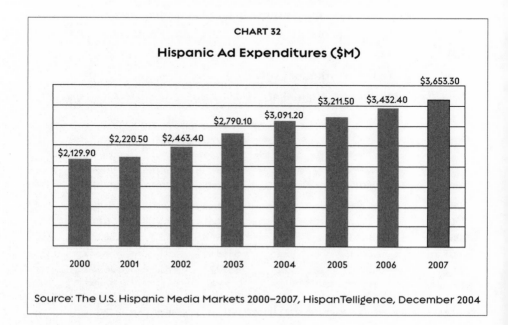

CHART 32

Hispanic Ad Expenditures ($M)

Source: The U.S. Hispanic Media Markets 2000–2007, HispanTelligence, December 2004

power of the African American community by 2009, are driving more companies to the Hispanic market. Again, the HispanTelligence report, *The U.S. Hispanic Media Market 2000–2007*, gives us a sense of the projected growth in Hispanic advertising expenditures (table 52).

It's like a Hispanic market gold rush! Agencies are telling their clients that they either need to get a greater piece of the pie or, at the very least, put a stake in the ground. And, of course, the driving force behind all the population growth is Hispanic youth. Since 2001, Hispanics have accounted for the largest growth in the two most coveted advertising segments. The number of Hispanics grew 40 percent in the adult 18–34 demographic and 24 percent in the adult 18–49 demographic. Clearly, Hispanic media have been enjoying gains in advertising over the past couple of years, especially Spanish-language TV, but the burgeoning Hispanic advertising market is still very difficult to track.

Only recently have Taylor Nelson Sofres (TNS), Competitive Media Reporting (CMR), and Publisher's Information Bureau (PIB), begun to track advertising expenditures in Spanish-language media. For lack of any official sources, the most reliable information at this time comes from *Hispanic Business Magazine*'s research arm, HispanTelligence, which annually tracks the top 50 advertisers in the market (table 53).

In April of 2004, *The Wall Street Journal* reported that the nation's top 671 advertisers, which account for 80 percent of the total ad spend-

TABLE 53 U.S. Hispanic Advertising by Medium ($M) 2002–2007

	2002	2003	2004	2005	2006	2007
Network/Nat'l TV	$1,014.0	$1,216.8	$1387.2	$1,414.0	$1,530.1	$1,646.2
Local TV	$507.4	$558.1	$602.8	$639.4	$680.8	$722.3
National Radio	$170.1	$180.3	$191.2	$213.1	$227.2	$241.3
Local Radio	$419.0	$448.3	$473.2	$509.4	$536.1	$562.9
Nat'l Newspaper	$90.5	$95.0	$110.2	$106.9	$111.8	$116.7
Local Newspaper	$135.7	$143.7	$161.9	$163.2	$171.5	$179.8
Magazines	$61.3	$73.6	$88.3	$82.6	$87.7	$92.8
Out of Home	$65.6	$74.3	$76.3	$83.1	$87.2	$91.4
Total	$2,463.4	$2,790.1	$3,091.2	$3,211.5	$3,432.4	$3,653.3
Annual % change	10.9	13.3	10.8	3.9	6.9	6.4

Source: *The U.S. Hispanic Media Market 2000–2007,* HispanTelligence, December 2004

ing in the United States, spent roughly $3 billion advertising in Spanish-language media in 2003, up from $2.8 billion the year before. By comparison, total ad spending by those same top advertisers in the United States increased 15 percent in 2003, to $56 billion from $48.7 billion in 2002.

SO, WHO'S GOT GAME?

Every year, *Hispanic Business* magazine publishes a list of the top sixty advertisers in the U.S. Hispanic market. Invariably, Procter & Gamble is always at the top of the list. This consumer product giant has been a leader in this market for the last twenty years, and as its spending increases, so does its share of the U.S. Hispanic market.

It is rare to find a company that has such a dedicated Hispanic marketing team. Usually, Hispanic marketing efforts will fall under the general marketing area, regardless of whether there is anyone on staff who actually knows what they are doing. That's why Hispanic advertising agencies play such an important role. More often than not, you'll find large multinational companies that have "multicultural" marketing divisions, but only occasionally do you find a company with a dedicated Hispanic effort, led by true experts in Hispanic marketing. This may

TABLE 54 TOP 10 HISPANIC ADVERTISERS
(Total Expenditures in Millions)

Rank	Company	2004	2003	% change	2000
1	Procter & Gamble	$85.56	$80.13	6.8	$46.2
2	Altria (Philip Morris)	$71.13	$60.74	17.1	$25.0
3	General Motors	$68.25	$55.29	23.4	$25.0
4	McDonald's	$44.44	$48.15	−7.7	NA
5	Coca-Cola	$44.17	$34.88	26.6	NA
6	Wal-Mart Stores	$38.91	$22.91	69.8	NA
7	Johnson & Johnson	$37.7	$32.83	15.0	NA
8	Sears, Roebuck	$36.15	$42.53	−15.0	$35.0
9	Pepsi-Cola Co.	$35.75	$38.93	−8.2	NA
10	AT&T	$34.88	$33.45	4.3	$35.0

Source: *The U.S. Hispanic Media Market, 2000–2007*, HispanTelligence, December 2004

account for some of the perceived failures in this market, but also indicates the current state of affairs. Frankly, it wasn't until the Census 2000 that people started to give this market the respect it deserves!

As the leader in this market, P&G has always had Hispanic brand managers handling the Hispanic budgets for some of its brands, and clearly that has worked well for them. But in 2000 P&G decided to consolidate its Hispanic efforts under one umbrella, creating a sixty-five-person team based in Puerto Rico which would be dedicated solely to increasing P&G's share of sales to Hispanic consumers in the United States and Puerto Rico. In 2003 that team managed twelve different P&G brands and even helped the company tailor some of its products more toward Latino tastes! For example, after conducting research in 2002, P&G found that 57 percent of Latinos like to smell their purchases, so the company added a new fragrance to its Gain brand detergent, "rainwater fresh." Sales of Gain in the Hispanic market have experienced a double-digit growth since then and currently outpace sales of Gain to non-Hispanics in the United States, according to *Hispanic Market Weekly*'s 2004 special report on Hispanic advertising.

And finally another interesting thing to note about the top ten list of advertisers in the U.S. Hispanic market is that every year you'll see some of the same companies. They know that advertising in this market pays off. But you also see some high-flying new arrivals that more often than not quickly fade away. Don't be a flash in the pan. Be smart and know that to make money in this market, you must spend money. Consistency has paid off for P&G, McDonald's, Coke, and others, so why shouldn't it work for you too?

MAKE A COMMITMENT

I don't know why clients expect to have success in the Hispanic market overnight. Those who have been in the market a long time will tell you that advertising to Hispanics works, but as with anything in business, you have to give it time and be consistent with your message. Far too often, American companies assume that because *they* have been doing business in the United States for a long time, Latinos will know who they are and will buy their products without their having to spend any money advertising to them. Does that make any sense to you? Of course not!

Well-known American products are often completely foreign to many Latinos, especially those who are foreign born. A good friend of mine, Filiberto Fernandez, once told me a great story that will illustrate this point. In the early '90s, when he was the senior vice president of marketing and business development at Telemundo, he was at a sales meeting with S. C. Johnson and Son Inc., and was trying to convince the marketing team to dedicate some of their advertising dollars to the Hispanic market. The brand manager of Pledge quite plainly told him that he didn't need to advertise one of the biggest brands in the category on Spanish-language TV because everyone knew what Pledge was. But Filiberto challenged him and said, "I'll give you ten spots for free on my network if that is true. Here's what I propose we do. Let's do some focus groups in Los Angeles with Latina housewives, and we will ask them if they are familiar with or use Pledge. If they don't [use Pledge], you have to commit to advertising on my network." A few weeks later, at the focus groups, the marketing delegation from S. C. Johnson was completely floored when a roomful of Spanish-speaking women not only didn't know what Pledge was, they barely could pronounce the name of the product! Needless to say, the marketers got the message and Filiberto got the account!

Cadbury Schweppes is another company that recently saw the power of Hispanic consumers. Sales of their Clamato juice had flattened out to about 2 million cases a year in 2000, so after conducting research in the market, the company decided to dedicate its entire marketing budget to the Hispanic market. It was a gamble, no doubt, to launch a Hispanic-only advertising effort to increase sales in a market they had never reached out to. But the gamble paid off. The company hired a Hispanic agency, which designed a targeted effort for this product, and only 24 months later, their sales had tripled. Today, sales of Clamato juice in the Hispanic market alone account for 2 million cases a year! Similarly, at Ford Motor Company, hiring Mexican actress Salma Hayek as the spokesperson for the

Lincoln Navigator has increased sales of this vehicle by 12 percent among Hispanics. Sales figures remain flat with non-Hispanics.

Examples like this abound in the market. What you don't want to do is hold the Hispanic market to a higher standard than you do other segments. Don't get me wrong. "Testing" is good, but what you "test" are marketing variables, like price point, language, or message, even media vehicles, to see what works best. But you don't "test the market" to see if you should make a commitment or not. That you must decide beforehand. As with any new business venture or product launch, you must do your due diligence. Do research and find out if there is a need for your product in the Hispanic market. Then put together a plan for a launch. But you must give your Hispanic efforts enough time and money to show results. If not, I can guarantee that you *will* fail. And please, whatever you do, don't think you can enter this market by just translating your current advertising campaigns into Spanish. You'd be surprised how many people actually do that only to make fools of themselves. For example, an airline company which shall remain nameless but that does business all over Latin America once decided to simply translate their newest advertising campaign announcing new leather seats on their flights to Latin America. I believe the English language ads simply said, "fly in leather." The connotation was, of course, one of luxury and comfort. In Spanish the word for "leather" is *cuero.* But if you add an "s" to the end of *cuero,* its meaning changes to "naked." Well, I don't know who they got to translate their slogan but, yes, for a while in Miami you could see huge billboards announcing that you could "fly naked" to Latin America on this airline. That's definitely the kind of "oops" you want to avoid. So, hire an expert or go to a Hispanic agency, and they will help you create an appropriate message and help you understand how best to sell your wares to this highly complex market.

HISPANIC AGENCY LANDSCAPE

It is easy to find the list of the top ten Hispanic agencies in the United States. It is much harder to find the right agency for your specific needs. The Association of Hispanic Advertising Agencies publishes a directory of its member agencies every year. This directory will help you understand what services are offered at each agency, which is very helpful. Remember, not all agencies are good at everything, so ask questions and make sure the agency you hire knows how to do what you need it to do. Because the Hispanic market is changing so quickly, the one-size-fits-all mentality no longer works. Some agencies are better at creative and strategic planning, while others excel at public relations or direct mail. In the Internet space, for example, the leaders in the market are The Vidal Partnership and Bromley Communications for the work they have done in this space. So you see, you need to ask questions and find out exactly what they can or *cannot* do for you.

Advertising Age has been covering the Hispanic market for the past twenty years, and every year it publishes a list of the top ten Hispanic agencies by revenue. In 2004, *Advertising Age* also published the first Hispanic Fact Pact, a great resource for those trying to get their hands on the most recent data on the market. In the fall of 2004, *Adweek* launched a new magazine, *Marketing y Medios,* dedicated to covering the Hispanic advertising and marketing industries. But their new magazine, which is published ten times a year, faces tough competition from *Advertising Age* and other leaders in the trade space, Hispanicad.com and *Hispanic Market Weekly*. So if you want to be informed about this market, there are plenty of sources for you to subscribe to, something that was not true ten years ago!

As mentioned earlier, every year, *Advertising Age* publishes the *Agency Report,* which is used by everyone in the industry to determine their ranking. This report includes a special section for multicultural agencies. Since most agencies actually don't have to report their billings or annual revenues, the majority of the revenues are estimated by *Ad Age,* so take them with a grain of salt, but table 55 will definitely give you a sense of who's on top.

Not surprisingly, the multinationals dominate the list. Why? Because big advertisers want a one-stop shop. I'm not sure that clients get better results with this one-stop shop mentality, but it does make the job of the brand manager easier. And, of course, consolidation continues. In

TABLE 55

Rank	Agency (parent/affiliate)	Headquarters	2003 Revenue ($Millions)	2002 Revenue ($ Millions)
1	Bromley Communications (Publicis)	San Antonio, TX	$32,937	$29,943
2	Bravo Group (WPP)	New York, NY	$31,775	$27,873
3	Dieste, Harmel & Partners (Omnicom)	Dallas, TX	$23,000	$16,700
4	Zubi Advertising Services	Coral Gables, FL	$16,400	$14,900
5	La Agencia de Orci & Asociados	Los Angeles, CA	$14,160	$13,474
6	Lapiz Integrated Hispanic Marketing (Publicis)	Chicago, IL	$12,432	$11,200
7	Lopez Negrete Communications	Houston, TX	$12,095	$11,200
8	Del Rivero Messianu DDB (Omnicom)	Coral Gables, FL	$11,215	$10,013
9	Mendoza, Dillon & Asociados (WPP)	Aliso Viejo, CA	$11,000	$12,907
10	Casanova Pendril (Interpublic)	Costa Mesa, CA	$10,689	$9,630

Source: *Advertising Age*, April 19, 2004 *Agency Report*

February 2004, a merger between Bromley Communications and Publicis Sanchez & Levitan was announced, catapulting the newly merged company to the number-one spot with an estimated $33 million in revenues and a reported $276 million in billings. I know what you're thinking: I'm not big enough to work with an agency. I don't have a million dollars in my advertising budget! Well, first of all, you don't need lots of money to work with an agency. And, second, if you have a small business and usually don't work with an agency, don't worry. You can still get help. Not every agency is listed in the AHAA directory, although I would recommend you stick to them, but check your local listings as well and find out who in your area might be able help you out!

FOOD FOR THOUGHT

As I said at the beginning of this chapter, the Hispanic advertising industry is facing a rapidly changing marketplace, forcing it to change as well. There are three main issues you will be hearing a lot more about in the next couple of years. The changing use of language and media in the Hispanic market is one key issue facing this industry. The redefining of the marketplace is another. Before, country of origin and Spanish-language usage defined the U.S. Hispanic market, but as this population grows and matures, it becomes more acculturated and more bilingual. The differences between U.S.-born Latinos and foreign-born Latinos may soon start to shape how you market to Latinos in the United States. And, finally, can the Hispanic market continue to fit under the "multicultural" umbrella? Is the concept of "multiculturalism" still viable in our day and age, or will each minority or ethnic group be so unique that it must exist on its own? These are the questions that marketers and advertisers will be grappling with over the next few years.

- **Language** The question is no longer whether you can use one universal Spanish to reach the Hispanic market (see Roberto Ruiz's sidebar "Are There Spanish Dialects?"). The question now is in which language, English or Spanish, should your advertising messages be? The answer, of course, depends on whom you are targeting within the Hispanic market, but chances are you will end up using both languages, because, as you have seen, Latinos consume media in both languages. This is something the "old guard" of Hispanic media companies and agencies has resisted for some time, but the reality is that with 60 percent of the future Latino population growth coming from U.S.-born Hispanics, English-language advertising geared toward Latinos will also have to grow. You already see some English-language ads featuring Latino stars, like Salma Hayek for Lincoln Navigator or Shakira for Pepsi, who give them a definite Hispanic twist. I suspect Hispanic agencies will start to break up into different groups: Those that do excellent work for English-dominant Latinos, and those who specialize in doing more work in Spanish, and those who try to do both. But the fragmentation of the market will continue, and soon you will find Hispanic agencies specializing in Latino subgroups. The Ruido Group, for example, specializes in bilingual Latino youth and, although relatively new, it is already working with corporate giants such as Coca-Cola.

- **Acculturation** Besides measuring return on investment (ROI), this is perhaps one of the most difficult issues facing the industry because there are so many factors that influence acculturation. Among them are whether Latinos are foreign born or U.S. born. If foreign born, at what age did they emigrate? How long have they been in the United States? Where do they live and work and, most important, what level of education do they have? All of these factors will vary from individual to individual and will also influence one's level of acculturation. Thankfully, certain characteristics, values, and behaviors can be associated with each level of acculturation, allowing marketers to more clearly define three distinct groups: isolated, acculturated, and assimilated. So acculturation is something all Latinos have in common, and experts predict this will become the key to further understanding the consumer behavior and media habits of Latinos in the United States. The Pew Hispanic Center is, in my opinion, one of the leading research organizations in this arena, and its studies constantly illuminate various aspects of this ongoing debate. Please visit its website at www.pewhispanic.org and support the Annenberg School for Communication at the University of Southern California or the Pew Charitable Trusts of Philadelphia in any way you can, because research like this is very important to have.

• **Hispanic versus Multicultural** Here you have a double-edged sword. One the one hand you have many corporations trying to neatly fit all minority groups under one "multicultural" umbrella, creating jobs for multicultural managers and trying to create marketing messages that include all ethnic groups. The thinking here is that all minorities are somehow similar because, well, they are viewed (mostly by white people) as "other." Second, minorities tend to cluster in the same large urban areas, constantly influencing one another's taste in music and clothes, among other things. Imagine, for a moment, that multinational companies decided to cluster all English-speaking people in one group and created only one message to sell their products to people in the United States, the United Kingdom, Australia, South Africa, Nigeria, and Jamaica. Imagine trying to create one message that will work with all of those different, English-speaking groups, and you will start to understand the difficulties facing "multicultural" marketing efforts. Indeed, minorities, especially blacks and Latinos, have become the new "trendsetters" of pop culture. But far too often corporate America embraces these multicultural efforts merely to escape having to create new campaigns for each subgroup: African American, Asian, and Latino. On the other hand you have marketers and advertising agencies who think this whole "multicultural" thing is a huge cop-out. How can the message for a Latino be the same as the one for an Asian or an African American? (For that matter how can a brand message be the same for a woman, a man, or a teenager?) Those are all distinct groups with very distinct cultural and linguistic differences who all deserve their own, proper messages. Some agencies see the whole "multicultural" thing as an excuse that continues to allow large corporations not to make a true commitment to minority markets. This is a hugely divisive issue and will not be easily resolved in the near future.

CASE STUDY: IT'S NOT ABOUT LANGUAGE, IT'S ABOUT THE MIND-SET
By Roberto Ruiz, Partner Consumer Contacts

It is tempting to try to generalize and make assumptions that help us generate efficiencies, but this can be a trap that will work against you. The key is to think specifically about your product or service and identify the mind-set that makes the most impact on its sales. In other words, what is the mind-set of the consumer when he or she uses your product or service? If you understand that mind-set, then the simpler demographic segmentation becomes less important.

A couple of years ago (when I was part of The Vidal Partnership) we helped a financial institution launch a product to transfer money internationally over the Internet. Latinos wire more than $10 billion abroad a year, so, of course, they were a key target market. Although smaller in size, Filipino and Indians were also frequent users of money-transfer services, and since they were also more computer savvy, they too were an important target market. While the Vidal Partnership was initially tasked with only the Hispanic strategy, we ended up creating a campaign for all three groups. Why? In the process of developing the strategy, we discovered that we were *not* dealing with people who, when using this product, are defined by their country of origin. We were really dealing with an immigrant "mind-set." And that specific mind-set was that of a person living in two worlds, with emotions for family overseas, working hard to achieve a goal, and fulfilling an emotional and financial duty by sending money. This immigrant "mind-set" went far beyond our original country of origin or language segmentation. Given that one of the key product benefits was convenience and ease of use, we ended up developing a campaign that resonated among all groups. The language was the last thing we worried about. It was the concept that had to be clearly articulated. The campaign was a success in all three markets, and I remember our print ads well: "Making money is hard enough, sending it back home should be easy." Now that's a message we all get, right?

Getting to understand the right mind-set takes time, money, and more than a few focus groups, but it is well worth it if it makes your message and your brand relevant.

THE BROUHAHA OVER NIELSEN PEOPLE METERS

Everyone knows that the Nielsen ratings are used to allocate millions of advertising dollars each year. What most people don't realize is that, until now, Spanish-dominant viewers have been excluded from the general market meter panels, and, instead, measured separately through the National Hispanic Television Index (NHTI). As we all know, separate but equal does not work! Rightfully, Spanish-language television networks have been complaining about this for years because by excluding Spanish-dominant viewers from the total ratings books, the Nielsen figures have favored English-language programs. Over the years, Nielsen Media Research has been slow to include Spanish-dominant viewers in their famous People Meters, always claiming it was a difficult and complicated task that needed to be done right. Although they took way too long to figure it out, in their defense, Nielsen worked with some of the finest minds in research and academia in order to develop a methodology that would stand up to everyone's scrutiny by taking into account several key variables:

- **Language shifts:** Nielsen found that the most common reasons for language shifts are additions or subtractions of people in the home.

- **Number of school-age children:** Researchers found that one child makes it more likely that the family will shift toward English, and that two or more school-age children influence the language of the family even more.

- **Age:** In order to accommodate English-language cable stations like Nickelodeon and MTV, who know they are being watched by Hispanic children, Nielsen decided to include two definitions of Hispanic TV households: Adults 18+ and Persons 2+.

In an interview with *Hispanic Market Weekly*, Nielsen's director of Hispanic services, Doug Darfield, said that while Hispanics may gain greater English ability over time, it may not change their preference to use Spanish at home, debunking the myth that Hispanics will eventually completely migrate to English-language television networks. As mentioned earlier, since it started tracking Hispanic television viewing in 1992, Nielsen has seen *increases* in Spanish-language television viewing, decreases in viewing of English-language networks, and a rise in the viewing of English-language cable networks such as HBO, TNT, Disney Toon, Nick, and TBS.

"When Spanish-dominant viewers are integrated into total market ratings reports, advertisers will have a holistic and accurate view of what people are watching," concludes *Hispanic Market Weekly*. What does this mean for the television and advertising industries? Stay tuned . . .

8

~~~

THE LATINO BABY BOOM

THE IMPACT OF GENERATION Ñ

For me, one of the most striking statistics that keeps on surfacing every time you talk about the growing Hispanic community is its youthfulness. As I mentioned at the beginning of this book, today one out of every five children born in this country is born to a Latina mother. In cities like Los Angeles and El Paso, those birth rates are even higher! Fifty percent of all children born in L.A. are Latino. In El Paso, Texas, that number goes up to 82 percent of all births! As has already been widely reported, one of the big surprises of the 2000 Census was that the size of the U.S. Hispanic community had been underestimated by nearly 10 percent (9.9 percent to be exact). The Census now predicts that the size of the U.S. Hispanic population will triple over the next fifty years, and that Hispanics will make up one-quarter of the total population in the United States by then. Closer range estimates put the Hispanic population at about 44 million by the year 2010 and 55 million by 2020. No doubt, these are huge numbers, which is why corporate America is suddenly waking up to the potential Hispanics have as consumers.

These new Hispanic population numbers have "the potential to reshape the marketing landscape [of the United States], influencing everything from media buys to new store locations," according to *Counting Change*, a special report published by *Advertising Age* in

May 2001. Another area where the 2000 Census proved previous estimates wrong was in the total number of persons between the ages of 18
and 29. Again, this age bracket happens to be one in which the Hispanic
community is growing at a much faster pace than that of any other community in the United States. Why is this important? Because these
numbers will have an impact on the workforce and, ultimately, the U.S.
economy. According to another Pew Hispanic Center study, *Jobs Lost,
Jobs Gained: The Latino Experience in the Recession and Recovery*,
Hispanics were the main source of new workers in the U.S. economy
between 2000 and 2002. According to this study, Latinos gained
379,199 jobs from 2000 to 2002, while African Americans lost 505,040
jobs and non-Hispanic whites lost 1.2 million jobs.

One of those states where Hispanics are going in search of jobs is
Kentucky, where a stagnant population growth has left the farming and
construction industries looking for more young labor. "Latinos have
moved on from working on tobacco farms to food-processing plants and
general construction. Kentucky Hispanics are moving into service
and retail jobs, and Hispanic entrepreneurs are opening grocery stores
and Latino restaurants that attract a predominantly non-Hispanic clien-
tele," Rob Crouch, a Kentucky state demographer, told Adrienne
Pulido for her special report in *Hispanic Market Weekly*. "Explosive
Latino labor growth started in 1995 and has intensified. Hispanics represented 32 percent of the U.S. labor growth during the boom from
1991 to 2000, according to the Bureau of Labor Statistics. And that figure has grown to 50 percent during the downturn from 2000 to 2002,"
reports Pulido.

THE EXPLOSIVE GROWTH OF LATINO YOUTH

Now, let's talk about teens. According to Nielsen Media, between 1993
and 2001, the Hispanic teen population grew 30 percent while the non-
Hispanic teen population grew by a mere 8 percent. According to the
latest Census data, there are 14 million Hispanic Americans under the
age of 18—the largest number of ethnic youth in the United States.
National proportions for Hispanic youth are also impressive—in 2000,

35 percent of all U.S. Hispanics were under the age of 18, compared with only 22.6% of non-Hispanic whites. But the real story can be seen at the local level. Already in certain cities, Latino kids represent the majority of the under-18 population. For example in San Antonio, Texas, 61 percent of the under-18 population is Latino. In Los Angeles, 53 percent of the under-18 population is Latino. When you look at the population age distribution data of the 2000 Census, you can clearly see how Hispanics compare with non-Hispanic whites (table 56).

TABLE 56 Population Age Distribution: Hispanic versus Non-Hispanic Whites

Age Distribution	Hispanic Population (000)	Percentage of Hispanic Population	White, non-Hispanic Population	Percentage of White non-Hispanic Population
Under 5 years	3,841	10.3	11,560	5.9
5 to 9 years	3,766	10.1	11,964	6.1
10 to 14 years	3,480	9.3	13,040	6.7
15 to 19 years	3,122	8.3	12,803	6.6
20 to 24 years	3,559	9.5	12,038	6.2
25 to 29 years	3,537	9.4	11,252	5.8
30 to 34 years	3,457	9.2	13,068	6.7
35 to 44 years	5,439	14.5	31,029	15.9
45 to 54 years	3,399	9.1	29,733	15.3
55 to 64 years	1,942	5.2	20,362	10.5
65 to 74 years	1,175	3.1	14,550	7.5
Total	37,438	100.0	194,822	100.0

Source: U.S. Census Bureau, Current Population Survey, March 2002

In the new millennium, the lure of reaching New Generation Latinos (ages 12–17), Latino Gen Xers (18–24), and the so-called Generation Ñ (25–49), will mimic the wave of consumerism that corporate America experienced with the Baby Boomers in the '70s, '80s, and '90s. Smart companies will want to capture this market while they are still young and keep them loyal to their brands as they get older. But corporate America will have to work hard at getting and keeping the Hispanic consumer hooked on its products. Hispanic consumers may be more brand loyal than general market consumers, but they are not stupid. If companies don't treat them right, they will go looking for a competitive product or service elsewhere. After all this is America, the land of opportunity!

According to the Selig Center for Economic Growth, Hispanics spend more, as a percentage of their total expendable income, than any other ethnic group on things such as groceries, telephone services, furniture, small appliances, children's clothing, and footwear. In spite of the fact that Hispanics overindex in these categories, companies in these sectors are still not allocating the appropriate amount of advertising dollars to reach them. According to the Association of Hispanic Advertising Agencies the industries that are currently "underdeveloped" in the Hispanic market include:

- Insurance

- Automotive

- Specialty/Retail

- Securities/Financial Services

- Travel/Entertainment

- Computers/Software

- U.S. Government

- Pharmaceutical

ACCULTURATION AND RETRO-ACCULTURATION

We've already talked about how the Hispanic community can be divided into three main groups: the "isolated" or Spanish-dominant, the "acculturated" or bilingual, and the "assimilated" or English-dominant. Depending on what research you use, the size and names given to each of these groups will differ, but what everyone does agree on is that the Hispanic market can be divided into three main "buckets" defined by level of acculturation and language use. Today, when you hear people talk about the Hispanic market, they are usually referring only to the

Spanish-dominant group. But in my opinion, bilinguals are the most important of these three groups. Not only are they the largest and fastest growing, they are also younger, more affluent, better educated, and *bicultural,* meaning that they live in both worlds. This group is unique because it *chooses* what language to use depending on its needs at the moment. This "language switching," in turn, shapes its consumer behavior and affects its values and attitudes as well. Most experts would agree that younger Latinos feel more comfortable in English, because that is the language they use most often in school and at work. But the fact that they *choose* to keep their Spanish language and culture alive while living in an English-dominant society clearly indicates that they value the Hispanic aspect of their identity too. It is in their formative years, when Hispanics are teenagers, that many of their social and cultural values as individuals are shaped. So in order to better understand the bilingual group, you must first understand two very important sociological phenomena: acculturation and retro-acculturation.

Make no mistake, acculturation, retro-acculturation, and assimilation are processes that *all* immigrants go through, not just Hispanics. Traditionally, immigrants who came to the United States left their homelands completely behind. Seldom did they return, because going back was often undesirable, difficult, and expensive. Then, as time passed, new generations of these immigrant groups adopted the values, beliefs, and behaviors of the U.S. culture. In other words, those immigrants become *assimilated* into American culture. This process usually takes two to three generations to complete. Unlike other immigrant groups, however, Hispanics are not assimilating as quickly into the American mainstream. For Hispanics in the United States, the process of assimilation has been slowed down significantly due to various factors: The geographic proximity of Latin America, the constant flow of immigration, the relative ease with which people can travel and communicate with friends and family back home, and the fact that Spanish-speaking immigrants concentrate in large ethnic enclaves within urban areas. *Acculturation* is defined as the process of transformation by which an individual originating from one culture adapts to another culture and begins to incorporate its values into his or her own. "The values of foreign-born immigrants are shaped by their country of origin and go back many generations," says an article on this subject published by Hispanicad.com in January 2000. "But the process of acculturation begins when they start modifying these values to accommodate to their new life in the United States. Traditionally, the longer an immigrant stays in the United States, the more acculturated they become."

In his 2003 study, *The Rise of the Second Generation, Changing Patterns in Hispanic Population Growth,* Roberto Suro, the director of research at the Pew Hispanic Center, adds yet another dimension to the definition of acculturation by stating that, in fact, both the individual and the host country are affected by this process. "Whereas assimilation describes this process on the individual level and focuses on members of one group adopting the cultural patterns of the majority or host culture, acculturation focuses on the impact that the two cultures have on each other." Most experts would agree that the principal measure of assimilation is language acquisition of the host culture, which in this case is English. So the fact that Latinos have chosen to keep the Spanish language alive from generation to generation has, in fact, changed the process of assimilation for this group. The question is to what extent does the retention of the Spanish language affect the values and attitudes of Hispanics in the United States? We'll get into that in just a bit, but first let's finish defining all these terms, so that we are all on the same page.

Retro-acculturation is the process by which usually second- or third-generation adults, the sons and daughters of immigrants, feel a need to reconnect to their cultural heritage and traditions. Again, this process takes place within *all* immigrant communities in the United States regardless of their ethnicity. Retro-acculturation usually affects children of immigrants who are in their twenties or thirties who suddenly feel the need to start reconnecting with their cultural roots. What is interesting is that we are starting to see the process of retro-acculturation in Hispanics happen at a much earlier age, especially with U.S.-born Latinos. Some experts have even observed retro-acculturation in Hispanics who are in their teens.

Remember, the number of Hispanic teens is expected to grow 62 percent by the year 2020, compared with a 10 percent growth in the teen population overall. U.S.-born Hispanics are usually raised in a home that has already undergone some partial acculturation. For the first ten to fifteen years of their lives, Hispanic children are going to school in English and feel more American than anything else. These kids don't want to be thought of as "different," even though the values that are instilled in them are often different from those of their counterparts. According to Hispanicad.com, when these kids reach their teens, they start defining themselves culturally. "At this age a burgeoning cultural pride begins to take hold and these teens begin the process of *retro-acculturation*. Across a number of categories, kids as young as eleven express the strong desire to learn more about their culture and the traditions that go along with it. Although it is much too early to tell, some researchers believe that this is due to two main factors:

1. Hispanic teens are undergoing a demographic awakening. They are becoming more aware of their number within their communities and across the United States. They are also better educated and more informed than their parents, and realize their enormous purchasing power.
2. There is no other way to say it. Being part of an ethnic group is *in*. In examining trends over the past five years, researchers have discovered that within most of the urban centers across the United States, it is the ethnic teens that set the trends."

Some marketers have tried to communicate with these kids by using a mixture of Spanish and English known as Spanglish, which is often what these kids speak. Spanglish, of course, is not a language per se, but it is unique to the U.S. Hispanic population. In his book, *Spanglish: The Making of a New American Language*, Professor Ilan Stavans defines Spanglish as "the constant clash between the two worlds, cultures and languages that Latinos live in." Although I have a newfound respect for Spanglish after reading this book, I am not in favor of inventing a new language (or, for that matter, destroying two perfectly good languages) in order to reach Latino youth. I believe that advertising and marketing messages can be properly crafted in English or in Spanish and still have the desired effect and cultural relevance. What is clear is that media and language choices play a very important role in shaping the attitudes and beliefs of the younger Latino generation who tend to be what Roberto Suro calls "language switchers."

THE IMPACT OF LANGUAGE AND MEDIA ON THE ASSIMILATION PROCESS

According to the U.S. Census, the number of Hispanics speaking Spanish at home has more than doubled in the past twenty years, from 10.2 million in 1980 to 24.7 million in 2000. "This growth has motivated concerns about the adoption of English by immigrants of Spanish-speaking nations," says Suro in his brief on bilingualism based on the *2002 National Survey of Latinos.* "It has also generated interest in the news media and among advertisers seeking the most efficient means to communicate with this growing population," he adds.

The *2002 National Survey of Latinos,* however, found that 46 percent of Hispanic adults speak *both* English and Spanish, meaning they are able to "carry on a conversation in either English or Spanish 'pretty well.' " Census 2000 data suggests that English-Spanish bilingualism is even more prevalent among Hispanic children than among Hispanic adults. In 2000, reportedly 59 percent of Hispanic children spoke Spanish at home, and spoke English either "well" or "very well" compared with only 53 percent of Hispanic adults.

But, as Suro points out, there is a difference between a person's ability to *speak* Spanish versus their ability to *read or write* Spanish. "Adults who are English/Spanish bilingual readers are bilingual speakers," he says. "However, the converse is not necessarily true. Not all Hispanics who have bilingual speaking abilities are necessarily able to read in both languages." Through a series of questions about language usage and ability, Suro was able to conclude that bilingual Hispanics were markedly different from the wider Hispanic adult population, especially in terms of mass media preferences.

In April 2004, the Pew Hispanic Center released another ground-

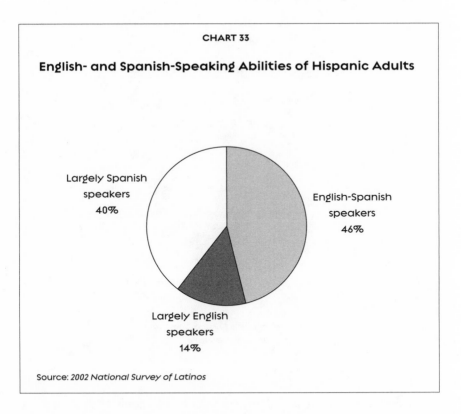

CHART 33

English- and Spanish-Speaking Abilities of Hispanic Adults

Largely Spanish
speakers
40%

English-Spanish
speakers
46%

Largely English
speakers
14%

Source: *2002 National Survey of Latinos*

breaking study, *Changing Channels and Crisscrossing Cultures: A Survey of Latinos on the News Media.* In this study Suro further explores the impact that media—in this case, particularly the news media—have on the assimilation process of Hispanics. "The language in which Latinos get their news significantly influences their opinions on issues ranging from immigration to the war in Iraq," writes Suro. In fact, he found that language substantially contributes to differences in attitudes, even after controlling for other factors such as age, gender, level of education, income, place of residence (urban, suburban, or rural), country of origin, political party, religion, citizenship, and generation in the United States. His findings on language usage of news media were similar to those he published in the *2002 National Survey of Latinos,* where a majority of adult Latinos reported getting their news in *both* English and Spanish (chart 34).

Contrary to the popular belief that Latinos are divided between those who consume media in English and those who consume media in

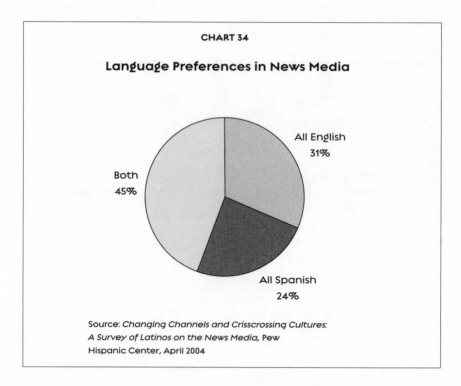

CHART 34

Language Preferences in News Media

All English
31%

Both
45%

All Spanish
24%

Source: *Changing Channels and Crisscrossing Cultures:
A Survey of Latinos on the News Media,* Pew
Hispanic Center, April 2004

Spanish, this study showed that nearly half of all adult Hispanics cross back and forth between the two languages and cultures. "Rather than two audiences sharply segmented by language, this study shows that many more Latinos get at least some of their news in both English and Spanish than in just one language or the other," adds Suro. This newer survey showed that 43 percent of second-generation Latinos are language "switchers," a surprisingly high percentage given their comfort with English. According to Suro, language "switching" occurs as a result of bilingual Latinos seeking out information in a certain language, depending on the subject of interest. For example, news from Latin America or sports tends to be consumed in Spanish mainly, but news about the presidential election would be consumed more in English. "Getting the news could be the single most extensive cross-cultural experience for the Hispanic population," says Suro. Now, let's look at some of the key differences the Pew Hispanic Center found among Latinos, according to their choice of language when consuming the news.

KEY CHARACTERISTICS OF THE LANGUAGE
PREFERENCE GROUPS:

Latinos who consume news all in English represent 31 percent of all adult Latinos. Of this group:

- 78% are U.S. born, 31% are high school graduates, 17% are college graduates

- 25% earn less than $30,000 a year, 44% earn more than $50,000 a year

Latinos who consume news all in Spanish represent 24 percent of all adult Latinos. Of this group:

- 96% are foreign born, 21% are high school graduates, 2% are college graduates

- 65% earn less than $30,000 a year, 2% earn more than $50,000 a year

Latinos who consume news in both languages represent 45 percent of all adult Latinos. Of this group:

- 31% are U.S. born, 69% are foreign born

- 35% are high school graduates, 9% are college graduates

- 46% earn less than $30,000 a year, 17% earn more than $50,000 a year

For me a surprising finding of this study was the extraordinary reach of English-language news media. According to this study, three-quarters of the Hispanic population gets at least some of its news in English versus two-thirds who get it in Spanish! "Exposure to news in English is greatly increased because so many Hispanic households are now bilingual with U.S.-born, English-speaking children living with Spanish-speaking immigrant parents," explains Suro. "Fully one-third of Latinos who get all their news in Spanish said that someone else in their household gets some news in English," he adds. More important, this study showed that the language in which Latinos get their news influences—and sometimes even changes—their opinions and views on a variety of social and political issues. This is important to note, since according to this study, the majority of Latino voters get the majority of their news *in English*. According to this study, 61 percent of those Latinos who are likely voters view only English-language programming, 28 percent watch programs in both languages, while the Spanish-only share of this audience is a mere 11 percent.

Finally, although not surprising to me, another important finding of this study is that the overwhelming majority of Latinos (78 percent) considered Spanish-language media very important to the economic and political development of the Hispanic population of the United States. In fact, according to the study, this view of the Spanish-language media as an important ethnic institution was shared by 61 percent of those Latinos who get all their news in English! "The significance of Spanish-language media as a social and cultural institu-

TABLE 57				
	Total	English	Spanish	Both
English language media contributes to a negative image	44%	51%	31%	46%
By too much emphasis on illegal or undocumented immigration	34	39	24	36
By too much emphasis on drug trafficking, gang violence, or other criminal activity	34	38	22	38
By not enough emphasis on economic accomplishments	28	40	14	28
By not enough recognition of Hispanic/Latino political community leaders	28	39	14	29
English language media contributes to a favorable image	46	39	54	47
Don't know	9	10	14	5
Refused	1	1	1	1

Source: *Changing Channels and Crisscrossing Cultures: A Survey of Latinos on the News Media,* Pew Hispanic Center, April 2004

tion is magnified by the widespread concern expressed by 44 percent of all Latinos that English-language media contributes to the negative image of the Hispanic population in the United States," says Suro (table 57). Here, of course, the culprits are not only the news media, but all of Hollywood as it continues to marginalize Hispanics both on TV and in film, perpetuating negative stereotypes of Latinos as sex-pots, housemaids, or criminals.

According to *Looking for Latino Regulars on Prime-Time Television: The Fall 2003 Season,* a study by UCLA's Chicano Studies Research Center, the percentage of regular Latino characters on prime-time TV has remained at 4.1 percent since 2002. Furthermore, the study indicated that Latino characters appeared in only five of the twelve dominant TV genres: crime, sitcoms, drama, science fiction, and sports. Latinos were most notably absent from teen shows, medical shows, musical shows, news, and reality TV. Researchers at UCLA also questioned why so few minority characters appeared on so many of the prime-time shows like *The O.C., CSI,* or *ER,* particularly since many of these series are actually set in urban areas where Latinos represent a large segment of the population! I'm still waiting for someone to explain that to me, because if Hollywood thinks Latinos aren't watching, it's wrong. Nielsen ratings show that, in fact, many Latinos are tuning in to these programs. Clearly, programs and advertising messages intended to reach the growing number of Latino youth can and should be done in both languages.

DEMOGRAPHIC AND CONSUMER PROFILES: ISOLATED, ACCULTURATED, AND ASSIMILATED

Although the 2003 Yankelovich MONITOR Multicultural Marketing Study uses slightly different names for the isolated, acculturated, and assimilated groups I described earlier, it, in essence, describes the same groups by using the terms "Hispanic dominant," "Intercultural," and "Assimilated." In their study, conducted in collaboration with Cheskin and Images USA, Yankelovich compares the three groups in ways that are very helpful to anyone trying to understand this market. Table 58 contains a sampling of the great data in this study.

TABLE 58

Demographic	Total	Hispanic Dominant	Inter-cultural	Assimi-lated
Average Size of Household	3.7	3.9	3.6	3.6
Median Annual Household Income	$32K	$25K	$34K	$48K
Never Married	28%	18%	30%	36%
Mean Age	37.3	40.6	36.9	34.4
Own Your Home or Apartment	48%	38%	48%	57%
Hispanic culture				
I am very proud of my Hispanic background	95%	99%	98%	89%
I would like to participate in more activities that celebrate my Hispanic culture and heritage	81%	95%	89%	61%
I need to preserve my family's cultural traditions	87%	93%	94%	76%
More and more I look to religion as a source of comfort in my life	77%	80%	79%	71%
Consumer				
Go online at least weekly	40%	28%	44%	49%
Have health insurance	68%	58%	73%	75%
Have a savings account	45%	33%	46%	56%
Have a checking account	61%	56%	58%	70%
Have a car loan	25%	14%	31%	32%
Have a 401(k)	23%	11%	27%	32%
Need to be hip/cool on the cutting edge	52%	68%	55%	34%

Source: 2003 Yankelovich MONITOR Multicultural Marketing Study: Management Summary Report

HOW TO GET STARTED: MENTOR FROM WITHIN

I know that these issues of language usage and acculturation can be intimidating to mainstream companies who are first venturing into this market. But if you keep in mind the median age of this market (25.8 years in 2000), and its projected growth in the next decade (to 44 million by 2010), and its purchasing power (more than $700 billion by 2007), there is no doubt of the promise this market holds. But only those companies that are willing to make a commitment to this market and create *new* business models will truly benefit. In order to do that, it is important to have people who truly understand this market and its complex issues at the highest levels of the decision-making process.

Look around and see who if anyone on your staff can be of help. If you can find a bright, young professional interested in the Hispanic market, mentor them, nurture them, and give them a chance to participate in your Hispanic projects. But don't be fooled by a surname. Just because someone who works for you may be of Hispanic descent does not mean she or he has the necessary skills, expertise, or knowledge to successfully work in the Hispanic market. Make sure you hire or promote people who have actually had working experience in this market whether they are Hispanic or not, and then please listen to what they have to say! Granted, there is a lot of new ground to break, especially in the English-language world, but don't assume that just because a manager of yours is Hispanic, she or he can do the job. You would be surprised to know how many companies actually make this mistake!

9

SO YOU WANT TO GET INTO THE HISPANIC MARKET?

Ten Mistakes You Should Avoid

1. Do not make assumptions about the Hispanic market.

Many companies still have a one-size-fits-all mentality. Your mass market strategy may have served you well for decades, but as the general market becomes more and more fragmented and less economically powerful, understanding how to sell your products and services to the emerging minorities (black, Hispanic, or Asian) becomes a business necessity. Minorities already represent 30 percent of all consumers in America. Now ask yourself, are 30 percent of your sales coming from these markets? Make no mistake, the future growth of your business will depend on your ability to penetrate an increasingly fragmented marketplace with more targeted products and services. Remember, by 2050 minorities will make up half of the total population, one-fourth of which will be Latino. So, the first thing you need to do is understand your target market(s) before you can successfully sell them your products.

In her book *Latinos Inc.*, Arlene Dávila gives a great example of the importance of understanding your target audience. For her book, Professor Dávila interviewed Alicia Conill, one of the pioneering women of the Hispanic advertising industry. Conill recalled how, in the early days of Hispanic advertising, American companies didn't understand how unique and different the Hispanic consumer was, so they were very reluctant to even conduct research in this market. In an effort to get the Campbell Soup Company account for her then-nascent agency, Conill Advertising, Alicia personally conducted more than 500 interviews with Latina women all over New York City to see if they knew the Campbell soup products and, if they did know the products, how they were using them in their homes. Through her research she discovered that Latina women did, in fact, know and use Campbell products, but not to make soup! The majority of the women she spoke to used cans of condensed Campbell soup without adding water to make *sofrito* instead. *Sofrito* is a seasoned food base commonly used in Latin America for cooking all sorts of dishes. So you see, Latinas were buying Campbell's soups, but they were using the product in ways that were unique to their culture.

Let's say you are a magazine publisher looking to expand your most successful brands into the Hispanic market. The knee-jerk reaction might be to simply translate your magazine into Spanish and put it on the newsstands. For example, let's assume you have a celebrity magazine. Everyone likes celebrity gossip, right? Sure. But not all celebrities have crossover appeal. Of course there are Hollywood celebrities who have worldwide appeal, but not all TV stars, sports stars, or even royalty that appeal to you also appeal to Latinos. With four or five Spanish-language TV networks, Hispanic soccer fanatics can watch any number of games. Latin women have access to a growing stable of Latino film stars. The community has, in fact, created a parallel universe in the world of entertainment. So, now how do you define who is a celebrity? It depends on who your target audience is. If your target readers are Latin women 35–55 who watch Spanish-language TV, you'd better know what is important to them: *telenovelas.* Can you name one *telenovela* star? I'll give you a hint. One of the most famous ones was married to Tommy Motola. Another famous *telenovela* star has already crossed over into Hollywood and is a big star known by all of you. I'm talking about Salma Hayek. That's right!

The same would be true for a sports magazine. You know the average male reader in the United States is mainly obsessed with football, basketball, hockey, NASCAR, and baseball. But what if your new target market is Hispanic? Well, you'd better start covering soccer, wrestling, and boxing too! (Do you even have the right staff to write intelligently about these other sports?) And if you already cover baseball, the sport with the most Latino players in the United States, you will definitely have to change the athletes interviewed in your main stories to make sure you are appealing to a Hispanic reader.

Okay. Now, let's assume that you do have a staff that can help you identify who are the right celebrities to cover in these new Hispanic magazines. How do you treat your celebrities in print? In Latin America and Spain, celebrity magazines rarely talk badly about their celebrities. Sure, they love their gossip, cover celebrity tragedies and indiscretions, but Latin celebrities are like your best friend, so mean-spirited, tabloid-style articles will not go over as well with your new Hispanic audience.

If you don't know who your target audience is, you will invariably fail to reach them by simply translating your product into Spanish. Never make assumptions about what Hispanics (or any other minority group, for that matter) know or like about your product. The best thing you can do before embarking on any marketing strategy for Hispanics is to spend some time and money trying to find out what your target market thinks about your product, which takes me to mistake number two: Do your own research.

2. Don't launch a product or campaign in the Hispanic market without doing research.

Understanding the differences between your current market and your new target market can make or break your project. You would NOT believe how many "Hispanic" products have been launched into the marketplace without doing any market research *at all*. I know what you're thinking. Market research is expensive and your boss is pushing for you to just "get it done." Well, unless you want egg on your face, you'd better push back and do some research.

Just because your product is well known in the Anglo, mainstream market, does *not* mean that it is known in the Hispanic market. In fact, you should treat this launch like a new product launch, with all that that entails. Would you launch a product in Canada without doing research?

I hope not. You must first find out what people know or think about your product. How do they feel about the product category in general? Are there cultural or linguistic nuances that you need to be aware of? The classic example here is the Chevy "Nova." Back in the 1970s when Chevrolet was launching this car in Latin America, they could not figure out why sales were so terrible until someone told them that in Spanish the words *no va* means "It doesn't work"!

Before 1980, research in the Hispanic market was practically nonexistent. The very first national studies on the Hispanic market, conducted in 1981 and then again in 1984, were funded entirely by the Spanish-language television network Univision—then known as SIN—in an effort to verify its national reach to its growing stable of advertisers. Strategy Research Corporation, today known as Synovate, got into the Hispanic research market in the mid-'80s and continues to be a leader in this space today. But to pay for their biannual research studies, Synovate had to get funding, and invariably its research studies have been funded by Spanish-language media companies or advertising agencies who have a vested interest in proving that Spanish-language media is a viable tool to reach the Hispanic market. Nevertheless, Synovate's "Blue Book" on the Hispanic market is still the most reliable source in the marketplace, since some of the other big names in the research industry did not get into this market until quite recently. Yankelovich has been publishing its Hispanic Monitor since 1988. Nielsen Media Research inaugurated its Hispanic Television Index in 1992 and Simmons introduced its studies of Hispanic purchasing patterns in 1995! As you can see, the amount of syndicated research that exists on the market is limited, so chances are that you will not find exactly what you need to know about your product.

If you are doing national research, make sure you pick neutral markets that mirror the marketplace, such as Chicago, where you get a good mix of Mexicans, Central and South Americans, as well as Latinos from the Caribbean. If you are doing research on Mexicans, don't do research in Miami or, for that matter, in east Los Angeles, because you will get a distorted picture. Also keep in mind issues of acculturation and location. If your business has stores only in Texas, keep in mind that a Mexican living in San Antonio may be completely different from a Mexican living in El Paso or Houston or McAllen. In many ways Hispanic consumers are the same as any other consumers, but understanding the little things that can turn them on or off will make the difference between success and failure when you launch your product in the Hispanic market.

Another important factor to keep in mind when talking about capturing the Latino consumer is that a large percentage of the Hispanic population is still foreign born. "It is important to note that brands that automatically suggest a product category for most U.S. customers may not carry the same association to recent immigrants," warns the 2003 Yankelovich study. "Thus, Spanish-language advertising may need to have more consumer education, clearer definitions and a different message than the general market ads for the same product." Keep in mind that your product may be at the end of its life cycle in a mature general market, yet at the very beginning of the curve for the Hispanic market. This fact alone should make your brand manager and your ad agency adapt their message to the appropriate stage for the Hispanic market.

Without spending oodles of money on research, you can figure out how best to approach this market. But if you don't at least understand how Hispanics perceive your brand or product, how are you going to successfully launch anything? When doing research make sure that the vendor you contract with specifically has experience in the U.S. Hispanic market, not in the Latin American market. If you don't, you could end up paying for their mistakes and your research will most likely suffer.

3. Do not enter the Hispanic market without making a commitment. One of the reasons why I have worked on so many start-ups is that often the company behind the start-up did not make a real commitment to the project. Without the commitment in terms of time and money, you will always fail. Once, I worked at a company that was launching two new magazines, one geared to the teen market and one for Hispanics. Although the markets were similar in size and growth potential, the teen magazine project was given a budget three times the size of the

Hispanic project. If your company is not committed to doing things right, you're better off recommending that they not do it at all!

If you have taken the time to understand your target market and done your own research, the worst thing you can do is "test the waters" with a half-hearted effort. Do you really want to enter this market with a mediocre effort? No, you want to put your best foot forward, right? I'm all for testing, but leave your market wanting more, not disgusted with their experience when trying you out for the first time. You only have one chance to make a good impression, and Latinos are very savvy consumers.

The second worst thing you can do is to hold the Hispanic market to a higher standard of business success. If it takes five years for a company to break even with the launch of a new product in the general market, why do these same executives think they can launch the same new product in the Hispanic market and break even or even make money in just one year? This expectation of a higher return on investment in this market truly dumbfounds me, but I encounter it all the time.

You must respect this market as much as you respect any other consumer market, so your commitment to the Hispanic market must go beyond what your company is going to get out of the Hispanic market and include efforts to "give back" to the community. Latinos are weary of companies that are looking to make a quick buck on them. If you want their support and loyalty, you must support the Latino community in other ways that are meaningful to them. If you "give back" to the community, they will take note and you will see that they will always give back to you too.

All State Insurance is a good example to follow. In the early 1990s, All State decided to expand its sales in the U.S. Hispanic market, which at the time were estimated at around $1 billion. In order to attract more Hispanic customers, they conducted research to find out how Hispanics felt about insurance issues. They then launched a dedicated effort in this market, which included hiring local Hispanic agents, sponsoring events, and donating money to the Hispanic community as well as advertising across all Spanish-language media. Over ten years, All State reportedly spent $60 million in their marketing efforts to Hispanics and its efforts paid off handsomely! By 2001, All State had doubled its sales in the Hispanic market and today, if you ask a Latino to name an insurance company, I would bet All State would be at the top of his list!

Unfortunately, shortsighted executives worried more about the price of their stock and this year's bottom line dominates the world of business. Executives with vision realize that the only way to deliver the long-term growth rates that Wall Street has become accustomed to is by expanding into new markets and giving them time to fully develop. Clearly, the emerging minorities in the United States are becoming a bigger and more important piece of the nation's economy. Among these minorities, Hispanics already represent the largest segment, and are growing faster than all other minorities in the United States with the exception of Asians! Because of immigration and high birth rates, our population grows by approximately 1 million persons each year. Add to that the number of Latino youth who enter the workforce, and the total number of Hispanic consumers in the United States increases by an estimated 2 *million* persons *each year.* These are big numbers and they demand real commitments.

4. Don't forget to get your message out.

This is perhaps the most egregious of all the mistakes on this list. If you have spent time and money understanding your target market, and you have created a new product or tweaked your old product to make sure it works for the Hispanic market, why would you *not* let people know that? If you don't have an advertising budget and you're not planning any special promotions or public relations campaigns, how on earth do you expect to sell your product? Any product launch in the Hispanic market must be treated as a *new* product launch, even with recognizable brands. Brand arrogance will get you nowhere.

The first thing you MUST do is hire a public relations specialist with experience in the Hispanic market or make sure the Hispanic advertising agency you are working with provides that service. If your company has a public relations department, chances are it doesn't really know what to do in this market. Again, simply translating a press release won't do. You need Hispanic press lists, contacts in Hispanic media, and the know-how to pitch your story for this market. For example, let's say a well known Latin star is going to be in L.A. to receive a local community award and appear on the CBS show *Hollywood Squares.* The "pitch" for the American press release would be "Latina star to appear on *Hollywood Squares.*" The "pitch" for the Hispanic press release would be "Latina star receives local community award." See what I mean?

Find out what's important about your product to this market and a well-thought-out public relations campaign is probably the cheapest way to get your message out. Give yourself time to create some brand awareness in the community and, most important, keep the buzz going. Of course if you have an advertising budget, hire a Hispanic agency that can not only craft the right message and positioning for your product, but can also help you with your media planning and buying. Make sure your advertising agency also works closely with your public relations specialist, so that all of your efforts are coordinated and consistent.

Proper media planning will be critical to your success. In today's growing and complex Hispanic media market, in-depth knowledge of network programming schedules and program demographics is required. Because the expertise does not exist at general market media buying companies, this was an area that Hispanic agencies were forced to develop in-house. There are also a few, very good independent media planners and buyers who specialize in the Hispanic market. You'd be surprised how much more you can get out of your advertising dollars if you spend them in the right places. If you've got a great product and a great message, what good does it do if it doesn't reach your audience?

5. Don't dilute your brand. That's all you've got.
Brands are powerful and yet delicate things. When you look at the list of the most powerful brands of the millennium that *Advertising Age* published in the year 2000, you can't help but be in awe. Every aspect of your

business is reflected in your brand. The product itself, the way you deal with customers, the charities and events your company gets behind, and that ever-changing thing called "perception" are all important elements of your brand. And, as we have seen recently with companies like Enron and Tyco, the perception of your brand can quickly change in the consumer's mind. You can go from the best to the worst in a very short span of time. You can also go from having a brand that is considered old and somewhat bland to having the coolest, hottest thing. Think Burberrys! If brands are so fragile, why would anyone in their right mind risk lending their brand to an experiment to which they are not fully committed?

"Brand is an important element in Hispanic product purchasing decisions," says the 2003 Yankelovich MONITOR Multicultural Marketing Study. "Not only is it used to assure quality and value, but Hispanics are also interested in brands that make them feel good about themselves." So the first question you must ask yourself is does my brand have any equity in this market? Is it well perceived or not?

If you are an international conglomerate that has been doing business in Latin America, you should know that many of the brand names used there are different. As mentioned earlier Pampers are called "Do-Dots" in Spain and "Arruchaditos" in Venezuela. In some cases you

TABLE 59		
Reasons for Selecting a Particular Brand (Summary of Describes Completely/Somewhat)	Hispanics	Non-Hispanic Whites
The brand assures me that a reliable company stands behind the product or service	71%	85%
The brand helps me to eliminate risk so I can avoid a bad decision	62%	72%
The brand makes it quicker and easier for me to buy	60%	75%
The brand keeps me in-the-know about what's new and trendy in the marketplace	44%	38%
The brand lets other people know where I am on the social ladder	25%	14%

Source: 2003 Yankelovich MONITOR Multicultural Marketing Study: Management Summary Report

might want to use the Latin American brand name when targeting the U.S. Hispanic market because it will have some built-in brand equity, at least with the foreign born or recently arrived, who are more Spanish dominant.

In the 1990s, the easiest way to brand a "Hispanic" version of any product was by adding the label "en Español" to the brand name. In some cases I think it worked, as in the case of *People en Español,* where the *People* brand immediately conveys to the reader what the magazine is about. But one of the reasons why *People en Español* continues to be so successful is that it is not a mere translation of a bunch of articles written for *People* magazine. The majority of the articles in *People en Español* are written originally in Spanish with a U.S. Hispanic audience in mind, which is something I pushed for very hard when launching that product to the market. So Time Inc. capitalized on its *People* brand name by extending it to this market, but changed the product content to accommodate the tastes of its new readers. Of course, that doesn't work with all brands.

6. Don't be fooled by a Hispanic surname. Work with real Hispanic "experts."

In the 1980s, as the burgeoning U.S. Hispanic market started to really develop, it was not uncommon to hear people selling themselves as "Hispanic experts" in the growing media and advertising industries simply by virtue of *being* Hispanic. "I'm a Latino, I know how Latinos think and what they do" was their motto. That was the beginning of the "professional Latino," a scary breed of executive who actually has made it quite far in corporate America. The "professional Latino" still exists, although I like to think that she or he is now a dying breed. But you must be careful not to be fooled by someone who claims she or he can do the job simply because they have a Hispanic surname.

What you want to find is a "Latino professional" and, guess what, they don't even need to be of Hispanic descent. There are a number of "Latino professionals" who are not ethnically Hispanic but who have worked in the U.S. Hispanic market for years and are well respected in their field. Gary Berman, for example, is one. He heads a very important market research firm in the Hispanic market. Another well-known Latino professional, who actually specializes in sports marketing for Latinos, is my friend Joe Schramm, a super nice *gringo* from Long Island, New York. When looking for the right person to help you out on a Latino project, or if you just want to beef up your team with someone who can provide your company with Hispanic market expertise, make sure he or she has had experience working with this market. If this person doesn't have experience with the U.S. Hispanic market, at the very least he or she should have some experience with Latin American markets. Although the United States and Latin American markets are very different, experience in Latin American markets will at least be helpful.

Latino professionals should also be fluent in Spanish, because to know the language is to know the culture. Knowledge of the Spanish language is critical, because so often in marketing it is more important to communicate "ideas" or "concepts" that might not even exist in the Spanish language or culture. And if a translation can be done, chances are it should not be literal because it probably won't make sense or won't be clear. For example, in the 1990s I worked for COLORS magazine, a racy youth magazine that was distributed world-wide, produced and sponsored by the Italian clothing company Benetton. Once we did a whole issue on sex. Well, when it came to translating "safe sex," if you do a literal translation, you get "sexo seguro." But, guess what, that doesn't mean safe sex in Spanish, it means quite the opposite, "I'm getting laid!" So we had to change the translation of safe sex to "sexo sin riesgos," which in English would be translated as "sex without risk." Your Latino professional will have to be able to judge if the marketing and advertising messages created for your company's product or services are effective in Spanish, which is why knowledge of the language is so important.

And, finally, if you cannot be the judge of someone's language ability, then ask someone who does know the difference to interview them too. Sounds obvious, but you'd be surprised how many people are fooled by Latino expert wannabes. And the problem only gets compounded if senior management can't tell the difference between what is done well in Spanish and what is not. In time the truth will come out, but do you want to waste time and money working with someone who doesn't really know what they are doing just because you're embarrassed to ask a few tough questions? I hope not.

7. Don't forget to educate your senior management.

One of the hardest things for any Latino professional to deal with in corporate America is debunking the myths and stereotypes about the Hispanic community that their colleagues and superiors may still harbor. It is a very tough job to do because you don't want to insult anyone's intelligence, but you also want them to understand the market properly so that you can get the support, financial or otherwise, that you need in order to get the job done right.

Don Francisco, the host of *Sabado Gigante*—the highest-rated television show on Spanish-language television—once told me a story that will illustrate this point. His show started airing on Univision in 1987, and although he had great ratings, the Hispanic market was still in its infancy and his salesmen had a very hard time convincing American companies to advertise on his show. Once at a big meeting with a national retail store—which shall remain nameless—the president of the company asked him, "Why should I advertise on your show when your viewers are my shoplifters?" Although that was almost 20 years ago, trust me, things have not changed that much. For example, in 1998 the Katz Radio Group, one of the leading sellers of radio time in the Hispanic market at the time, got in trouble when a memo containing derogatory remarks about blacks and Latinos was leaked to the press. The infamous memo implied that advertising to these audiences was appealing to "suspects not prospects." Stereotypes and ignorance are still pervasive. I kid you not when I tell you that once one of my bosses at a big Fortune 500 corporation asked me if the streets in Latin America were actually paved!

The best way to debunk many of these myths is by constantly educating your senior management about the market. If you are in charge of a Latino initiative, I recommend that you often pass along information that you get on the market. Get them involved in your Hispanic effort early on, so that as you learn more about what needs to get done to do the job right, they will be right there with you. If you attend a conference on the market or an event, try to bring them along. Educate, educate, educate! For many high-level executives their only contact with Latinos are their nanny, their doorman, or their gardeners, so to meet other Latino executives and learn about the market will help them be more supportive of your Latino efforts.

And, of course, learn to manage their expectations. Often, when new Latino projects are started, there is a lot of enthusiasm among upper management because they see the potential and want to cash in on the opportunity as soon as possible! But the enthusiasm starts to wane quickly when you start telling them all the things that have to be done or changed in order to make this new project work for the Hispanic market. So keep them apprised of your progress. Take baby steps, and have a clear understanding of what your company needs to do to keep on moving forward with the Hispanic market. If you manage expectations well, you will look good and, more important, you will make *them* look good too!

8. Don't assume that Latin projects must be cheaper to get done.

Who was a better dancer, Fred Astaire or Ginger Rogers? Most people would automatically assume it was Fred Astaire, but in fact the better dancer was Ginger Rogers, because she had to dance backward, in a dress and high heels!

In this case Spanish-language media are like Ginger Rogers. Both Nielsen and Arbitron have been tracking this market for more than a decade now, and even though Spanish-language media often beat English language media with audience ratings, the fact remains that they are forced to charge less for their advertising time than comparable English-language media. According to a 1999 study conducted by the Federal Communications Commission, advertisers that regularly pay $1 per listener for general market radio stations pay only 78 cents for minority-formatted stations and 71 cents for stations that are both minority-owned and minority-formatted. The perception that reaching Hispanic households is somehow worth less than reaching non-

Hispanic households needs to change, especially given everything you have learned about Hispanic consumers and how they actually shop more than non-Hispanic consumers.

Selling advertising time is different than actually producing a product, especially a Spanish-language media product (TV, radio, print, or Internet). But for some reason the same mentality prevails: It must be cheaper in Spanish. I don't know why people who are in the business of producing content think that if you're producing something in Spanish, it will cost less or be cheaper to produce than if you are doing it in English. Do you think the electric company or an airline company charges Hispanics less than other customers? No, we pay the same as everyone else!

When I worked for Spanish-language print media, I often got asked to work with smaller editorial budgets and yet get qualified personnel to do the job right. For example, if an English editor would get paid $35 an hour, a Spanish-language editor would be budgeted at $25 an hour. But that made no sense to me, so I learned to push back. One day I went up to the managing editor of the English-language magazine I was working for and said, "I can't find anyone to do this work for the money you are willing to pay, so give this article to your best editor and have him edit this." Of course, the article was in Spanish, so even his best editor could not do the job. He got the point and upped my budget.

9. Don't treat the Hispanic market as if it were a "quota" you must reach.

When I ask companies to tell me what percentage of their customer base is Hispanic, they usually won't know. If you don't know who is buying your product, then your company may be wasting money with its current marketing and advertising efforts. Usually the basic consumer information companies keep track of will not go beyond name, address, and telephone number, if that! If you have a database of names of your customers, a quick way of getting a sense of how many Latinos may be in your database is by doing a Spanish surname overlay. This means that your database will be screened through a computer program that identifies last names ending, for example, in "uez," like Rodriguez, or "iz," like Ruiz, or other typical endings that characterize Hispanic surnames. Although this is better than nothing, a Hispanic surname overlay will not be enough to really tell you how many Latinos are buying your product, since many Latinos have surnames that are not typically Spanish, due to the mixture of people of various cultural backgrounds that have historically converged in the Americas. O'Farril, Saltzberger, Movradinov, are just a few examples of Hispanic last names I've come across over the years. So if you really want to know how many Hispanics may be in your database, there are companies that specialize in identifying them through a series of more sophisticated overlays that include Census and ZIP code data, among other proprietary software.

Once you have determined how many Latinos you have consuming your product, you might want to determine how much human capital you have on your staff to help you capitalize on any new efforts you may engage in to penetrate the Hispanic market. Successfully growing your sales in the Hispanic market may require that your operation be tweaked. Think of every consumer touch point in the life cycle of your product or service, and ask yourself if you are properly set up to service your Hispanic customers. Advertising and marketing departments are obvious, but there are other critically important areas in a company that are often overlooked, such as customer service, training manuals, billings (should your invoices and statements be bilingual?), and collections. Before you launch any new marketing efforts, you must ask yourself if your company is really ready to do business in the Hispanic market.

Another very common mistake people make when thinking about minority markets is to think in terms of "quotas." Since Mexicans represent 60 percent of the Hispanic market, we should devote 60 percent of our Hispanic advertising budget to Mexicans, the thinking goes. If you pick up a Hispanic magazine, do you expect to find 60 percent of the stories to be about Mexicans. God, no! Good stories are good stories, no matter what the ethnic background of the person, Mexican, Puerto Rican, or Chinese. On TV we have yet to go beyond one-dimensional Latino characters, but shows like ABC's *George Lopez,* which has an all-Hispanic cast, allow the viewer to start noticing the slight differences among Latinos. George is Mexican American, his wife is second generation Cuban, and the tension between these two Latino cultures, their old guard parents, and their acculturated kids are the basis for the show's humor. Remember, Latinos can be targeted either in English or in Spanish with universal messages, so your advertising efforts should try to encompass the whole market, not just a segment of it.

Another common mistake is that the management tends to ghettoize minorities. Before launching *People en Español, People* magazine, like any other mass-market publication, would only occasionally cover Latino celebrities or other Latinos in human-interest stories. But as we worked on the development and launch of *People en Español,* awareness of the Hispanic market at *People* magazine started growing at the same time that artists like Ricky Martin, Jennifer Lopez, and Marc Anthony started crossing over to the general market. Yet after *People en Español* launched in 1997, if felt as if *People* magazine practically stopped covering Latinos, because anything Hispanic was immediately sent over to their Spanish-language title. As a result, the coverage and visibility of Latinos in the mainstream magazine actually decreased!

10. Don't assume you know who is a Hispanic celebrity.
Even if you have managed to avoid all the other mistakes mentioned in this chapter, understanding who is a Latino celebrity and how to use them effectively will be important, especially if you are looking for a spokesperson to promote your product in the Hispanic market. Because Spanish-language media are so developed in the United States, there exists a parallel universe of Latino stars. Yes, there are a handful of Latino stars whose names you may recognize because they have made it in Hollywood. George Lopez, Jimmy Smits, Edward James Olmos, Oscar de la Hoya, Jennifer Lopez, Antonio Banderas, Salma Hayek, Ricky Martin, and Marc Anthony are probably the stars you think of when you talk about the Hispanic market. But not all of these artists actually have crossover appeal in the Hispanic market. You see, the

198 | LATINO BOOM!

problem with Hollywood stars is that they mainly work on English-language projects, so they are not necessarily known to huge segments of the Spanish-speaking Latino population. Some stars, such as Marc Anthony or Ricky Martin, keep their popularity in both markets by releasing albums or making movies in both languages. But others are really not well known in the Hispanic market, even though they are Hispanic.

Similarly, some of the biggest names in the world of Spanish-language entertainment may not be known to you, but are much more recognizable in your average Latino household than Jimmy Smits or George Lopez, for example. Do you recognize any of these names: Don Francisco, Cristina Saralegui, Myrka de Llanos, Raul de Molina, Lilly Estefan, Maria Celeste Arrarás, Chayanne, Juan Soler, Sofia Vergara, Fernando Colungna, Alejandro Fernandez, Lucero, Juanes, Los Tigres del Norte, Marco Antonio Solis, or Paulina Rubio? All of them are superstars in the world of Latin entertainment, and in some cases would be much more effective in communicating your message to the Spanish-speaking market than most of the "famous" Latino Hollywood stars mentioned earlier. There are many more Latino television and film stars, of course, and the great thing about using these stars as spokespersons for your product is that they tend to be much more approachable and probably more "affordable" than the Hispanic stars in Hollywood you may be familiar with.

According to the 2003 Yankelovich MONITOR Multicultural Marketing Study, the power of a celebrity spokesperson in this market should not be underestimated. "For Non-Hispanic Whites, the sight of a celebrity of their race pitching a product is nothing whatsoever out of the ordinary and does not generate any special interest," says the report. "For Hispanics, however, it represents a sign of mainstream success and acceptance. The presence of a Hispanic celebrity will not necessarily generate an immediate sale, but the fact that a particular company or brand values and respects these customers sufficiently to use one of their celebrities as a spokesperson will be remembered."

So, there are a couple things you need to keep in mind when choosing a Latino celebrity to work with. Don't make a decision based on who *you* think is a Latino celebrity. Let your Hispanic expert or your Hispanic agency guide you in order to help you find the right celebrity spokesperson for your product. Just because you don't know who this person is doesn't mean that your target market won't know.

10

THE BIG PICTURE

There is no doubt that the United States is experiencing a demographic transformation like no other before in its history, and that the Hispanic population is not assimilating as quickly as other immigrant groups have in the past. Although research studies indicate that second- and third-generation Latinos are well on their way to assimilation, the constant influx of new Spanish-speaking immigrants and the growing economic ties between the United States and its Latin American neighbors will probably keep the Spanish language and culture alive in the United States for many years to come. The explosive growth of the Latino population, which is mainly driven by high birth rates and immigration, has already made Hispanics the largest minority group in the country, surpassing the African-American community two years ahead of the Census Bureau's initial projection. "Certainly, the Latino boom brings a welcome charge to the economy at a time when others' population growth has slowed to a crawl," says Brian Grow in a special report on the Hispanic market published by *BusinessWeek* in March 2004. According to newly released Census Bureau projections, the Hispanic population will triple in size—surpassing the 100 million mark—by 2050, when Latinos will represent one-quarter of the population of the United States and when, for the first time ever, the white non-Hispanic share of the population will fall to 50.1 percent of the total.

With this growth also comes increasing economic power, especially as an increasing number of Latinos are born and raised in the United States. According to Global Insight, by 2020, the disposable income of the Hispanic population is expected to triple from an estimated $743 billion in 2005 to more than $2.5 trillion. Economists are already calling the Hispanic population the "key catalyst" of future economic growth as their consumer spending, employment, and home ownership rates are expected to grow steadily year after year. Critics, however, argue that poorly educated, non-English speaking immigrants don't help the economy but rather undermine it. "Although a steady influx of low-skilled workers helps keep America's gardens tended and floors cleaned, those workers also exert downward pressure on wages across the lower end of the pay structure," says *BusinessWeek*. "Already this is causing friction with African Americans, who see their jobs and pay being hit."

Hispanic immigrants are no different from their Irish or Russian counterparts in the nineteenth and early twentieth century. They come to this country fleeing the economic difficulties of their homelands and end up doing the jobs that other Americans simply do not want to do. The downward economic pressure on these low-paying jobs will always be there, whether the jobs are taken by Mexicans or Chinese immigrants. The fact is they will be taken by someone who is willing to do the job. What critics seem to forget is that second-generation Latinos are also exerting a positive influence on the job market. According to the Pew Hispanic Center, college-educated Hispanics saw the greatest percentage gains in labor growth from 2000 to 2002. And while the preservation of the Spanish language has been the most obvious way of differentiating this market in the past, the reality is that today's Hispanic market is equally divided into three distinct language groups: Spanish-dominant, bilingual, and English-dominant Latinos. Beyond language, however, the glue that keeps this market together is the strong ties Latinos have with Hispanic *culture*. Another bond comes from our shared immigrant experience in the United States, where Latinos of different countries intermingle more freely than they would back in their homelands. The fact that Spanish language usage may be growing among bilingual and English-dominant Latinos is a testament to the pride they feel for their culture, which undoubtedly shapes their Hispanic identity in many ways.

But the *culture* Latinos inherit or bring with them from Latin America has both good and bad elements. On the positive side, Latinos have inherited a strong entrepreneurial spirit and strong family values coupled with a desire to get ahead and make a better life for themselves and their children. On the negative side, Latinos largely distrust financial institutions, expect government to take care of them, and often have a fatalistic view of life. In this chapter we will go over some of the current obstacles facing the Latino community in the United States today. I will also outline some of the important market trends to look out for in the near future.

EDUCATION

As I mentioned briefly in chapter 2, an alarming number of children are disappearing from the United States' educational system every year. According to the Civil Rights Project at Harvard University, half of all black and Hispanic ninth graders will drop out of high school before graduating. While official government figures put graduation rates at 88 percent for non-Hispanic whites, 80 percent for blacks, and only 57 percent for Hispanics, the reality is that the figures are actually much lower. According to the Civil Rights Project, the "official" high school graduation rates are higher because most official graduation rates are estimates based on inaccurate data. "Both the two most commonly used measures—the modified National Center for Education Statistics (NCES) formula and the Census Bureau CPS data— produce data that often dramatically underestimate the numbers of students who leave school without high school diplomas," says the Civil Rights Project in its report, *Losing Our Future: How Minority Youth Are Being Left Behind by the Graduation Rate Crisis.* "The NCES is what most states use to calculate their graduation rates. However, large numbers of students that leave school and are unaccounted for are often left out of the NCES calculations. Most districts do not 'chase' students who disappear, often assuming they have relocated," says the report.

According to the Urban Institute, the federal *No Child Left Behind* law now holds schools more accountable for test scores but not for students who drop out. So some schools are actually encouraging their "weaker" students to take the G.E.D. instead. In April 2004, an article in *The New York Times* said that "nationally, teenagers accounted for 49 percent of those earning G.E.D.'s in 2002, up from 33 percent a decade earlier." In terms of actual graduation rates, the Civil Rights Project estimates that on average only 75 percent of white students, 50.1 percent of black and 53 percent of Hispanic students actually graduate from high school. These graduation rates were derived using the Cumulative Promotion Index (CPI), which was developed by the Urban Institute, a nonprofit, nonpartisan policy research and educational organization that examines America's social, economic, and governance problems. According to the Civil Rights Project, "the CPI, which relies on actual enrollment and diploma data, is the most accurate of current methods for estimating graduation rates. The CPI allows comparisons across years, across districts, and across states using a common metric and a constant statistical treatment." Table 60 shows the states with the worst graduation rates for whites, blacks, and Hispanics. I think you will agree that the numbers are truly alarming.

We are facing an educational crisis that is completely unacceptable for a superpower such as the United States. And as more and more American jobs go offshore, how are our children going to make a living if they can barely read and write? On the brighter side of this dismal picture are U.S.-born Latinos, who will be a major force behind the

TABLE 60 Four Lowest Graduation Rates by State and Group

	Worst	2nd Worst	3rd Worst	4th Worst
Race/Ethnicity	State : Rate	State : Rate	State : Rate	State : Rate
Black	NY : 35.1	Ohio : 39.6	Nevada : 40.5	Florida : 41.0
Hispanic	NY : 31.9	Mass. : 36.1	Michigan : 36.3	Nevada : 37.6
White	Florida : 57.9	Nevada : 62.0	Georgia : 62.4	Miss. : 63.3

Source: Urban Institute: Analysis of graduation rates in 50 states

future Latino population growth. According to the Pew Hispanic Center's 2002 *National Survey of Latinos,* U.S.-born Latinos demonstrate significant improvements in educational achievement, with only 23 percent not completing high school versus 55 percent of foreign-born Latinos. I hope we can expect this trend to continue as second- and third-generation U.S.-born Latinos go through the educational system of the United States.

THE DIGITAL DIVIDE

Although Hispanics are the fastest growing online population, Latino computer ownership and access to the Internet still lag behind the general population's. According to first unified *National Consumer Survey* released by Simmons in the fall of 2003, Latino PC ownership is at 55.6 percent versus 77.2 percent for non-Hispanics. However, among the Spanish-dominant group, PC ownership rates go down to 46 percent. The Westhill Partners/*Poder* magazine survey, published in January 2004, puts Latino PC ownership at 59 percent and access to the Internet at 57 percent, while Synovate indicates that overall only 45 percent of all Latinos have access to the Internet. The 2004 AOL/Roper ASW Hispanic Cyberstudy does not give figures on Latino PC ownership or access to the Internet, but it does say that 20 percent of at-home Hispanic Internet users have been online for less than six months versus only 6 percent of the general at-home online population. Furthermore, the AOL/Roper ASW study found that the high cost of computers and high Internet service fees are two important reasons why the majority of off-line Hispanics still do not have access to the information superhighway at home. Access to good Spanish and/or English-language content that appeals to Hispanics is another reason why off-line Latinos have not ventured online. But perhaps the most disturbing finding of the AOL/Roper ASW study is the utter lack of knowledge about the Internet. Almost seven in ten (68 percent) of off-line Hispanics said they would not know how to use the Internet! "America's largest ethnic group lacks familiarity and access to key information-age resources," says Alexander Jutkowitz, president of Westhill Partners in his article

"What Latinos Think," published by *Poder* magazine. "This situation presents a potentially serious handicap for Hispanics in today's knowledge economy."

LATINO EARNING POWER

Although Latino entrepreneurship is alive and well—with projections that one out of every ten small businesses will be Hispanic-owned by 2007, according to Merrill Lynch—building a nest egg is something Latinos don't generally know how to do. As long as foreign-born Latinos continue to drag down overall household incomes, Latino earning power will be another issue facing this market. But I believe this is only a short-term issue because, as we have seen, within certain segments of the Latino population, earning power is growing by leaps and bounds, and Latinos are joining the ranks of the American middle class faster than ever before. According to the Pew Hispanic Center's *2002 National Survey of Latinos,* 50 percent of Latinos are earning less than $30,000 a year compared with only 29 percent of whites and 44 percent of blacks. But again, when you break down the Hispanic market by foreign-born versus U.S.-born Latinos, you see that only 37 percent of U.S.-born Latinos are earning less than $30,000 a year versus 57 percent of those who are foreign born.

Keep in mind that 35 percent of all Hispanics are under the age of 18! As more and more of these younger Latinos enter the workforce, overall Latino earning power will increase. Already 28 percent of U.S.-born Latinos are earning between $30,000 and $50,000 a year while 27 percent are earning $50,000 or more. By comparison, 27 percent of whites and 30 percent of blacks earn between $30,000 and $50,000 a year, according to the Pew Hispanic Center, while 42 percent of whites and 22 percent of blacks are earning more than $50,000 a year.

But a general ignorance about financial tools and a cultural distrust of securities is another big issue facing the Latino community that deeply affects its overall ability to generate long-term wealth. "Hispanics are far behind the curve when it comes to utilizing the principal vehicle for generating long-term wealth: the financial markets," as

Jutkowitz points out. "According to a recent Schwab study, only 22% of U.S. Hispanics are invested in stocks and bonds, compared to 79% of Non-Hispanic Caucasians. And of invested Latinos, 48% have less than the equivalent of 5% of their annual incomes in the markets," he adds.

IGNORANCE ABOUT FINANCIAL TOOLS AND INSTITUTIONS

Before Latinos can access the financial markets to create real wealth for themselves, they still have a lot to learn about the basic financial tools available to them in America. Unfortunately, most Hispanics come from countries where financial institutions have historically been highly unstable, so there is a barrier, born of hard experience, regarding the best way to manage your finances. A significant number of Latinos in the United States are currently "unbanked" (meaning they have no relationship with a bank) or "underbanked" (they have a limited relationship with a bank, such as a savings account or an IRA account only). According to the Pew Hispanic Center, about three-fourths (76 percent) of African-Americans and two-thirds (65 percent) of Latinos say they have a bank account, while virtually all whites (95 percent) have an account with a bank. Although in the past couple of years more and more banks are allowing people to open accounts with "consular IDs," only 50 percent of Spanish-dominant Latino households have a bank account compared to 77 percent of bilingual Latinos and 79 percent of English-dominant Latinos, according to the Pew Hispanic Center. Ignorance of the benefits of financial tools is the biggest obstacle facing this market. I believe that even many of those Latinos who *do* have relationships with banks don't understand how best to use these financial tools to their benefit. Banks and other financial institutions need to realize the huge information gap that exists with Latinos in this area. Although some are starting to develop programs in both Spanish and English to help educate the Latino market about important financial tools, *much more needs to be done.*

In his article, "What Latinos Think," Jutkowitz gives us a great example of the need for more education regarding basic financial tools.

One of my corporate clients has a large Hispanic workforce, but, inexplicably, they just weren't contributing to his firm's 401(k) plan. And he feared it would soon be declared top-heavy and invalid. We sat down and talked with his employees and we quickly discovered that my client had done a poor job communicating the benefits of the plan. So we turned around and addressed these underlying concerns fast. Not via a Spanish-language version of a smiley brokerage firm handout, but in language that dealt with what mattered: the real benefits and the relative risks. The result: contributions rose nearly immediately.

ACCESS TO CREDIT

According to the Pew Hispanic Center, five in ten (51 percent) Latinos report they have a credit card compared with nearly eight in ten (77%) non-Hispanic whites. Among Spanish-dominant Latinos, only 40 percent report having a credit card compared with 64 percent of bilinguals and 58 percent of English-dominant Latinos. Just like with other banking services, educating Latinos about credit and how to use it properly is going to be another critical issue for this market in the short term. This country is built on credit, and everything one does—from signing a lease on an apartment to getting a car loan or applying for a store discount card at The Home Depot—is tied to one's credit record! Again, Hispanic culture lacks the proper understanding of the concept of "personal credit." In Spain and Latin America, personal loans from banks are relatively rare. Although things are slowly changing, much of the lending is strictly commercial. I would venture to say that most Latinos are scared to death of credit, because they don't understand how to use it and they really need to be educated about the perils of misusing it. Credit card issuers and mortgage brokers must realize that in order to capitalize on the booming Hispanic market, they must educate Latinos every step of the way. Many Latinos don't even have a FICO score, the basic measurement used for extending credit in the United States. And while this could lead some people to believe that Latinos are a credit risk, representatives of various financial institutions that service loans to Latinos have told me on various occasions that Latinos are, in fact, some of their best customers! Because Latinos don't like the idea of being in debt and risking losing everything they have worked so hard for, they often will pay their loans ahead of schedule!

If you are in the business of extending credit, you should think about ways to change the way you measure the credit worthiness of Latinos. Because so many Latinos constantly pay their bills in cash or by money order, they have a hard time establishing a credit history. Look for other ways of establishing good payment behavior. Think of services in which Latinos overindex, like cable services, satellite TV, or long-distance telephone, as proxies for more traditional creditworthiness tools. Whatever you do, make sure you don't get in the business of rejecting potentially good Latino customers.

REDEFINING THE FUTURE HISPANIC MARKET

Census 2000 was the wake-up call corporate America needed to finally realize the importance of the growing Latino community. Only fifteen years ago, media coverage of this market was virtually nonexistent. Today, articles constantly appear in newspapers and trade magazines. Research studies about the many varied aspects of this market are growing in quantity and quality. More and better information about this market is absolutely key, but another challenge Hispanic marketers will face in the next five years is the changing definition of the Latino market. Whereas before the Hispanic market was portrayed as a homogeneous group of people defined mainly by their usage of Spanish and consumption of Spanish-language media, today's Hispanic market is much more complex. The umbrella under which all Latinos fit is starting to be defined by their distinct Hispanic *identity* and *culture*. But among Latinos there are also important differences to acknowledge and embrace. While the usage of the Spanish language and of Spanish-language media will continue to grow among Hispanics in the United States, a universally accepted definition of "Spanish-language usage or preference" needs to be created so that we can all accurately measure the size of each group. This will allow the government, researchers, and marketers to compare important data on this market on an apples-to-apples basis. Demographic and consumer differences between foreign-born Latinos and U.S.-born Latinos, as well as issues such as bilingualism, changing patterns of consumer behavior based on levels of acculturation, and consumption of English-language media will also become increasingly important. Research companies are now leading the way in acknowledging the complexity of the Latino market and are trying to help marketers and advertisers address the differences as well as the similarities among Latinos. Right now, it seems like there is a lot of contradictory information about the Hispanic market. "Such contradictory pictures are not limited to 'Hispanic research' but are endemic to marketing research as an industry and to the technology of knowledge," warns Professor Arlene Dávila in her book *Latinos Inc.* As this market grows in size and importance, universally accepted ways of measuring different aspects of the Hispanic market will help validate it.

WHAT LIES AHEAD?

On the political front, there has always been a "presumed alliance" between blacks and Latinos that dates back to the civil rights movement, if not before. Some say that a shared history of suffering and discrimination has, in the past, translated into shared political goals and interests. But over the past two decades voices on both sides have been accusing each other of not being supportive of their "issues." Already Latino population growth has led to competition on the employment front. Black-Latino solidarity has recently been challenged by divisive mayoral and gubernatorial elections from New York to Los Angeles. In boardrooms across the country, African-American executives are fighting tooth and nail not to lose ground to their younger, and often whiter, Latino counterparts. Companies who pit one minority against the other will be the ones who lose in the long run, since *all* minority markets continue to grow in importance. To succeed in the future, corporations will necessarily have to have more minorities in their boardrooms, not less. The question of how black-brown relations will develop on the national level as Latinos grow economically and politically is one that I am particularly interested in following.

Resentment toward the Hispanic community is also growing in certain circles in America. Hatred and fear of the impact of Latinos in the United States have been fueled in part by the writings of Harvard Professor Samuel P. Huntington, whose latest work, *Who Are We: The Challenges to America's National Identity,* identifies the growing Hispanic community as a serious challenge to the Anglo-Protestant culture of the United States. "Will the United States remain a country with a single national language and a core Anglo-Protestant culture?" he asks in an essay entitled "The Hispanic Challenge," published in the journal *Foreign Policy.* "By ignoring this question, Americans acquiesce to their eventual transformation into two peoples with two cultures and two languages." Although the press was quick to criticize his book as fueling racist flames across America, and to dismiss his arguments as misanthropic zeal when the book came out in May 2004, the reality is that, unfortunately, there are many for whom Huntington's arguments resonate.

From a media perspective, there will be two interesting trends to follow: the potential acquisition of more Spanish-language media companies by American media giants and the explosive development of English-language media geared toward Latinos. After NBC purchased Telemundo in 2002, rumors were flying around about the possible acquisition of Univision. Buyers mentioned at the time were Viacom, Disney, and Time Warner. Will there be another major Spanish-language network acquisition by one of the big three media giants? If so, how will this change in ownership affect the production of Spanish-language content? Can American media giants successfully manage Spanish-language media? So far their track record is not very good at all.

On the other hand, there has been a virtual explosion of English-language programs geared toward Latinos—mainly on cable TV—including the launch of a 24-hour, English-language cable network dedicated to Latinos: SíTV and the announcement of a major Hispanic push by MTV and VH1. When will the big broadcast networks come to realize that in order to stop the hemorrhaging of their television viewing audiences they are going to have to start developing programs that reflect the reality of America? Latino and Asian characters are still severely underrepresented on TV and in film. And when they are presented on screen, they are still horribly stereotyped, because the producers, writers, and directors working on these shows are still predominantly white. Advertisers may have to force the networks' hand, because they know better than anyone else who their consumers are.

Finally, will the predominantly brown Hispanic market help break America's obsession with thinking about everything in terms of black and white in the United States? I mean, really, in the end, isn't green the only color that really matters in business?

Resource Guide

~~~~~~~~~~~~~~~~

RESEARCH COMPANIES

Arbitron
Headquarters
142 West 57th Street
New York, NY 10019-3300
212-887-1300
www.arbitron.com

Cheskin
Headquarters
255 Shoreline Drive, Suite 350
Redwood Shores, CA 94065
650-802-2100
Fax: 650-593-1125
www.cheskin.com

ComScore Networks
Richard L. Israel
Vice President, Regional & Hispanic Account Services
601 Gateway Blvd., Suite 1050
South San Francisco, CA 94080
925-648-7207
Fax: 940-234-3423

E-mail: risrael@comscore.com
www.comscore.com

Creative & Response Research Services Inc.
Headquarters
500 North Michigan Avenue
Chicago, IL 60611-3781
312-828-9200
Fax: 312-527-3113
www.crresearch.com

C&R LatinoEyes
1111 Brickell Avenue, 11th Floor
Miami, FL 33131
305-913-7178
Fax: 305-913-4733
E-mail: info@latinoeyes.com

Cultural Access Group
5150 El Camino Real, Suite B-15
Los Altos, CA 94022
650-965-3859
www.accesscag.com

Global Insight
1000 Winter Street
Waltham, MA 02451-1241
781-487-2100
Fax: 781-890-6187
www.globalinsight.com

Horowitz Associates
1971 Palmer Avenue
Larchmont, NY 10538
914-834-5999
www.horowitzassociates.com

Nielsen Media Research
Hispanic Services
375 Patricia Avenue
Dunedin, FL 34698
727-738-3133
www.nielsenmedia.com

Roslow Research Group
939 Port Washington Blvd., Suite 2
Port Washington, NY 11050
516-883-1110
www.roslowresearch.com

Simmons Market Research Bureau
230 Park Avenue South, 5th Floor
New York, NY 10003
212-598-5400
Hispanic Market Sales: 305-774-6208
www.smrb.com

Synovate (formerly known as Strategy Research Corporation)
Head office in the Americas
222 South Riverside Plaza
Chicago, IL 60606
312-526-4000
Fax: 312-526-4099

Synovate
Hispanic Service
8600 NW 17th Street
Miami, FL 33126
305-716-6800
Fax: 305-716-6756
www.synovate.com

TNS Media Intelligence (formerly CMR)
Headquarters
100 Park Avenue, 4th Floor
New York, NY 10017
212-991-6000
www.tns-mi.com

The Santiago Solutions Group
Main Office
895 Broadway, 5th Floor
New York, NY 10003-1226
212-420-5948
Fax: 212-420-5915
California Office:
1405 Huntington, Suite 130
South San Francisco, CA 94080
650-588-4884
Fax: 650-588-4885
www.santiagosolutionsgroup.com

Utilis Research & Consulting
1001 Avenue of the Americas, 12th Floor
New York, NY 10018
212-939-0077
Fax: 212-862-2706
www.utilis-research.com

Yankelovich Partners
Headquarters
400 Meadowmont Village Circle, Suite 431
Chapel Hill, NC 27517
919-932-8600
Fax: 919-932-8829
www.yankelovich.com

HISPANIC MARKET SPECIALISTS

Consumer Contacts provides marketing consulting and strategies to capitalize on the Hispanic market. Specialists in nontraditional channels such as interactive, direct-mail, and guerrilla marketing.

560 Sylvan Avenue
Englewood Cliffs, NJ 07632
201-735-2153
Fax: 201-221-8736
www.consumercontacts.com

Ethnic Business Partners connects you with the Hispanic market in New England through a Hispanic Market conference series, the Hispanic Market Report, and a team of strategic and marketing consultants that deliver information, practical advice, and guidance packaged to meet your needs.

Attn: Vanessa Toledo
580 Thames Street # 233
Newport, RI 02840
401-847-3715
www.ethnicbusiness.com

EQS Partners helps companies and talent reach their potential through business advisory, management, talent organizational development, and executive and career coaching.
Contact: Fern Espino or Jim Szurek
3544 Eastham Road
Dearborn, MI 48120
313-350-1869
Fax: 312-399-4980

Hispanicad.com provides daily news and information, including photos and data from the United States, Latin America, and the Caribbean.

It contains news updates regarding Hispanic advertising, creative, marketing, media, promotions, and research.

1 Chardonnay Road
Cortlandt Manor, NY 10567
914-734-8264
Fax: 914-737-3234
www.hispanicad.com

Hispanic Business Magazine is the flagship publication of Hispanic Business Inc. Launched in 1979, Hispanic Business covers the growth of the U.S. Hispanic market, economic trends within the Americas, best business practices, and career development opportunities. Hispanic Business reaches CEOs, business owners, corporate decision makers, and professionals in all sectors, including business, law, accounting, health care, government, and engineering.

425 Pine Avenue
Santa Barbara, CA 93117
805-964-4554
Fax: 805-964-5539
www.hispanicbusiness.com

Hispanic Market Weekly is a must-read for all media and marketing executives interested in the ever-growing and fast-changing Hispanic market. It is an e-mail newsletter that already reaches the most important players across all media industries.

2625 Ponce de Leon Blvd., Suite 285
Coral Gables, FL 33134
305-448-5838
Fax: 305-448-6573
www.hmweekly.com

Hispanic Magazine Monitor is a leading advertising, monitoring, and intelligence service focused exclusively on Hispanic print media in the

United States. It provides intelligence to help you sell, buy, and plan Hispanic advertising—or make strategic decisions.

Info@hispmagmonitor

IQPC provides millions of business executives with tailored practical conferences, keeping them up-to-date with industry trends, technological developments and the regulatory landscape.

Corporate Office
535 Fifth Avenue, 8th Floor
New York, NY 10017
212-885-2700
Fax: 212-885-2703
E-mail: info@iqpc.com
www.iqpc.com

Latino Media Source Inc. is a marketing-driven media company that assists clients in all categories with the development and execution of their advertising campaigns.

530 West 25th Street
New York, NY 10001
646-638-4898
Diane Librizzi, president
E-mail: latmedia@yahoo.com

Marketing y Medios: The only trade magazine with a monthly publication dedicated to covering the growing Hispanic marketing and advertising community.

VNU Business Publications
770 Broadway, 7th Floor
New York, N.Y. 10003
646-654-7510
www.marketingymedios.com

Meredith Integrated Marketing (MIM) utilizes a results-driven process called R.O.P. (Results Optimization Process) to develop a deeper understanding of your customers' needs, and how best to meet them through Relationship Media.

Chiqui Cartagena
Managing Director, Multicultural Communications
125 Park Avenue
New York, N.Y. 10017
212-557-6600
Fax: 212-551-7116
www.meredithmim.com

Multicultural Marketing Resources Inc. (MMR) is a public relations and marketing company that represents corporations with multicultural and diversity news and is the nation's leading expert in marketing to Hispanic, Asian American, African American, women, and other cultural markets.

286 Spring Street, Suite 201
New York, NY 10013
212-242-3351
Fax: 212-691-5969
www.multicultural.com

SPANUSA is the executive search firm specializing in the placement of bilingual Spanish-English-speaking professionals and executives of every ethnic background in the United States and Latin America.

1415 Boston Post Road
Larchmont, N.Y. 10538
914-381-5555
www.spanusa.net

Strategic Research Institute creates, produces, and manages conferences covering industry-specific business-to-business topics. These conferences also provide a forum for face-to-face networking between industry leaders, potential strategic partners, prospects, and customers. Its mission is to provide relevant and strategically focused information at professionally managed events.

New York (Head Office)
333 Seventh Avenue, 9th Floor
New York, NY 10001-5004
212-967-0095 / 800-599-4950
Fax: 212-967-7973/74
E-mail: info@srinstitute.com

TRADE ASSOCIATIONS

• *AHAA—Association of Hispanic Advertising Agencies*
The mission of AHAA is "to grow, strengthen and protect the Hispanic marketing and advertising industry by providing leadership in raising awareness of the value of the Hispanic market opportunities and enhancing the professionalism of the industry."

AHAA is fostering understanding among top corporate decision makers of the economic value of Hispanic advertising and marketing and the need to use the specialized agencies most qualified to reach this massive market. If you're serious about doing business in the Hispanic market, then you should do business with an AHAA member agency.

AHAA (Headquarters)
8201 Greensboro Drive, Suite 300
McLean, Virginia 22102
703-610-9014
Fax: 703-610-9005
www.ahaa.org

• *CAB—Cabletelevision Advertising Bureau*
Cabletelevision Advertising Bureau
830 Third Avenue

New York, NY 10022
212-508-1200
www.cabletvadbureau.com
Multicultural Marketing Resource Center
www.cabletvadbureau.com/mmrc

• *MPA—Magazine Publishers of America*
Magazine Publishers of America (MPA) is the industry association for consumer magazines. Established in 1919, the MPA represents more than 240 domestic publishing companies with approximately 1,400 titles, more than 80 international companies, and more than 100 associate members. Staffed by magazine industry specialists, the MPA is headquartered in New York City, with an office of government affairs in Washington, D.C.

Magazine Publishers of America
810 Seventh Avenue, 24th Floor
New York, NY 10019
www.magazine.org

• *NAHJ—National Association of Hispanic Journalists*
The National Association of Hispanic Journalists (NAHJ) is dedicated to the recognition and professional advancement of Hispanics in the news industry. Established in April 1984, NAHJ created a national voice and unified vision for all Hispanic journalists.

National Association of Hispanic Journalists
1000 National Press Building
529 14th Street NW
Washington, D.C. 20045-2001
202-662-7145 / 888-346-NAHJ
Fax: 202-662-7144
E-mail: nahj@nahj.org

• *NAHP—National Association of Hispanic Publications*
The National Association of Hispanic Publications Inc. (NAHP) is a

nonprofit trade advocacy organization representing more than 200 Hispanic publications serving more than 55 markets in 28 states and Puerto Rico with a combined circulation of more than 14 million.

NAHP
National Press Building
529 14th Street NW, Suite 1085
Washington, D.C. 20045
202-662-7250
Fax: 202-662-7251
www.nahp.org

HISPANIC ASSOCIATIONS

• *ASPIRA*

The mission of ASPIRA is to empower the Puerto Rican and Latino community through advocacy and the education and leadership development of its youth.

ASPIRA (National Offices)
1444 I Street NW, Suite 800
Washington, D.C. 20005
202-835-3600
Fax: 202-835-3613
E-mail: info@aspira.org

• *CHCI—Congressional Hispanic Caucus Institute*

The mission of the Congressional Hispanic Caucus Institute (CHCI) is to develop the next generation of Latino leaders. CHCI seeks to accomplish its mission by offering educational and leadership development programs, services, and activities that promote the growth of participants as effective professionals and strong leaders. In the spirit of building coalitions, CHCI seeks to establish partnerships with other Latino and non-Latino organizations.

Congressional Hispanic Caucus Institute
911 2nd Street NE

Washington, D.C. 20002
202-543-1771
800-EXCEL-DC
Fax: 202-546-2143
www.chci.org

• *HACR—Hispanic Association on Corporate Responsibility*
HACR's mission is to ensure the inclusion of Hispanics in corporate America at a level commensurate with our economic contributions. HACR focuses on four areas of corporate economic activity and refers to them as indicators of corporate responsibility and "Market Reciprocity." They are: Employment, Procurement, Philanthropy, and Governance.

In pursuit of its mission, HACR offers corporate America access to the Hispanic community—its talents, its entrepreneurs, and its leadership—creating a forum to ensure corporate responsibility and market reciprocity for the nation's Hispanic population.

Hispanic Association on Corporate Responsibility
1444 I Street NW, Suite 850
Washington, D.C. 20005
202-835-9672
Fax: 202-457-0455
E-mail: hacr@hacr.org

• *HSF—Hispanic Scholarship Fund*
The Hispanic Scholarship Fund (HSF) is the nation's leading organization supporting Hispanic higher education. Its goal is to strengthen our country by advancing the college education of Hispanic Americans.

Its mission is to double the number of Hispanics earning a college degree. Since 1975, HSF has awarded more than 68,000 scholarships in excess of $144 million to Hispanic students from all 50 states, Puerto Rico, and the U.S. Virgin Islands. These students have attended more than 1,700 colleges and universities.

Hispanic Scholarship Fund (Headquarters Office)
55 Second Street, Suite 1500
San Francisco, CA 94105
877-HSF-INFO (877-473-4636)
Fax: 415-808-2302
www.hsf.net

- *LULAC—League of United Latin American Citizens*
The mission of the League of United Latin American Citizens is to advance the economic condition, educational attainment, political influence, health, and civil rights of the Hispanic population of the United States.

LULAC (National Office)
2000 L Street NW, Suite 610
Washington, D.C. 20036
202-833-6130
www.LULAC.org

- *MALDEF—Mexican American Legal Defense and Educational Fund*
MALDEF is the leading nonprofit Latino litigation, advocacy, and educational outreach institution in the United States. Its mission is to foster sound public policies, laws, and programs to safeguard the civil rights of the 40 million Latinos living in the United States and to empower the Latino community to fully participate in society.

MALDEF (National Headquarters)
634 S. Spring Street
Los Angeles, CA 90014
213-629-2512
www.maldef.org

- *NALEO—National Association of Latino Elected Officials*
The National Association of Latino Elected and Appointed Officials Educational Fund is the leading organization that empowers Latinos

to participate fully in the American political process, from citizenship to public service.

NALEO Educational Fund
1122 West Washington Blvd., 3rd Floor
Los Angeles, CA 90015
213-747-7606
Fax: 213-747-7664
E-mail: info@naleo.org

• *National Alliance for Hispanic Health*
The National Alliance for Hispanic Health (the Alliance) is the nation's oldest and largest network of Hispanic health and human services providers. The Alliance provides key leadership and advocacy to ensure accountability in these priority areas, resulting in improved health for all throughout the Americas.

The National Alliance for Hispanic Health
1501 16th Street NW
Washington, D.C. 20036
202-387-5000
E-mail: alliance@hispanichealth.org

• *NCLR—National Council of La Raza*
The National Council of La Raza (NCLR) is a private, nonprofit, nonpartisan, tax-exempt organization established in 1968 to reduce poverty and discrimination and improve life opportunities for Hispanic Americans. NCLR is the largest constituency-based national Hispanic organization, serving all Hispanic nationality groups in all regions of the country.

NCLR (Los Angeles Office)
523 West 6th Street, Suite 801
Los Angeles, CA 90014
213-489-3428
Fax: 213-489-1167

NONPROFIT RESEARCH CENTERS

- *The Pew Hispanic Center*

  The Pew Hispanic Center, based in Washington, D.C., is a nonpartisan research center supported by a grant from the Pew Charitable Trusts of Philadelphia. The Center is a project of the University of Southern California Annenberg School for Communication. The Pew Hispanic Center's mission is to improve understanding of the diverse Hispanic population in the United States and to chronicle Latinos' growing impact on the nation. The Center strives to inform debate on critical issues through dissemination of its research to policy makers, business leaders, academic institutions, and the media.

  Pew Hispanic Center
  Kaiser Family Foundation
  1615 L Street NW, Suite 700
  Washington, D.C. 20036
  202-419-3600
  Media & Information Line: 202-419-3608
  Fax: 202-785-8282
  www.pewhispanic.org

- *Selig Center for Economic Growth*

  Created to convey economic expertise to Georgia businesses and entrepreneurs, the Selig Center for Economic Growth is primarily responsible for conducting research on economic, demographic, and social issues. Through its range of projects—major economic impact studies, economic forecasts, publications, information services, and data products—the Center's efforts help to guide business decisions and the direction of public policy.

  Terry College of Business
  University of Georgia
  Bank of America Building
  110 E. Clayton Street

Athens, GA 30602-5269
706-542-4085
www.selig.uga.edu

- *TRPI—Tomás Rivera Policy Institute*
  The Tomás Rivera Policy Institute (TRPI) is a freestanding, nonprofit, policy research organization that has attained a reputation as the nation's "premier Latino think tank." One of TRPI's critical strengths is survey research—ranging from questionnaire and sample frame development to survey interviewing—which allows TRPI to gauge the attitudes held by diverse Latino populations vis-à-vis salient policy issues.

  The Tomás Rivera Policy Institute (California Office)
  University of Southern California
  School of Policy, Planning & Development
  650 Childs Way, Lewis Hall, Suite 102
  Los Angeles, CA 90089-0626
  213-821-5615
  Fax: 213-821-1976
  www.trpi.org

GOVERNMENT OFFICES

- *U.S. Census Bureau*
  The best source of information for just about anything in the United States. The Census Bureau carries the latest demographic, economic, and geographic information in the United States.

  U.S. Census Bureau
  Public Information Office
  301-763-3030
  www.census.gov

- *USHCC—United States Hispanic Chamber of Commerce*
  Since its inception, the USHCC has worked toward bringing the
  issues and concerns of the nation's more than 1.6 million Hispanic-
  owned businesses to the forefront of the national economic agenda.
  Through its network of more than 130 local Hispanic Chambers of
  Commerce and Hispanic business organizations, the USHCC effectively communicates the needs and potential of Hispanic enterprise
  to the public and private sector.

  U.S. Hispanic Chamber of Commerce
  2175 K Street NW, Suite 100
  Washington, D.C. 20037
  800-USHCC86
  202-842-1212
  Fax: 202-842-3221
  E-mail: ushcc@ushcc.com

Acknowledgments

This book could not have been possible without the input and help of many, many people. First and foremost to my parents, María José Mercader and Norberto Cartagena, who always taught me to believe I could do anything I set out to do. *Gracias!* To my partner in life and love, Jennifer Knight, who had the idea in the first place for me to write this book and who patiently read every draft I wrote and listened to me talk about this market for the past six years. Thanks must be given as well to Anne Mollegan Smith, who has shepherded many a writer during her fabulous career, and who helped me shape my ideas into a real book. Special thanks go to my dear friend Victoria Watkins, who helped me cull through seemingly endless reams of data from the Census Bureau and who put what I needed into charts that make sense. My warmest thanks go to my friends and colleagues Laurel Wentz, Filiberto Fernandez, Julio Rumbaut, Ed Miller, Lucia Ballas-Traynor, Manuel Garcia Lascurian, Betty del Rio, Loreyne Alicea, Richard Israel, Peter Blacker, Sonia Maria Green, Jim Szurek, Gilbert Dávila, and Gene Bryan, who all read the book in manuscript form and whose incredible feedback and comments made it much better. A huge debt of gratitude goes to my brilliant friend Roberto Ruiz, who wrote all of the case studies in the book simply because he wanted to be a part of it and help me out.

As a first-time writer I must admit I had no idea what I was getting into when I wrote this book. First, I want to acknowledge Larry Dunn, who introduced me to the great Fred Ciporen, who was the first one to see what I saw in *Latino Boom!* Of course, I couldn't have done any of this without the guidance of my agent, Alfredo Santana, so a special thanks to you and to our mutual friend, José Pérez, for introducing us! At Random House, a huge *abrazo* to Melody Guy for believing in this book from the get-go. But there aren't enough words in English or Spanish to thank my editor, Danielle Durkin, and to my copyeditor, Joyce Yasner, who patiently corrected my manuscript and asked all the right questions. Thanks must also go to my favorite photographer in the world, Emérito Pujol, for taking my picture for this book, and to my colleague at *Advertising Age* Rahmin Pavlovic, who created my beautiful website www.latinoboom.com. And finally, thanks to all the people and institutions who graciously allowed me to use their data for this book.

Chiqui Cartagena

HISPANIC MEDIA & MARKETING EXPERT

CHIQUI CARTAGENA, managing director of multicultural communications for Meredith Integrated Marketing, is a media pioneer with twenty years of experience developing, contributing to, and launching some of America's most successful Spanish-language products, including *People en Español, TV Guide en Español,* and many others.

Prior to joining Meredith, Ms. Cartagena was the business development director for the Ad Age Group. In 1996 she was part of the team that developed and launched the Spanish version of *People* magazine. *People en Español* is still the most successful Spanish-language magazine, and continues to dominate the Hispanic print market today. In 1998 Cartagena left Time Inc. to become executive editor of the Spanish-language version of *TV Guide.* She has also worked as a senior director of Club Música Latina, the Latin music club of Columbia House.

Having grown up in Madrid, Spain, Cartagena returned to the United States to study at the University of Miami, where she became a *cum laude* graduate with a bachelor of arts in journalism and Latin American studies in 1985. Ms. Cartagena has received many honors for her pioneering work in Hispanic marketing, including *El Diario/La Prensa*'s Woman of the Year in 1998 for her work on the launch of *People en Español* and a Special Achievement Award from the United States Postal Service for her achievements in Direct Marketing while at the helm of Club Música Latina, the largest direct marketing club geared toward Latinos in the United States.

Caledonia was designed by William A. Dwiggins in 1939 and originally appeared under the name Cornelia with the Mergenthaler typesetting machine factory in Berlin. Conceived as a reworking of the Scotch Roman which was designed for Mergenthaler Linotype in New York, the neotransitional Caledonia has serene, vertical forms, unflexed serifs, and a transitional style italic. Linotype reworked the typeface in 1982 and released it as New Caledonia. This large typeface family is perfect for large amounts of text due to the fine weight differences it allows. Caledonia's cool, classic look can be used in almost any application.